W9-AQI-832

DATE DUE

Ganga

Ganga

A Journey Down the Ganges River

Julian Crandall Hollick

● ISLANDPRESS / Washington • Covelo • London

ISLAND PRESS is a trademark of the Center for Resource Economics.

Library of Congress Cataloging-in-Publication Data

Crandall Hollick, Julian.
  Ganga : a journey down the Ganges River / Julian Crandall Hollick.
      p. cm.
  Includes bibliographical references and index.
  ISBN-13: 978-1-59726-386-3 (cloth : alk. paper)
  ISBN-10: 1-59726-386-9 (cloth : alk. paper)
  1. Ganges River (India and Bangladesh)—Description and travel.
  2. Crandall Hollick, Julian—Travel—Ganges River (India and
Bangladesh) I. Title.
  DS485.G25H65 2007
  915.4'1—dc22
                                    2007034424

Printed on recycled, acid-free paper ⊕

Manufactured in the United States of America
10 9 8 7 6 5 4 3 2 1

Keywords: India, Hinduism, environment, religion, mythology, travel,
Himalaya mountains, urbanization, water

To
Martine
friend, lover, companion, wife

Note to Readers

No two maps or atlases about India, wherever they are published, ever agree on the spellings of place names. For better or worse we have therefore chosen to follow the spellings found in the *Road Atlas of India*, published by Eicher Goodearth Ltd in strategic alliance with the Survey of India 2006, copyrighted by the government of India in 2006.

Similarly, spellings for just about everything else in the text, whether god, animal, vegetable, or mineral, vary; Shiva can be spelt Siv or Siva (depending on whether the speaker is using Hindi, Sanskrit, or an anglicized spelling). A follower of the god Vishnu will refer to Haridwar as Haridwar, but a follower of Shiva calls it "Hardwar." Banaras can be called Benares, Varanasi, or Kashi. For every person who swears that a name, place, object or idiom can only be spelled *one* way there exists somewhere another Indian to affirm just the opposite! My solution has been to choose one spelling and stick with it throughout the text.

Indian words have not been italicized apart from a few Sanskrit phrases which may not be understood by the reader.

A comprehensive photo gallery of the trip on which this book is based is available at: http://www.ibaradio.org/India/ganga/index.htm, where you can also listen to a series of radio documentaries, additional web-only audio, and the theme music *Om Jaya Ganga Mata,* recorded and performed by the jazz trio Sangam in San Francisco, November 3, 2006. The members of Sangam are Zakir Hussain (tabla), Charles Lloyd (saxophone, flute, taragato), and Eric Harland (percussion).

Contents

Maps

All maps drawn by Christopher Beacock,© IBA, Inc. 2007

Introduction

How can Indians pollute Ganga yet at the same time worship her as a goddess? How can so many millions take a "holy dip" every morning to wash away their sins in a river that is polluted by so much waste, both human and industrial? How does one explain this paradox?

~

The seeds of my obsession were sown at a very early age. When I was a child, my grandmother used to read me to sleep on those long, dark, dreary winter nights in England, with stories about far-off places — mountains, deserts, and rivers such as the Amazon, Mississippi, Nile, and Yangtze. They made my own river, the Thames, look like an apology. But Ganga stood out, even then. She was two continents away, but different from the others because she was a holy river that carried you to heaven, like the Styx in Greek mythology.

It was the mythology of Ganga that made her special, not just to me as a little boy but to countless Indians who consider her waters to be amrit and dream of dying on her banks to attain moksha. Many rivers on other continents are indeed sacred or holy but no other river in the world is worshipped as a goddess. This is why Ganga is unique.

In fact it's hard at first glance to figure out why the physical river should be so venerated. The Ganges River[1] is not especially long — thirty-four rivers are longer. Its entire course is only 2510 kilometers

---

[1] Ganges is the anglicized name for the river, which is called Ganga in Hindi and most other Indian languages.

1516 miles) from source to sea. The Nile, Amazon, Yangtze, and Mississippi are each more than twice as long. No great capital is generally associated with Ganga, nor has she ever really been the center of a famous kingdom.[2] Few, if any, important battles have been fought for her control. Yet, it was Ganga that remained my favorite, the river that never stopped calling to me.

Fast forward to 1986, when I found myself for the first time physically on the river: I was distinctly underwhelmed. I was in Varanasi making a documentary series for NPR (National Public Radio, the American equivalent of the BBC).[3] At dawn, just like every other visitor, Indian or foreign, I was rowed up and down the river. I observed Hindu men and women wading into the water, cupping their outstretched palms together, and praying to the sun that rose over the sand dunes on the river's southern bank.

I wasn't to return to Varanasi for another twenty years, but I saw Ganga again often in the course of my travels without ever really contemplating her presence; she was just always there. In 1987, I drove beyond Tehri to spend time with Sunderlal Bahaguna[4] in his ashram in the Himalayas.

Way below us ran one of the turbulent mountain streams which flows into the Bhagirathi, a tributary that joins the Alaknanda river to form Ganga. Again, I didn't pay it too much attention. My immediate concern was the appalling state of the road near Tehri; two cars could pass simultaneously only at their own peril. I sat in the middle of our vehicle so I would not have to gaze down at the sheer drop into the valley that is now the lake behind the Tehri dam.

In 1995 and 1996, I spent three months in the northern industrial city of Kanpur making a documentary on the monsoon. Several days each week, I traveled to the banks of Ganga in what was strictly a working

---

[2] Both great cities and kingdoms (Pataliputra, various Bengali kingdoms) have, of course, existed on her banks, but it cannot be argued that Ganga was the primary cause of their power or wealth.

[3] Born and raised in Oxford, England, I have spent many years in France and much of the last twenty years in India. Currently, I divide my time between France and the US.

[4] Environmentalist and founder of the Chipko movement that successfully slowed down the deforestation of the High Himalayas, Bahaguna has opposed the Tehri dam project on Ganga's tributaries for years.

relationship. I met with farmers and fishermen in the village of Bithur, which calls itself the "center of the universe" because Brahma was said to have rested here after creating the world.

It was high summer, just before the monsoon was due to break. The river was very low and no more than a hundred yards wide. We would cross the pontoon bridge in a car or on a motorbike, riding a quarter of a mile across sand dunes to the far bank where a friend had a farm. Fishermen harvested watermelons that had been planted in the sand dunes in February, when the river had begun to shrink. It seemed hard to imagine that this modest, placid river would become a veritable sea just a month later.

Five years later, I got to know a very different Ganga. I was in the delta country in southwestern Bangladesh and West Bengal where land, river, and sky bleed hazily into one another. The river here was so vast I could not see to the other shore. It was hard to equate this large, calm body of water with the sacred yet muddy waters of Ganga at Bithur or Varanasi, or the fierce torrents of the Himalayas. Yet it was all one and the same — the same Ganga!

I was hooked. How can the same river have such disparate personalities, I wondered. I realized I knew next to nothing about the physical reality of the river. Indeed, not too many people do. Travel writers, novelists, even distinguished academics, have focussed either on high culture or on the obvious tourist sites — Varanasi, Allahabad, Rishikesh — and their picturesque mythologies. None of them have attempted to make any real connections between mythology and geography. Scientists, hydrologists, and geographers all look at the river from within their specializations — nobody has studied the river holistically.

I was also intrigued by the idea that the river was the embodiment of the goddess Ganga. In the West, we've separated sacred from secular so the very notion of them being one seems absurd. However, bathing in Ganga's waters is a combination of spiritual necessity and simple practicality; one worships and washes at the same site. Thus, the question arose — if Indians worship Ganga as sacred, how can they also pollute her so off-handedly? The questions I had and the contradictions they posed seemed to spin around me without the possibility of a final resolution.

~

It was to answer some of these questions that I decided to do a radio documentary while traveling down the entire river. After all, could anyone really claim to know Ganga unless they'd actually explored her length and breadth? Could it even be done?

It had been done, but only by a very few people, and none of them recently. Very few people — Indians or non-Indians — know Ganga in its entirety today. Millions know small stretches — at Gangotri, at Haridwar or Rishikesh, Allahabad, Varanasi, Kolkata, maybe even Sagar Island where the river enters the Bay of Bengal in India.

But you can probably count on the fingers of both hands the number of people — non-Indians as well as Indians — who actually know the whole river. Indian scientists are no help either; they are usually familiar only with the area that concerns the immediate subject of their research. I've met just one scientist who has traveled the river to the extent of the area in the plains between Haridwar and Sagar Island, and that was only because he was making a survey of the Gangetic dolphin.

The logistical difficulties are daunting throughout. Roads do not run consistently alongside Ganga; often just getting to the river is next to impossible. Much of the northern half of the river isn't even deep enough for anything other than shallow-draft, non-mechanized boats. Channels are numerous and confusing; you desperately need the knowledge of local boatmen. Moreover, there are few towns along the river, outside of the obvious tourist spots, where one can stay to recharge one's batteries. It was tough enough for Eric and Wanda Newby in their 1964 voyage down Ganga.[5] In 2004, with interpreters, guides and photographers to make a radio series? Forget it!

But I decided to embark on this journey. My operations would have to be low-key — I'd use country boats, camp every night on the river bank — yet geared to make radio. This would eventually involve a rugged Mahendra Scorpio — the Indian SUV — to carry tents, cooking equipment, supplies, recording equipment, a portable generator, local cell phones that would work on the river, and two simple GPS[6] units so we could meet up every evening. In Varanasi, Kanpur, Haridwar and Kolkata we stayed in hotels — or ashrams. (It is almost impossible to camp in any Indian town, let alone a city; little security and no campgrounds. The humble ashram, however, offers both.)

As it is impossible to travel down Ganga by boat in a single journey, my travels spread out over eighteen months. When the snows have finally melted in the Himalayas the plains are already a furnace, the river bed may have dried up, and vice versa. Thus we did our voyage in

---

[5] Newby, Eric: *Slowly Down the Ganges*, Picador, London, 1983 (1963).

[6] Global Positioning System.

three parts; a two-week prologue in the Himalayas in late April 2004, the main journey from October 10, 2004 to January 20, 2005, and a coda at the end of the year, after Ganga misbehaved outrageously in West Bengal.

While I was the only person who actually traveled the entire river, I was most definitely never alone. At all times there was a small team of drivers, boatmen, trusted guides (different people in the mountains and the plains), at least one interpreter, various photographers (who appeared, then vanished to return to urban civilization), and Martine, my wife. She accompanied me all but the final one hundred kilometers from Kolkata to Sagar Island.

Also, while the trip was mine, it alternated between the eyes of Ganga's worshipers and the slightly different lens of scientists and environmentalists — the ecstasies of the "holy dip" and the lamentations of the exasperated scientist.

~

When you eventually travel the entire Ganga there are two added complications. First, Ganga has two quite distinct personalities. Its religious aspect dominates from the river's source in the Himalayas down to Varanasi. This is the Ganga of mythology, the Ganga who came down to earth from the Milky Way through the locks of the god Shiva's hair. Ganga ma is a generous goddess who gives life to the fields, cleanses the body of disease and the soul of sins, and opens the way to the next life.[7]

The spiritual benefits of Ganga jal — Ganga water — go hand in glove with the physical benefits of bathing in and drinking this water. From Gaumukh down to Varanasi, Ganga is worshipped everywhere at tirthas,[8] sacred crossing points between the world of the gods and that of human beings. People in the north are most concerned with this river of their minds.

But beyond Varanasi everything changes. Ganga gets much bigger and becomes an overwhelmingly physical presence. The monsoon completes this transformation of Ganga into a destroyer of land and life. Reality in Bihar and West Bengal means dealing daily with the sheer physicality of Ganga, not her spiritual generosity. Of course, millions do still worship Ganga as goddess, but they usually pray with one eye open for the fury of floods and storms.

---

[7] Casting someone's ashes in Ganga is said to help avoid reincarnation as she flows directly to the sea, down into the next world, taking his soul with her.

[8] See Chapter 4.

So far, so simple — two personalities.

How about *three* forms of Ganga? Three distinct rivers, all with the same name, although I prefer to call each river by its dominant source of water.[9] I think understanding Ganga as three distinct rivers is helpful in trying to solve many of the river's long-term environmental problems, because each section seems to require its own solution.

Himalayan Ganga flows all the way down from Gaumukh to Allahabad, where it's just about on its last legs. In the nick of time it meets the mighty Yamuna, which more than doubles its size. Himalayan Ganga is approximately one thousand kilometers long and runs from Gaumukh in the Himalayas, near the border with Tibet, down to Allahabad in the heart of the northern plains in Uttar Pradesh. It consists of a fierce and quite substantial braiding of various mountain streams, tumbling head over heels down three thousand meters within just three hundred kilometers; over ten meters per kilometer. (Try and visualize it - the height of a three story house every three thousand feet!) Few people travel the purely Himalayan stretch by boat, although Sir Edmund Hillary did get up as far as Devaprayag in a jet boat in the early 1970s.[10]

At Rishikesh and Haridwar the river is still fast-flowing, but it broadens and flattens out as it enters the flat northern plains. It also becomes much shallower. Himalayan Ganga gets most of its water from the melting snows of the Himalayas. But from Haridwar to Allahabad (seven hundred kilometers) the only substantial new sources of water are runoff from the Shivalik range and the Ramganga river, both on the lower slopes of the Himalayas. Much of the reach between Haridwar and Kanpur (five hundred kilometers) is fascinating, yet it is all but unknown except to those who live along its banks. The river is not big at all here, frequently dividing and sub-dividing into a multitude of different channels — many of which turn out to be dead-ends.

By now Himalayan Ganga is less than two meters deep and flows at less than five kilometers an hour. There's not much new water entering Ganga and a huge amount is pumped out by farmers, their fields thirsty and usually growing sugar cane. Ganga can get quite feeble here, and in places (Kanpur) its water is almost dead due to heavy pollution, often caused by toxic industrial wastes the Indian government is trying to clean. The lack of sufficient water (except during the monsoon months) exacerbates this pollution, which cannot be flushed away.

---

[9] There may be a link between the personalities and the physical characteristics of these three rivers, but I'm not yet ready to make that leap.

[10] Hillary, Edmund: *From the Ocean to the Sky*, Viking Press, New York, 1979.

But just when Ganga appears out for the count it gets a massive infusion from the river Yamuna — the most unlikely of sources because in Delhi the same river is practically brain-dead for lack of oxygen. Yamuna is one-and-a-half times as big as Ganga when they merge — in strictly hydrological terms the new river should now be called Yamuna, but almost nobody does.[11] For this is the sacred heartland of Ganga the goddess, where every village and creek is the scene of devotion that combines oral traditions, great and small, with worship of Ganga ma.

Yamuna Ganga, on the other hand, is merely a short bridging river. Revitalized and no longer on life support, this second form of the river flows on to Varanasi, then into Bihar, where it yet again changes physiognomy and becomes the *Nepalese* Ganga, its third avatar.

At least four huge rivers — the Son from the Deccan plateau to the south, and the Ghaghara, Gandak, and Kosi from the Nepalese Himalaya — now pour into Ganga. Yamuna Ganga completes its metamorphosis from mountain stream into a giant river between the Bihar border and Farakka (just four to five hundred kilometers) thanks to massive rivers flowing down from Nepal and elsewhere.[12] By the time it reaches Farakka, Nepalese Ganga is more than three times the size of Yamuna Ganga and eight times the size of Himalayan Ganga when she entered the northern Indian plains at Haridwar.

Farakka marks the beginning of the descent into the Gangetic delta and the Bay of Bengal. Very few Indians outside Bihar know this Nepalese Ganga, and with reason. Roads are few and far between and Bihar has a very bad reputation for lawlessness. Also, the river is huge, sometimes so broad you can't even see the opposite bank. While it is very flat, during the monsoon the quantity of water flowing down this stretch is so immense it carries away animals, humans, and entire fields.

Paradoxically, the silt it shifts and deposits is highly fertile. Nepalese Ganga thus takes away with one hand and gives back with the other, characteristic of Shiva, who originally brought Ganga down to earth from the heavens. Shiva is never the life and soul of a party at the best of times, and he puts his mark all over Ganga both as creator and destroyer — or as both at the same time.

---

[11] Two men I know — one in Kanpur, the other in Allahabad — have dared to give it this name. I think their reasons are convincing (see Chapter 4).

[12] Nepalese Ganga also gets most of its water from the Himalayas, only from the Nepalese part of the mountain range.

Farakka, where Nepalese Ganga turns to make its final descent to the sea, also marks the place where man has successfully de-sexed Ganga. If you think this is too harsh a judgement go and see for yourselves! The Indian government, in its infinite wisdom, has interfered with nature, for generous but misguided reasons. Its original intentions were good: to build a barrage to control the river's natural course into Bangladesh, where it becomes the river known as Padma.

Much of Nepalese Ganga was to be diverted down a man-made canal into a smaller river that flows through Kolkata, the idea being to boost the amount of water in this area and keep Kolkata a viable deep-water port. Not only has this not happened — Bangladesh screams bloody murder because it is frequently deprived of sufficient water — but the whole character of the river down to the sea has been altered.

Indeed, the final four hundred kilometers of Nepalese Ganga often resemble a Bengali river Thames, flowing daintily through the pastoral scene of the countryside. It's still Nepalese Ganga of course, but the linking canal has smoothed out any irregularities in flows.

Supreme irony: only in Kolkata where the water is basically too shallow for anything except commuter ferries, does the river finally assume a majesty befitting her status as both goddess and river. Her different avatars finally fade away. She is at last Ganga, flowing through the heart of an ex-capital city. Unfortunately, it's a case of too little too late.

The Sundarbans delta below Kolkata, which also stretches into Bangladesh, is almost the complete antithesis of everything that's gone before. Totally silent. No sound of a diesel engine, not even a cell phone. The Bangladeshi part of the Sundarbans is inaccessible except by boat and is probably one of the last wonders of the world, precisely because it is one of the last places on earth man has yet to develop.

~

While the paradox of Ganga has been at the forefront of my imagination, the key to this riddle — of how Ganga can be both goddess and river — probably lies elsewhere, in the Indian mind. Many Indians simply do not see any riddle. It is just so obvious to most Indians that a river can be both in the mind and a very physical reality. Yet, for the many Indians who have to live along Ganga's banks this apparent contradiction — of how a river can be both sacred, yet poisoned by human indifference — has very real and often tragic consequences. Ganga today is threatened in all directions. In the mountains, the Tehri Dam diverts most of her waters; in the plains, dangerous quantities of toxic chemicals are dumped into her; and further down there is Farakka.

The ability of Ganga's countrymen to live with these multiple realities is perhaps necessary for survival, but may be adding to the problem. In places, the river may actually die because of common apathy or indifference, despite the best intentions of environmentalists, scientists, or concerned Indians. In the minds and hearts of her devotees, the solution to the riddle is simple: what's the problem if we pour our garbage into the river or suck her dry? Ganga can always survive and purify herself, precisely because she is a goddess.

Ironically, some of the tools to clean up pollution lie within Indian culture. "They are very much there if we choose to use them," says Vinod Tare, an environmental science professor at IIT-Kanpur. He believes Indians have been spending far too much time looking at Ganga's problems through Western lenses, that successive Indian governments have chosen Western parameters and technologies often unsuited to Indian realities. Appealing as these imported methods may be to environmentalists and idealists, I wonder if today's India is really in tune with these traditional values?

While the scientific method is universal, what a scientist chooses to examine may be determined by his or her culture. The danger is that the dominance of Western science within India has caused a corresponding loss of knowledge of and confidence in India's own scientific values and heritage.

Ganga is a good example: if there was a problem, what exactly was it? Back in the 1980s, Indian government scientists and their international consultants decided pollution was Ganga's main problem. This in turn dictated the parameters of the 1986 Ganga Action Plan — Dissolved Oxygen and Biological Oxygen Demand — chosen to measure success or failure. It also largely dictated the method they would adopt to tackle the problem, although there were and still are less expensive alternative and indigenous solutions — variations on low cost settling ponds that use the sun, another of India's great natural assets, to let nature do much of the work at a fraction of the cost.[13] It's not that the

---

[13] Vinod Tare's proposed settling ponds in Kanpur or the Sankat Mochan's Advanced Integrated Wastewater Pond Systems (AIWPS) in Varanasi are examples (see Chapter 3).

choice of parameters was necessarily wrong. They just may not have been the most sensible or immediately useful ones to consider when devising solutions for a river in a tropical country.

In any case, the issue of pollution may be secondary to that of the lack of water; solving the riddle might not salvage the physical condition of Ganga, even if pollution is brought under control. For the real problem today is flow, the actual amount of water in the river. India simply cannot go on taking so much water out of Ganga and expect her to somehow survive. It's always possible that wisdom may prevail and get the people to understand that there has to be a balance between supply and demand. But economic pressures may prove too great. How much water will increasingly demanding agricultural enterprises, urbanization, and a rapid modernization require? Some ambitious proposals have been put forth in response to this need. But are river-linking or the prospect of more dams really viable solutions in the long run?

Importantly, are the sources of Ganga stable, sufficient, or in decline? Not all the dangers come from within India. The most serious one may be global warming, whose possible effects on Himalayan glaciers is a cause for real worry in the long term. In the short term melting glaciers mean more runoff into rivers such as Ganga. In the long term it may mean much less snow-melt and less water in rivers. The best-laid plans for the generation of hydro-electricity may literally dry up.[14]

What does all this mean for Ganga? These are questions I have heard far too few scientists within India ask. Why? Because the solution is too large for them to even contemplate? Because it's safer to concentrate on more narrowly-defined questions? Because they expect the central government in New Delhi to always take the initiative?

There's the awful possibility that too many Indians will simply continue on regardless, ignoring meaningful conservation and sucking Ganga dry, drawing her down, convinced that the goddess will somehow find ways to renew her liquid form. But what if Ganga ma cannot and does not?

*****

---

[14] Cf Syed Iqbal Hasnain's warning in *New Scientist,* May 8, 2004, or "The Big Meltdown" in *India Today,* November 6, 2006.

Garhwal Himalayas

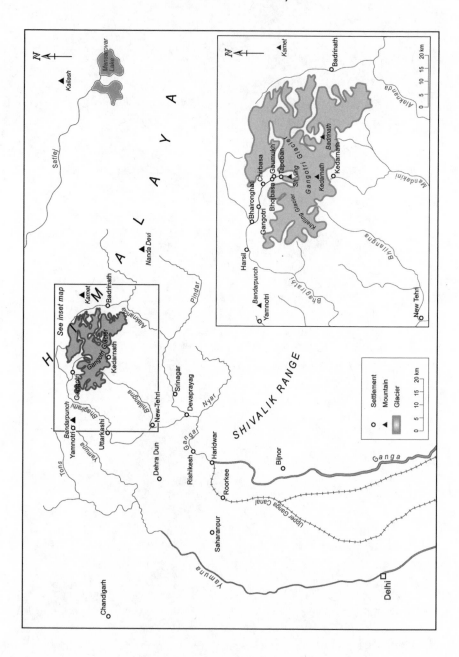

CHAPTER 1

Himalayan Adventures

I can go straight ahead or take a right across the split log that straddles the tiny stream. I choose right. And then where? The backpack weighs a ton and my hiking boots feel as if they are filled with sand. Visibility is no better than ten yards; a raw wind is buffeting wet spring snow against me. Anish and Aditi are too far ahead; Martine and Neal too far behind. None of them can possibly hear my shouts for help. I am wet, cold, and lost.

Luckily I've forgotten Hugh. He suddenly appears out of nowhere, skipping lightly across the rocks like a tahr, the Himalayan mountain goat. "Follow me. We've kept hot chai for you. Go up to that rock and turn left. I'll wait behind for Martine and Neal."

Neal Jackson and Hugh Stevens are lawyers from North Carolina. Anish Andheria is an environmentalist and photographer from Mumbai. Aditi Thorat is my assistant/interpreter, also from Mumbai. Martine and Neal eventually appear and we follow Hugh down a path invisible to our bedraggled selves, through pines, to our tents, assembled and covered with wet snow. This is Chirbasa, the first stage of the climb to the source of the Ganga at Gaumukh—the cow's mouth—at the edge of the Gangotri glacier in the Indian Himalayas, a few kilometers from the border with Tibet.

~

When most people, Indians or foreigners, consider the source of Ganga in the Himalayas, they usually think of the mythological origins of the river. The physical setting of these origins—mountains, clear streams tumbling down fiercely over huge, rough-hewn boulders— enhances the sensation of having wandered up into dev bhoomi, the land of the gods. The ideal of river as goddess makes perfect sense here. Yet all the pressures that weigh the river down further on, in the plains, are already present here in microcosm.

The most famous legend tells of how Ganga came down from the Milky Way in answer to the prayers of King Bhagirath. He wanted her to use her powers to release the souls of his grandfather's sixty thousand sons; they had been cast into this state in a fit of anger by a sage called Kapil, on the shores of the Bay of Bengal (more of this later). The river at its source[1] is therefore called Bhagirathi in his honor.

Because the river's descent would have shattered the earth, the great god Shiva agreed to soften its impact by allowing her to climb down through the long locks of his hair. Bhagirath then escorted Ganga through the plains of India to the Bay of Bengal to restore the souls of his ancestors to life and allow them to enter heaven. They often stopped along the way, and these resting points became especially sacred.

My friend Sharada Nayak[2] in Delhi says you can understand the story, with a little imagination, from a wing seat in a Boeing 737 at thirty thousand feet.

"Just look at a contour map, even. If you look at all the rivers that flow from the Himalayas and join the Ganga as tributaries, they really look like the matted hair of Shiva; like locks of hair coming together to be braided into a gentle stream."

Same thing in the delta in Bengal; so many rivers braided together to flow into the sea. The imagery of matted hair is very evocative. Sharada says, "All the images come from stories. The geography of the country is explained through mythology to people in other parts of India where the Ganga doesn't flow." In the oral cultures of India, people have been telling the story of how Bhagirathi asked the gods to send Ganga down to Gangotri for centuries. It has become so real that a peasant in Kerala or Tamil Nadu would know where Gangotri is—he'll never see the Himalayas but he knows where the mighty river starts. You can also find this imagery in the poems of Kalidas or in any of the other great Sanskrit

---

[1] This is actually one of several sources. The others are Mandakini and Alaknanda near Kedarnath (abode of Shiva) and Badrinath (abode of Vishnu) respectively. It's generally assumed that the water of Bhagirathi somehow represents the essence of true Ganga jal, but either of the other two has respectable claims to containing that magical element, Mysterious Factor X. It would be silly to dismiss either Kedarnath or Badrinath as lesser shrines than Gangotri, but it happens all the time. Popular culture has chosen Gaumukh and Bhagirathi to venerate, so that's the way it is.

[2] Sharada Nayak was the longtime director of the Fulbright program in India and now heads the Educational Resources Centre Trust in Delhi.

texts. The description of the country is astonishingly evocative of the geography of the land.

Myth therefore defines the geography of India. How could it be otherwise in such a vast land? How else could someone in Tamil Nadu—who has never seen high mountains—have any knowledge of Mount Kailash or the Himalayas or Ganga without the works of Kalidas? Sharada is convinced that India is knitted together into a concept of oneness in the mind of the average Indian through mythology and stories.

Sharada says, "Every south Indian I know wants to make a pilgrimage to Varanasi. Why Varanasi? You could go closer, you could come to Delhi, you could go anywhere along Ganga's length." She's right: there are a lot of other places far more convenient for a pilgrim or a religious tourist. It's true Varanasi claims to be the oldest continuous human settlement, which ranks it ahead of places in the Middle East. But Sharada thinks there's another reason: "It's the only place where you can stand by the river and pray to the rising sun. It is the only place where the river flows north and pays obeisance to Kailash, which is directly north of it. That's why Varanasi is so significant." I make a mental note to ask some other south Indians to verify Sharada's thesis.

When I first became fascinated by Ganga, I used to discount the mythology that surrounded her. And then my disdain slowly softened to sceptical acceptance. These fantastic stories are indeed often ways of explaining complex scientific phenomena (famine, floods, meteors, earthquakes) in language and imagery an ordinary Indian peasant, whose world is tightly circumscribed by geography— rivers, mountains, deserts, or jungle—and the distance he or she can travel on foot between sunrise and sundown, can comprehend. Indian scientists now accept that myths might have some basis in fact.

Mythology is omnipresent as a daily reality up here. Many, for example, make a pilgrimage to the three villages at Yamnotri, Kedarnath, and Badrinath.[3] Together with Gangotri they form the four great shrines in the char dham yatra.[4] Lower down the Himalayas are Devaprayag[5]

---

[3] Vishnu's foot is supposed to have accidentally cracked the heavens. His footprint is allegedly preserved inside the tiny temple next to the Brahmakund at Hari-ki-pairi Ghat in Haridwar. I am skeptical because I would have expected any self-respecting god to have a bigger foot than size 10 English or 45 European.

[4] In the *Mahabharata,* the five Pandava brothers and their joint wife Draupudi are condemned to wander these four peaks for thirteen years in search of the gods and their eventual release.

[5] Devaprayag is said to be Vishnu's navel and therefore especially sacred. The other vital body parts are to be found at Badrinath and Gaya in Bihar.

and Haridwar. Devaprayag, about a hundred fifty kilometers south of Gangotri, is a sangam where Bhagirathi and Alaknanda finally merge to form Ganga. Haridwar is sacred because it marks one of four places where drops of magic nectar fell in a cosmic wrestling match between the gods and demons.[6]

As we head up to Gangotri now, in late April, we're going not just to see the source of Ganga, but specifically to witness Ganga Dussehra (the locals also call it Akshay Tritiya)—the reinstallation of goddess Ganga in her summer quarters at the temple in Gangotri.

The snows have finally melted. We start out from Dehra Dun in the foothills of the Himalayas where Nidish Sharma lives. Nidish is the quintessential Garhwali—stocky, incredibly fit, loyal, and with a twinkling sense of humor. Martine complains one day of feeling exhausted. Martine trusts Nidish. He's worked with us in the mountains for almost twenty years. And she knows he knows his Himalayas—he's climbed Nanda Devi, one of the area's highest peaks. So when Nidish asks her, "Would you like some high-altitude medicine?" (we were at twelve thousand feet), she readily agrees. Nidish produces a small bottle in a brown paper bag from his rucksack and tells her to swallow hard. She does and explodes —"It's pure rum!"

~

We climb for two days in low gear up winding valleys, via the towns of Chamba and Tehri. Twenty years previously we had traveled up to Silyara beyond Tehri to stay with Sunderlal Bahugana. At that time the Tehri dam was in its early stages. The road was not yet wide enough for two vehicles to pass. The gears on our driver's Ambassador were progressively packing up. First the third gear went, then the second— only the first and fourth remained. He therefore couldn't use the gears to brake as we went down mountain roads. If a lorry or bus was coming up we either had to hope we could find an indentation in the granite wall of the mountain, or pray we wouldn't be forced over the edge. Martine said the fall was a thousand feet. I was seated in the middle of the backseat, eyes firmly closed shut.

No such problems this time. Harbijan Singh (he looks old enough to be the father or even grandfather of the cricket player Harbhajan Singh) drives confidently and safely. The road is in good shape, lined with giant rhododendron trees. The river shimmers far below. I never feel panic, though scared of heights. That first night we stay in Uttarkashi

---

[6] See the glossary for a brief description of the various Kumbh melas.

at a clean and comfortable rest house run by the Garhwal Mandal Vikas Nigam (Garhwal Regional Development Agency). In the garden a big sign admonishes us:

> **Every drop of water is precious—don't waste it.**
> **You are in the abode of the gods.**
> **Respect the Ganga and Yamuna.**
> **Garbage-free Himalaya, Heavenly Himalaya.**
> **Serve the Himalaya — keep it clean.**
> **Flora-fauna, soil and water are the very Essence of life—**
> **conserve them and be conserved.**

The next day we set out for Bhaironghati, a few miles short of Gangotri. Much of the trip is idyllic. The road runs through a canopy of chir pines, deodar, and birch trees. The Bhagirathi runs playfully through shallows and I almost expect to see trout and salmon jumping. The river also marks the division of Garhwal: to the left is Pauri Garhwal, to the right Tehri Garhwal. In the Gurkha War of 1814–1816, the ruler of Garhwal needed British military help. He made a bargain and ceded them all his kingdom to the right side of the Bhagirathi, provided he got to hold on to the land to the left. Even today, if you ask a villager up here where he comes from, he'll still make this distinction: Puri (or Pauri) versus Tehri Garhwal.

In the olden days pilgrims used to make their yatra to Gangotri on foot. The road has apparently wiped out the path, but it follows the old routes. What it no longer offers are the chattis and chaans where the pilgrims could seek shelter. When pilgrimages were made on foot pandas would accompany pilgrims all the way from Uttarkashi, offering a non-stop travel commentary en route, retelling the myths and legends of the various shrines along the yatra. Today, Indian families take private cars or buses up to Gangotri. They watch reruns of the two immensely popular television series based on Hindu mythology, the *Ramayana* and the *Mahabharata*.

I'm essentially asking Nidish to play a variation of this age-old role of panda: to supply a running commentary on the various shrines, retelling legends, because when all's said and done a tour operator is also a modern form of panda. I doubt Nidish would agree. I have the sense he feels my expectations of him already go beyond the normal. Not only do I want good idiomatic English for the microphone, I also expect accurate, concise storytelling. He hadn't bargained for that. By the end of our time together in Kanpur I realize I may have pushed him beyond other limits, in more ways than one.[7]

Just before the final climb we pass through the town of Harsil, which means "stone of God." Nidish tells us it was here that Shiva slew King Jasodha, who had challenged the authority of the gods. The township on the right bank of the river is now an army camp.[8] A modern footbridge crosses the river to the other half of the village on the slopes. A small group of six men carry an empty palanquin on their shoulders across the bridge and up a path to a temple complex.

During World War II, Harsil served as an internment camp for enemy aliens captured on imperial (i.e. British) territory. One of them was a German called Heinrich Harrer who escaped and managed to cross the Himalayas into Tibet, where he befriended the young Dalai Lama. (Harrer's book about his escape was made into the Hollywood film *Seven Years in Tibet*.) When Nidish was a young man, he and Harrer had explored these mountains together, back in 1977. The landscape above Gangotri was very different then. "We were able to cross Ganga above Gangotri by a snow bridge. We got to the other bank and then we climbed up to Tapoban." Nidish is no friend of the commercial development of the mountains, "Nowadays there is not enough snow. How can you have snow when there are no trees? There's so much building going on now. It's like a concrete jungle. Our environment is being ruined and nobody cares."

~

And then we too start to climb sharply and steeply. Each hairpin bend is littered with warnings from the Border Roads Organization. Tibet is only twenty or so kilometers away and after the 1962 war with China, New Delhi started taking security seriously. Roads had to be built to carry troops and guns to the frontier. Never again would India take her frontiers for granted.

A good deal of the doggerel is also to warn drivers of the dangers of the road:

Life is a Journey, Complete it;
Road is Hilly, Don't Drive Silly;

---

[7] Nidish guided us on the next stage of our yatra, by boat down to Kanpur. He volunteered to cook the evening meals with decidedly mixed results.

[8] The village is called Mukhba. This is where Ganga spends the winter. Nidish claims tourists therefore can't stay at Harsil. But tourist brochures all seem to offer nights here, so presumably these are outside the restricted area.

Keep Your Nerves on Sharp Curves;
Going Faster Can Lead to Disaster;
No Hurry, No Worry;
That is Deep, Don't Go to Sleep;
Eager to Last? Don't Drive Fast;
If You Are Married, Divorce Speed.

The air becomes lighter, purer. And then the final push up through pine forests until we cross a single-span metal bridge at Lanka, crossing the Jadhganga gorge. This is where the road used to end. One had to make the last ten kilometers to Gangotri on foot.

In the nineteenth century, you crossed the Jadhganga gorge by a rope suspension bridge, possibly built by an eccentric English adventurer, Pahari Wilson, who lorded it over the valley. The bridge consisted of a trolley on grass ropes that was pulled across the gorge with pulleys, one pilgrim at a time. It presumably worked well until one of the wives of the Maharajah of Tehri, expecting a child, decided to make a pilgrimage to Gangotri to seek the blessings of the goddess Ganga. The Maharani made the fatal mistake of looking down from the trolley, panicked and miscarried. The Maharajah ordered the pulley bridge torn down. If pilgrims wanted to cross and go on to Gangotri they had to take a footpath down one side of the gorge, cross the river and then climb several hundred feet up the other almost-sheer cliff. Now, thank God, there is a proper bridge. It advertises itself as the highest bridge in the world. I believe it.

Somewhere down in the gorge Jadhganga joins the Bhagirathi. Just beyond the gorge at a tiny pit stop called Bhaironghati we will get our first glimpse of the goddess Ganga. The palanquin we saw in Harsil this morning was in fact going up to the temple at Mukhba to fetch Ganga down from her winter quarters. They're carrying her now on foot up through the pine forests, following the motor road. Tonight she'll be sleeping next to Lord Bhairav in his shrine here at Bhaironghati, before making her final trek up to her summer residence in Gangotri at six next morning. Tomorrow is Ganga Dussehra, a joyous occasion for all, when the temple officially reopens.

Brahmin cooks are preparing the langar to feed the devotees who are accompanying the goddess on her journey — huge metal cooking pots are being scraped clean, ready for chawal (rice) and dal (lentils). Most Garhwalis are strictly vegetarian, abstaining even from eggs. Nidish is an exception.

Bhairav crops up in all the main pilgrimage sites in Uttarakhand. A young man called Krishna wearing a black leather jacket and sporting slicked-back hair tells me Lord Bhairav is Shiva's helper/companion.

Bhairav saved Shiva when he was being chased round the Himalayas by a rakshas or demon. Shiva was headed for Kedarnath, but before he left he gave Bhairav this spot, hence the name.

Krishna is one of fifteen sachivs or priests from Mukhya Mutth — the main temple at Harsil. Many centuries ago, a rishi called Mritang appointed five families — Semwals from south India — to stay at Mukhya Mutth and serve Ganga. Mritang Rishi established the custom of closing the temple at Gangotri on bhai dooj — the day after Diwali — when the goddess starts the journey down to her winter quarters at Harsil, until tomorrow — Akshay Tritiya — when she returns to take up summer residence again in Gangotri. This means the goddess is accessible to her devotees all year round in tangible idol form.

Krishna's come on ahead to check out the preparations because the priest who should be here is sick. Tomorrow he'll change out of his black leather jacket into more appropriate clothes and accompany the goddess for the ceremony in Gangotri. From far below I can hear a very distant rhythmical thud — drums. How far away? Impossible to say. Sounds carry over such huge distances, even in the plains. There is nothing to do but sit and wait. It begins to rain and I seek shelter inside Lord Bhairav's temple. A group of donkeys waiting patiently outside the shrine gets restless and moves off to investigate or seek shelter under the trees, bells tinkling brightly in the mountain air. The sound of the distant cortege fades in and out, like the signal of a mobile phone, as the goddess negotiates the many hairpins. The thud of the dhol is louder, nearer, now punctuated by the occasional bleat of a mountain horn and shouts of "Ganga ki jai."

And then, she is upon us all at once, taking a shortcut through the pines. Two drummers emerge: a man playing a two-sided dhol and a kid traipsing along with a small, tambourine-like drum called a damaum. They're followed by a massive, curled, serpent-like hunting horn. This ran singhar[9] is very old, patched in gold, and carried by an equally venerable man wearing huge spectacles with mismatched glass pieces, a patched Harris tweed jacket, and dhoti. Right behind them is the goddess Ganga, no more than three feet high, swathed in red and gold cloth and borne forth on her palanquin, on the shoulders of four young men. Straggling behind are an assortment of devotees, the occasional policeman, and a handful of families, with small children riding on their fathers' shoulders.

Ganga is carried up the steps into the sanctum sanctorum, already occupied by Lord Bhairav. Thirty minutes of mantras, bhajans, and then a full-throated recitation of the fifty-two slokas of the full 'Ganga Lahiri' ('the waves of the Ganga'), a poem written by the seventeenth-century

---

[9] The ran singhar looks very much like the equally ancient Jewish shofar.

Sanskrit poet and scholar Jagannathan in Varanasi.[10] Jagannathan was a south Indian Brahmin who is said to have contracted leprosy as a result of a liaison with a married Muslim woman. (Popular Indian belief views leprosy as the physical evidence of moral corruption.) So Jagannathan came to Varanasi to be cured of his leprosy by the waters of Ganga. Legend claims that each verse corresponds to the waters of Ganga, rising a step at a time up Panchganga Ghat until the water reached the final step and Jagannathan and his Muslim lover drowned.[11]

The river is very much a goddess here. Ashok Semwal, the president of the temple committee, says, "Narayan means God. Nar is our word for water and water forms the base of our life. So water equals God." Mr Semwal admits the river is highly polluted down in the plains. "But not here in the Himalayas. Ganga is not like other rivers, like the Yamuna or the Satluj. It can kill germs within ten minutes because it has unique self-purifying powers."

I ask him, "Is it true that if I drink Ganga jal at Gaumukh I'll live a hundred years but if I drink it at Gangotri I'll only live for ten years?" Roars of laughter answer me. But he confirms the rumor.

"Yes, it's true that if you drink the Ganga jal at Gaumukh you'll live a hundred years. There's a poem that describes the olden days when our forefathers came for pilgrimage to Gaumukh and Gangotri. It says they came kaffan bandh ke [which means 'with your coffin tied to your back']. They left all their worldly belongings behind because they didn't know whether they would ever return or not." But he has not really answered my question about how long I can expect to live if I only drink the water at Gangotri.

Next morning, even though we're up early Ganga's beaten us to it: she already left at six o'clock for her final climb to Gangotri. Today also marks the official reopening of the town from winter hibernation. Telephones will start working again, much to my assistant Aditi's relief — she's desperate to call home to her mother in Mumbai.

The temple itself is curiously small. The present one was built in 1800 by a Sikh general, Amar Thapar Singh, and is said to be constructed on top of a stone where King Bhagirath performed his tapasya, standing on one leg for a thousand years. It's a very small, squat building built of blocks of granite with a roof of tin (the guidebooks say metal). In front

---

[10] I am fully indebted to John Cort of Denison College, Indiana for sharing his monograph and translation of the "Ganga Lahiri" with me. The poem is also known as "Piyush Lahiri" ("the waves of fresh milk").

[11] There are two problems with this legend. Firstly, Ganga is not tidal at Varanasi and secondly, Jagannathan's suicide has to be allegorical, because he died several years after composing this poem.

of it is a courtyard paved with slate flagstones and encircled by a wall set into the hillside. The other side leads down to the river, which is churning happily down its rocky bed.

~

Nidish is basking in the sun and chatting with one of his porters, seated on a low wall at the back of the courtyard. The goddess arrived at eight o'clock from Bhaironghati. Now she's being washed and adorned before the installation, which starts at 10:30. Men are strewing marigolds on the lane leading down from the bazaar. A few people are chatting idly at the edges of the courtyard. The tall metal grills guarding the steps that lead up to the temple are firmly locked. We have time to kill, so Nidish starts to tell me more of the story of how King Bhagirath brought Ganga down to earth.

"There was a king called Sagar. He was a very great king and his biggest desire was to become the king of kings. So he organized an Ashwamedh Yagna — the horse sacrifice. Here, the horse was left on his own and the army followed the horse. Whoever caught the horse could challenge King Sagar and his army and become the king of kings."

"So he gets the kingdom?" I interrupt very briefly.

Nidish swats my question away: "He gets the kingdom." And returns to his storytelling.

"Anyway, the horse was set loose. Now King Sagar also had two wives — one wife had sixty thousand sons, the other just one son. The sixty thousand sons of the first wife told their father, 'There's no need to send your army after the horse. We'll do the job instead.' King Sagar agreed and the sixty thousand sons set out in pursuit of the horse.

"One day the horse wandered into the forest. Inside the forest there was a saint called Kapil. He was meditating so the horse sensibly kept quiet. Meanwhile the sixty thousand sons burst through the trees into the clearing where Kapil sat, and what do you imagine they saw? Kapil rishi next to the horse and this could mean only one thing — this rishi was throwing down a challenge to their father. So they made a racket to let Kapil know they were around. The rishi was angry as they'd disturbed his meditation. So he opened his eyes and turned them all to ashes.

"Months passed. No horse and no news back at court. King Sagar got worried. Should I send my army to look for them, he wondered. Anshuman, the son of the second wife said, 'Wait, let me go and see if I can find them.' His father reluctantly agreed. Finally, Anshuman arrived at the hermitage of Kapil rishi. What did he see but the horse grazing peacefully and the rishi meditating — and in front of the rishi a huge pile of ashes."

Nidish is warming to his task, baseball cap pulled down, really into his story. "He couldn't understand what had happened but he smelt the [sic] rat. So he waited and waited till Kapil rishi opened his eyes and saw this stranger in front of him.

" 'What's brought you here?' he asked him. So Anshuman told him the whole story and when he was done said, 'I can see the horse right here. But where are my brothers?' The saint said, 'Oh, you are a sensible man, but your sixty thousand brothers were not — they came and disturbed me and I have burned them into ashes and now I cannot do anything.'

"The son replied, 'I'm sorry on behalf of my brothers, but in our religion it's very important that the souls of my brothers should go to heaven. What can we do?'

"Kapil replied that something could be done. He explained, 'But first you'll have to please Mother Ganga who flows in the heavens. If Ganga can be brought down into the earth, she will wash away all these ashes. Then only can their souls go to heaven.'

"Anshuman thanked Kapil rishi and headed back to his father's kingdom, the bearer of both good and bad news. King Sagar was shocked and saddened at the stupid behaviour of his sons and went off into the forest to meditate, without much result. He died, his son and his grandson also meditated and in turn died, and now we come to his great-grandson Bhagirath, who also meditated right here where we're sitting. Bhagirath performed his tapasya standing on one leg for a thousand years on a rock said to lie under the present-day temple.

"And Mother Ganga was finally happy. She appeared and said, 'Oh son! What do you want?' So Bhagirath told her the whole story all over again, and at the end turned to her, saying 'Now we need you down here so that the ashes can be washed away.'

"Mother Ganga replied, 'Yes, I'm very happy about the way you have meditated. But there's a very real problem. If I come down from heaven to earth I will flood the entire earth and no one will survive.' Bhagirath asked her what the alternative was. Ganga had a suggestion. 'I'm willing to come down but I don't know how we'll keep my waters in check. As far as I know there's only one person who can control them and that's Lord Shiva. So go and make Lord Shiva happy and if he says he can do this, I'll come.'

"Bhagirath went back to meditation for another very long period. Finally, Shiva appeared and was told the whole story. He said, 'Yes, this is a noble purpose and I'm willing to help.'

"Mother Ganga was called and Shiva took her into his hair. He then unwrapped one of his locks and let Ganga down from the heavens to earth, right here at Gangotri. So from the source till Devaprayag the river is known as Bhagirathi (though it is really Ganga) because the credit has been given to King Bhagirath, and from Devaprayag onwards we call it Ganga. And this place, this very place Gangotri, is where King Bhagirath meditated. This is the story of how Ganga was brought down to the earth."

And here, Nidish ends his long tale. There are details about Indra and Shiva's involvement in the whole story I only learn about at the end of my yatra at Sagar Island, but for now he's done.

Interestingly, the first two shrines in the char dham yatra — Yamnotri and Gangotri — are sacred because they are the origins of two rivers, Yamuna and Ganga. The latter two — Kedarnath and Badrinath — are sacred as well of course, though not because they're the sources of two important rivers (the Mandakini and Alaknanda) that subsequently flow into Ganga at Rudraprayag and Devaprayag, but because they are venerated as the abodes of Shiva and Vishnu respectively.

Nidish has a nice story about Yamnotri I later hear retold by the priest in the Viswanath temple in Uttarkashi. "In the early days [presumably at least two thousand years ago]," he narrates, "there used to be just one priest for Yamnotri and Gangotri. This priest used to cross the pass, come over to this temple on the Ganga, take a dip, perform aarti and then cross the pass again back to Yamnotri to perform aarti there with Ganga jal. This was his job everyday. The years went by and the priest became old, too old. One day he was here, taking a dip, and he prayed to Ganga: 'Mother, I'm getting old and I'm finding it increasingly difficult to cross the pass and get back to Yamnotri. Please do something so I can stay in Yamnotri and there can be a separate priest here in Gangotri.'

"Anyway, that evening when he struggled back to Yamnotri he discovered a waterfall at the temple there. It hadn't been there that morning when he'd set out. A very small waterfall, but the water had the same qualities as Ganga here. Since that day Gangotri and Yamnotri have both had their own priests."

~

I can now hear the distant thud of the drums. The procession is on its way down the long bazaar. It enters through an archway from the bazaar, led by bagpipers from the Garhwal Rifles. Behind them is the palanquin, in which rides the deity, freshly adorned with marigolds, irises, roses and red silk. In statues and paintings Ganga is usually depicted as a very feminine goddess in earthly form. But the goddess who's being reinstated today doesn't look like that goddess at all. Underneath her silks she's a highly abstract modern sculpture, a silver rectangle on end with an attached chimney, the whole ensemble no more than three feet tall. The ornate burgundy-red skirts offer the only clue to her gender.

Unless, of course, this is merely her traveling case, while the real goddess is snugly cocooned inside, totally hidden from human gaze.

She's followed by the faithful from Harsil who brought her up to Bhaironghati the previous evening, the two drummers, the venerable ran singhar and its equally ancient performer, now supplemented by several other drums. The good, the great, and everyone else, with sadhus bundled up in warm clothes, bring up the rear. They march round behind the temple to the main gates. The pipes move off to the edge of the courtyard, the dhol, damaum, and ran singhar a safe distance away so each can play to a different section of the crowd — which by now is quite large — while the deity is solemnly carried through the iron gates, up steps and into the sanctum sanctorum of the temple. Anyone with any sort of camera is trying to climb the wrought-iron bars and get a shot of the goddess. Two queues form — VIPs to the left, others to the right. VIPs get to go in first for darshan. It will take at least an hour. The sun is warm, the crowd good-natured— the right day for a holy occasion.

The four pipers and a big bass drum launch into a spirited medley of Garhwal Highland marching songs. Over a crackling PA system the priests are chanting their slokas inside while the crowd waits, trays of offerings held in anticipation.

To one side a group of villagers — mostly women, it appears — are sitting on the flagstones chatting round a small deity called Bhauknath, who's seated in a silver carriage set into a long palanquin covered with blood-red cloth. Their village is Kaufnal, near Uttarkashi, and they've brought their goddess just to see Ganga. They bathed her at four o'clock this morning and this afternoon they'll head back home. The village poojari Kamal Singh starts retelling the whole story of King Sagar and Bhagirath. Meanwhile, people are lining up to receive darshan inside the temple. One woman, Runu De from Chandannagar, just north of Kolkata, has brought her two daughters. She says, "The Ganga flows in front of my house. It's so much a part of my everyday life. We bathe in her, we cross her every day in a launch. So we had to come and see where it all starts."

I mingle with the crowds, waiting to get darshan. I spot the old man who's been playing the ran singhar serpent horn. His name is Mangaldas and he's been playing the instrument since he was twelve years old when it must have been bigger than him. He says he's now over eighty. Next to him stands a sadhu called Krishna Anand from Vrindavan. He regularly makes the char dham yatra.

"Why do you come here?" I ask him. His reply will sound very profound on radio, later: "Someone calls me here. In the summer I go up to Gaumukh and Tapoban." Ten minutes later we run into Krishna Anand again. This time he wants me to give him 500 rupees to buy a shawl to keep himself warm. I decline with a clear conscience — I only have forty rupees in my kurta.

While I've been talking to Mangaldas and Krishna Anand, Aditi and I lose contact with Nidish and the others, temporarily. In search of him, Aditi and I wander down to the river to shallow concrete bathing ghats where a handful of hardy souls are bathing in the fast-flowing water that can't be much above freezing point. Beside them stands a large bell hanging from a wooden frame.

Back home I have a print of a famous lithograph by the nineteenth-century British painter William Simpson of this exact same scene — pilgrims getting dressed at the edge of the Bhagirathi, a similar bell in the foreground. The river is a fierce and shallow mountain stream pouring down over boulders, not something anyone can really stand up in away from the shore. I know: I tried to ford it and was swept over. (In the plains Ganga is also shallow, but muddy and slow-moving.) To his credit, Simpson's lithograph shows the river as it is, not a broad Himalayan Thames as others depict it. These colonial paintings and drawings are interesting in their approach because, like the Hudson River Valley School in Upstate New York, they often recast landscapes into familiar landscapes European viewers could relate to. Many of Simpson's contemporaries depict the valleys here as gentle but gloomy cousins of a Scottish glen. They downplay the altitude (after all, we're at more than ten thousand feet here), in favor of recreating the feel of the rolling hills of the Scottish Highlands (between one and three thousand feet maximum). Not Simpson.

Should I undress and take a dip or find out first how cold it really is? I choose my victim with care — Sriram Thappar — a middle-aged man just coming out of the water and not shivering noticeably. "How cold is the water?" "Minus two celsius," he replies. Forget it. Sriram Thappar comes from Mumbai, and is up here with five other families. This afternoon they'll head back by car to Uttarkashi, then by bus from Haridwar to Delhi, and by overnight train back to Mumbai.

"Why do you come and bathe in this water, when it's so cold?" I ask.

"Because I believe in Ganga. I believe Ganga is God. I have a bath because it is our tradition. Here if you have a bath you are purified. I believe this river is another form of God."

Has Gangotri lived up to his expectations? "I had this desire in my heart to come and worship here. That has been fulfilled." Another man from the same party — Harish Kumar — is busy filling plastic bottles with Ganga jal. Harish Kumar has come for a very specific medical purpose. He has Type 1 Diabetes. He swears Ganga jal lowers blood sugar: "I've been staying in Haridwar for the past fifteen days, taking Ganga jal regularly. My diabetes is hereditary and I know what it can do later on; my father died when he was just fifty-five. Normally my blood sugar after meals is one eighty, which is high. Here it's down to one thirty."

We cross back over a wooden bridge to another Garhwal Mandal Vikas Nigam resthouse; our booking here got bumped off the list so some VIPs could rest before today's ceremony. From the bridge I gaze down at the extraordinary series of pale granite cataracts that have been carved into surrealist shapes by the sheer force of the river. Both in colour and texture they look like whipped meringue, even though they're as hard as bone, official Gangotri leucogranite. Below them are three pools — Brahmkund, Gaurikund, Vishnukund. Ganga is said to have descended at this precise spot. These pools are therefore the most sacred places to bathe, though how you get down to them is a mystery. When the water's clear, you can see submerged lingams, reminding me that Shiva must indeed have been here.

That evening, when it's dark, Aditi and I return to the temple. There are only a handful of people about. The evening aarti is unusual — five different bells rung in sequence like English church bells, the ubiquitous thud of the dhol and the plaintive call of the ran singhar. While the priest is chanting slokas, something unusual (and very auspicious according to Aditi) occurs. A grey dove flies out of the sanctum sanctorum, takes a turn around the temple, and then returns inside. A perfect end to a very special day.

~

If mythologically these three pools are the source of Ganga, where is the actual physical source? The river emerges from under a glacier at Gaumukh but it's already fully formed — more than a foot deep and thirty feet wide. Scarcely a spring. So does it make sense to continue to refer to Gaumukh as the source? Does it come from somewhere further away under the Gangotri glacier? Nearer Badrinath? Could the ancients conceivably have been right all along? This would mean that it actually comes from the slopes of Mount Kailash and Lake Mansarovar (over the border in Tibet) and flows underground through the drainage divide of the High Himalayas, in defiance of all-known laws of modern science.

Can anyone ever really pinpoint the original spot, the original drop of liquid? The bigger question: is it ultimately that important?

The question *was* important to Europeans of very early times. Prior to the sixteenth century, European geographers such as Ptolemy and early Italian and Dutch cartographers tried to indicate the source of the river on their maps. Jesuit missionaries somehow traveled to Lake Mansarovar in the early seventeenth century and brought back the legend that this was the

source of Ganga.[12] Chinese cartographers were sent to Tibet and came
back with much the same story, and it received an official stamp of
approval when this was published in 1733 as part of the four-volume
Description de l'Empire de la Chine, and later in James Rennel's *Memoir
of a Map of Hindoostan* in 1783.[13] But this was pretty tenuous scholarship
at best.

So the East India Company sent Captain Webb in 1808 to "survey
the Ganges from Hurdwar to Gungoutri (or the Cow's Mouth), where
that River is stated by Major Rennell to force its way through the Himalaia
Mountains by a Subterraneous passage but it is said by some natives who
have visited the spot to fall from an eminence in the form of a cascade."[14]
The expedition never made it as far as Gangotri. But they did gather
reliable information that "the Source of the River is more remote than
the place called Gung outri, which is merely the point where it issues
from the Himalaia, not as is related, through a Secret passage or Cavern
bearing any similitude to a cow's mouth...although the access be so
obstructed as to exclude all further research."[15]

James Baillie Fraser was the first European to actually reach
Gangotri in 1815, followed two years later by Captain J.A. Hodgson,
who continued up to Gaumukh and officially discovered the source of
Ganga. Tomorrow, we make that same journey.

We set out at six o'clock in the morning from the guesthouse,
cross the bazaar behind the car park, clamber up a short path and on to a
well-maintained hiking trail strewn with pine needles. After a few hundred
yards we come to a gate and a big sign — HIMALAYAN CODE OF
CONDUCT — which asks us to refrain from giving money to any children
because it will encourage begging and to leave the area as clean as we
found it. It is issued by Board of Trustees of the Himalayan Environment
Trust, whose names include Edmund Hillary, Reinhold Messner, Maurice
Herzog, and Chris Bonnington.

Nidish read in a local newspaper at Uttarkashi three days ago
that they had collected two hundred sacks of garbage in Gangotri alone.
While we were waiting for the reinstallation ceremony to begin, he'd
gone off to see for himself. The paper said the garbage had been gathered

---

[12] Cf p 130 in Jagmohan Mahajan's *Ganga Observed*, Indica Books, Varanasi 1994 &
2003.

[13] Jagmohan Mahajan also edited a very similar large-format book, *The Ganga Trail-
Foreign Accounts and Sketches of the River Scene*, Indica Books, Varanasi 1984 & 2004,
pp 97–107.

[14] Ibid.
[15] Ibid.

behind the bus station. The locals roared with laughter when he asked where the two hundred sacks were — presumably they had been abandoned somewhere to rot.

~

I can't remember when it happened. One moment a hundred yards separated us and the porters were sprinting ahead with the camping and cooking equipment on their backs to get to the camp site at Chirbasa ahead of us; the next moment it started sleeting and they disappeared from sight; and the moment after that, there was a hard, driving fall of snow. Several of us met up at a chai stall, basically plastic sheeting and benches, but when we set out again the weather worsened. The snow became heavier, visibility decreased to less than five meters, and we got hopelessly spread out.

I know Martine and Neal are plodding along somewhere not far behind me, but there is no sign of anyone ahead. I am hopelessly lost until Hugh turns up and guides the three of us down to our camp site at Chirbasa — the place of the pines — where tents, hot chai, and Nidish's "high altitude medicine" awaits us. We all go to bed that night fully-clothed, taking refuge inside extreme weather sleeping bags and the wet snow crushes the sides of the tent, increasing our sense of claustrophobia. But what's the alternative — to go out? Not until the snowfall has ceased.

Next morning, the sky is clear. The mountain sides appear to be dusted with a light coating of icing sugar, their peaks gleaming pale gold in the morning sun. Outside a group of young students, dressed just in track suits and sneakers, are playing volleyball. Well-prepared, unlike us who have one book and a bottle of rum between us, as well as several digital cameras. But you can't eat cameras.

~

Nidish decides to play it safe; we'll stay here at Chirbasa, dry our clothes and get rested to make an all-out assault on Gaumukh the next day — there and back between sunrise and sundown. This sounds fine but the weather at this time of year is so unpredictable, and there are no trees at the next camp Bhojbasa. A sadhu called Sadhu Lal Bihari runs an ashram up there and his supporters have cut down all the silver birches to heat the chai they serve to people like us. When Nidish first came up here in 1977 Bhojbasa was still a thick forest, he tells us.

"We used to camp up there. It was very nice there, a good field. But now the field does not exist. A lady mountaineer called Harshvanthi

Bishth tried to grow baby birch saplings ten years ago, but nothing has happened since then because there is no one to look after the nursery."

Birches are sacred in Indian mythology. Great sages have retreated deep into the forests to compose oral epics on the tree's bark, which is like papyrus; Vyasa and Valmiki used it to record the *Mahabharata* and *Ramayana*.

Nidish, Aditi, and I wander down to the Bhagirathi, a hundred meters from our campsite. We sit by the fast-flowing stream. Scattered at the edges are more huge, meringue cream rocks, some as big as small houses, littered haphazardly after the gods had finished rolling their dice. I'm intrigued. Does Nidish, a man who has traveled the world, really believe the river came down in the locks of Shiva's matted hair?

Nidish is emphatic. "Based on what I have read I would say yes. Ganga was brought down to earth from heaven, and I'll tell you why. Only Ganga has this unique property that its water can never get contaminated. Yamuna is holy but it doesn't have these properties. Indian scientists attribute this to the properties of minerals and herbs in the water. But there are other rivers such as the Alaknanda or the Mandakini that rise here and contain mountain herbs and minerals and their water gets contaminated. So yes, Ganga is unique and it must be so because she comes straight from heaven. We are basically a god-fearing people. Whenever we find something unusual, we attribute this to our gods."

I still find it surprising that a well-traveled man like Nidish believes this story of the origins of Ganga. Maybe I should just sit back and enjoy being in the company of a friend who can go where I cannot?

I go back to the tents, which are drying out in the sun, and fetch a couple of thick plastic water bottles and two Ziploc bags to take samples of Ganga jal. After all, it can't get much purer than here, expect up at the source itself. The sediments settle immediately but the water itself stays cloudy. Nidish says the water in winter is absolutely clear, presumably because there are no monsoon deluges to wash sediment down the mountain sides.

"Have you drunk Ganga jal?" I ask Nidish. Sometimes the simplest questions produce unexpected revelations, and he doesn't disappoint: "Many times. Without Ganga jal we cannot survive. Ganga jal is everything for a Hindu, and I'm very much a Hindu."

Looking at my cloudy bottle, I object: "But it must taste of sand?" Nidish doesn't buy this at all: "This water is far better than the Ganges water people are drinking in Varanasi. That looks like sewage water. I'm drinking the water from the source. No matter it is cloudy or sandy or whatever. Nothing happens to us."

"And you've never been ill?" Nidish's answer is firm: "Never."

Same thing with his parents, whom I've met on several occasions. His father is still an active mountaineer at seventy-three, and his father before him lived to a ripe old age. Nidish attributes this to a swig of Ganga jal first thing every morning. Also, a few drops of Ganga jal mixed with ordinary tap water to perform his morning pooja.

"I remember the day he died," Nidish tells me. "We took his body — he was still alive — opened his mouth, and placed two drops of Ganga jal in his mouth, and then he died."

I've never seen Nidish bathe or pray to any idol, unlike say Indu[16] in Mumbai. He travels to Europe regularly, takes tour parties from the West up into different parts of Garhwal, and is very fond of high altitude medicine. So beyond the usual pieties what does it really mean for him to be a Hindu?

"I believe in all religions, even though by birth I'm a Hindu — of course I come to the temple and respect my gods and perform the few rituals I know well. I think Hinduism is the most flexible religion in the world, where everything is accepted — everything." So far nothing unexceptional. But that last phrase "where everything is accepted — everything" has real practical meaning for Nidish in his everyday life. In fact, I wonder if he came to his understanding of Hinduism recently as a way of justifying his habits to his wife Kalyani.

"In Garhwal — in this part of it which is the abode of Shiva - we always say there are many gods and goddesses and you have to please them accordingly. We have gods for everything, for food, for weather, we have a god for mountains, for wealth, we even have a god for sex."

I shouldn't have been surprised; Hindu mythology never strays far from fertility and sex. "So who's the god of sex?" I ask.

"That's Kam devta," answers Aditi, quick as a flash. She's obviously quite animated at this turn of the conversation and chips in her two cents worth: "Kama is a very powerful god. He's supposed to have ignited Shiva's third eye. It actually burnt him to ashes because he was trying to create desire in Shiva when the other gods wanted Shiva to get more involved in what was happening here on earth."

I steer the conversation towards another potential god. "Is there a god or goddess of wine?"

This time it's Nidish who jumps in: "Ah Shiva! It was Shiva who actually drank..." He searches for the word. "Amrit," suggests Aditi.

Nidish doesn't miss a beat. "There are certain Hindu temples in Punjab where you have to take an offering of a bottle of alcohol."

---

[16] Indu Agarwal who will join us in Varanasi.

But Aditi is more interested in our previous topic. "Did you know that the southern goddess Lord Kamakshi, also in some traditions seen as a consort of Shiva, is one of the forms of Kama? She is the devi version of the god of desire — in other words, the goddess of sex. In fact she's the deity my father worships, and I have a big idol of her at home."

Nidish and Aditi discuss their family gods. Nidish explains, "At home our family deity is Narsingh — the lion [one of the avatars of Vishnu]. And every family, at least in the mountains, has its own family god. We offer our prayers to Shiva, Lakshmi, or Krishna. But the main one in our family poojas is Narsingh."

Aditi almost falls into the water in her excitement. "Like Nidish, we also have a family god, Lord Jyotirba, who was actually a version of Shiva. Just outside Kohlapur, which is my ancestral town, there's a Jyotirba temple. He's a very powerful warrior god, not a Brahmin god, a Kshatriya god. So the offerings are meat and all kinds of sacrilegious items."

And sex is still on Aditi's mind: "The very beautiful idol we have at home is of Devi Kamakshi with an actual yoni [vagina], made in Kanchipuram. She is completely black, made of granite, and she glistens when oil is put on her. She is absolutely gorgeous."

We head back to our camp. The schoolgirls have finished their volleyball game and they run back to their tents after two blasts on a whistle from their teacher. Ten minutes later they reemerge in tracksuit tops and with backpacks, form a single file, and hop, skip, and jump off up the path. Thank goodness they don't see us the next morning when we set off at six thirty, a group of geriatric tourists plodding along in hiking boots and three layers of pullovers, feeling the rocks ahead with the very latest in blue hiking poles.

~

The trek starts well enough, the trail level and covered with pine needles for the first kilometer. Then it gets rougher; progress slows as we advance from stone to stone. Donkeys trip past us on the way up, with cases of soft drinks in panniers on either side. Once, we come to what appears to be a simple mountain stream. You can either cross it on a narrow wooden tree trunk or take your chances skipping from rock to rock. I choose the latter method and am across in no time. Most of the others opt for the tree trunk and have to be guided across by a porter, or risk a fall into the icy stream and subsequent paralysis. It takes half an hour for all of us to get across this otherwise insignificant stream. Twice more we have to edge forward on hands and knees, trekking poles extended towards helping hands because of rock slides. Lose your balance and you can fall a thousand feet down into the valley.

Beyond Bhojbasa, which indeed is totally denuded of all vegetation and would make a marvelous soccer or even cricket pitch, the path deteriorates yet again. We walk past what must have been the tree farm. A few stunted saplings are all that remain of the experiment. But there's a big metal sign:

A REQUEST

It is a religious ritual to collect the holy water of the river Ganga from its proverbial source, Gaumukh. But to conserve the flora, fauna, water and soil and not to litter around Gaumukh area is not merely the religious ritual but true religiousness. Hence you should go beyond the religious ritual and be truly religious. Don't ever forget: God and nature are synonymous with each other. Revering nature is revering God.

~

The mountains are indeed magnificent, worthy of all their clichés, peaks covered in snow, framed by deep blue skies, sun warming the entire valley. Ahead are the three Bhagirathi peaks, the other side of the valley with huge landslides in the foreground, Shivling behind.

Every writer refers to its phallic shape, smooth, round, and aggressive. The base is indeed phallic, but its peak has been bent back like the swing tip nose of the Concorde jetliner that can be adjusted forward for takeoff, then straightened out for cruising at altitude. Anish suddenly goes bounding up the scree beyond the path like some mountain goat. For five minutes we watch and wait as he leaps and crouches from boulder to rock, and then just as swiftly, he runs back down.

"Did you see them?" Complete blank. "See what?"

"Bharal. Five of them. Look to the left of that bush."

"I don't see anything." Anish is getting impatient with me. But Martine knows what he's talking about. "I can see them," she exclaims. "It's incredible how well they blend in with the rocks."

Finally, a slight collective movement and the blue mountain sheep move five yards across the moraine, perfectly camouflaged against snow leopards and other predators.

The going is rough and slow now. On a big boulder on the side of the trail is written "1935 200' SW SNOUT POSITION." We wonder, has the glacier really retreated that far in such a short time? Nidish says he read in yesterday's paper that it officially retreated twenty-three meters last year. Geographers calculate it to have retreated six hundred meters between 1935 and 1976. At this rate the Gangotri glacier will have shrunk back all the way to Badrinath over thirty-five kilometers due east, unless the warming trend turns out not to be irreversible global warning, but merely cyclical warming and cooling.

We shed two layers of thermal sweaters and Indian pilgrims regularly pass us in chappals and dhotis. Aditi had been freezing when we set out; she'd packed only a light anorak and sailing pants. Now she's perfectly attired for the full midday sun and skips along like the schoolgirls who must be up on the glacier, on their way to Tapoban.

The rocks here have been set into a bed of cement, so we have to stretch to move from rock to rock. This is a Himalayan Calvary, I think. On Good Friday, Jesus Christ, wearing a crown of thorns, had to drag both his body and a cross up a rocky path to Calvary, where he was to be crucified later that day. I turn a corner on our path, and there he is — Jesus Christ! Arms outstretched minus the cross, facing the sun. Must be a scarecrow. Martine thinks it could be a statue. I move closer and details come into focus; curly blond hair, closed eyes, blue running shorts, red sleeveless undershirt, backpack behind, yellow towel laid out on the ground, plastic flip flops neatly to one side. What we have here is a six-foot, thin as a rail Aryan from my part of the world worshipping the Vedic sun god Surya in the abode of the gods.

Next, I pass what looks like a stone graveyard of various shaped stones decorated in paint and cloth. They are Shiva lingams. Beside them sits a bearded Indian in orange turban and dhoti, wearing what appears to be a pair of Ray-Ban sunglasses and sunning himself. He gives us a Vietnam era sign of peace.

And then, there it is —Gaumukh. It's veined like a marbled cheese, tilting forward as if drunk, whole chunks ready to collapse into the river bed — not at all as I'd imagined. No pure, white, sheer wall, like an iceberg. But I've never seen a glacier before. It looks old and tired from rough working snow, grinding and chewing rocks up, spitting them out like some giant natural earthmover. Maybe this is how they do strip mining in lands where man has little respect for the earth?

Captain J.A. Hodgson in 1815 may have been in awe, but he was also all business, a good surveyor. He describes: "A most wonderful scene. The Bhagirathi or Ganges issues from under a very low arch at the foot of the grand snow bed." Hodgson estimated the face of the glacier to be three hundred feet high. Nothing here resembles a cow's mouth, there's just a glacier and a stream twenty-five feet wide and about fifteen inches deep. I like Hodgson's conclusion: "Believing this to be the first appearance of the famous and true Ganges in day light, I saluted her with a Bugle march."[17]

---

[17] Captain J.A. Hodgson, "Journal of a Survey to the Heads of the Rivers Ganges and Jumna," *Asiatik Research*, Vol XIV, 1922. Quoted in Jagmohan op. cit. pp 102.

I take out my tape recorder and interview Babaji Samarth Das instead.

Samarth Das comes from Rishikesh. He's been here before. Barefoot, dressed only in dhoti and grey shawl, he's come to collect Ganga jal in a white glass jar that he'll carry all the way down to Rameshwaram, the southernmost tip of India. There, he'll do a pooja to Bholenath, a form of Shiva, because he believes that if he takes Ganga jal to Rameshwaram and performs pooja there, boons will be granted to him.

"I have no personal desires. My only desire is that in every life that I will be born I will be able to worship God and be near him," he says. Gaumukh is important for him because it is the pure unadulterated Ganga — no mixing, no joining with other rivers. I wonder if there are any other sacred rivers in India?

"Yes there are, Narmada is Shiva's daughter." So what is Ganga? Samarth Das retells the basic story of Shiva's locks and Bhagirath's penance. He gets some of the details wrong but the essentials right — she is the supreme river, pure and sacred. His faith is simple and basic: "If you drink Ganga jal it purifies the soul in spite of all the pollution."

I wish him godspeed. It's well past midday and we have to get back to our camp before nightfall. But before we leave I fill my water bottle with Ganga jal and take a good swig to guarantee my hundred years. You never know. I gaze up at the glacier, then back down the valley. The river runs down the valley: after a quarter of a mile it just falls out of sight, drops off the earth, leaving the valley and those snow-covered peaks. I remember learning to ski down Alpine mountains where I would become terrified when the slope fell so steeply I could no longer see the bottom. Yet here I have never felt afraid.

But it will be downhill from here on, and in more ways than one. Ganga is her most pristine state here in Gaumukh. She is not only a victim of global warming, but over the course of the next twenty-five hundred kilometers she will also be raped, pillaged, and de-sexed, until she staggers exhausted into the Bay of Bengal at Sagar Island.

~

The problems start to appear as soon as we start back down to Dehra Dun. Man always dumps waste into Ganga, and to add to this, he interferes with the river, constantly diverting her waters to generate electricity. Less than one hundred kilometers south, just north of Uttarkashi, the river has been dammed up and diverted through pipes to feed turbines to generate electricity. Below the dam the river bed is bone-dry for several kilometers until the water is allowed back, just near the town. Downstream from the town a cement factory pours slurry into the river. These are not isolated instances; the demand for hydroelectricity is just too pressing.

The mother and father of all dams is being built at Tehri, just below the junction of the Bhilang river and the Bhagirathi. Nehru would have called the Tehri dam a "temple of the future." Today, many call it "a form of sacrilege, obstructing the inexorable current of a holy river that symbolizes the cosmos."[18]

An entire valley is now being flooded by a huge, earthen dam to generate electricity for Delhi (six hundred kilometers to the south) and the state of Uttar Pradesh (population 180 million and rising). The lake will stretch back thirty-five kilometres, be five kilometers wide. It will drown whole villages and productive farmland. Much of Bhagirathi–Bhilang will be diverted through three giant turbines set into the mountainside, then carried through a tunnel in the mountain and spat out again lower down.

Worse still, Tehri is in a major earthquake zone — it sits on the same fault line as the site of the 2005 Kashmir earthquake. But the Indian government stubbornly ignores environmental warnings because this project is already forty-plus years in the making and has built up such bureaucratic momentum that they are not about to abandon it now.

Nidish takes us to a spot high above the actual dam. Down below thousands of construction workers — ant-like figures — are scurrying to top off the dam. Stephen Alter compares them to King Sagar's sixty-thousand sons.[19] A different historical analogy springs to my mind: it's like watching a diorama of the building of the Egyptian pyramids in a science museum: scores, hundreds of dump trucks move ant-like up a series of zigzag ramps cut into the dam face, carrying their precious loads to the summit of this twenty-first century pyramid, just as the slaves somehow pushed hundreds of thousands of giant stone cubes up to the summit of the pharaonic mausoleums.

Another thing that intrigues me is that I've yet to see anyone fishing in Ganga. I'm used to West Bengal where fishing is in the air one breathes. Nidish says people in Garhwal are not fish-eaters. And even if you wanted to fish they won't give you a permit. The Forestry Department classifies fish as wildlife, and wildlife has to be preserved.

I ask Nidish whether the Ganga jal I drink lower down will have the same magical properties as Gaumukh and Gangotri's waters.

---

[18] Stephen Alter, *Sacred Waters—A Pilgrimage Up the Ganges River to the Source of Hindu Culture*, Harcourt, New York, 2001, p. 65.

[19] Ibid, p. 66.

"I don't know," he replies. "But as a Hindu I would say that after this dam starts functioning I think the real Ganga will only be found down to Uttarkashi."

So that does mean the Ganga below somehow won't be the real Ganga? Nidish yo-yos all over the place. In the same sentence he can wear two different hats; as a respected environmentalist (he's a member of the government's Advisory Panel on Ecology and Tourism), and then back to his old line as a devout Hindu whose faith trumps his knowledge of Himalayan ecology.

"I'm not a scientist, but this is what I believe. At Varanasi the water is already like a sewer and people are drinking it and bathing in it, and they are alive and well. So the faith will always be there, but I don't think the water will have the same properties."

Nidish says he's never been in favor of this dam. He's lived through the earthquake in 1991 that levelled Uttarkashi. It measured 7.8 on the Richter scale and killed three thousand people. As he reminds me: "Uttarkashi from Tehri is just about one and a half hours drive." Anyway, what will happen to the silt that will build up behind the dam? No one seems to have taken that into account. And if the dam does break, Rishikesh, Haridwar, even Bijnor (site of yet another dam), a hundred kilometers south of Haridwar will be washed away.

Nidish's solution would be to encourage the building of small check dams and local energy generation through micro-turbines. "In Switzerland I have seen small turbines that can generate electricity for fifty, a hundred houses, a small village, and it doesn't cost much. Just two people to look after the turbine. Whereas here you have thousands of people working. And for what? This is not safe for this size project."

He says this alternative is already being used here in Garhwal. "There's a place in Garhwal we call the Valley of Flowers. There's a lot of water there, there's a river, and the Government of India has done a wonderful job. They installed small turbines and they generated electricity. Now I admit the people who maintain the turbines are not engineers and so when the turbines break down there's no one to fix them, but the idea is good."

Small is indeed still beautiful. But engineers usually prefer the grandeur and glory, the politicians and contractors moolah — lots of it.[20] Where's the profit in sustainable development? This is something that really gets Nidish going.

"Tehri Dam is going to be a disaster for the country in the coming years. To run a hydroelectricity project you need water, not sand. One

---

[20] Moolah is nineteenth century American slang for money.

day that whole lake will be full of silt. And then where the hell is my government is going to throw all that sand? Tehri is going to become a white elephant. Concrete jungles are not balanced ecology."

~

Harbijan Singh, our driver, becomes rather excitable on the road from Tehri to Devaprayag. Maybe it's the hairpin bends, but he seems to imagine himself behind the wheel of a Formula One racing car. Much squealing of brakes in protest when Harbijan insists on trying to pass slower vehicles on blind corners without any guard rails. Martine is uncharacteristically nervous and resorts to gallows humour. I feel unusually calm — maybe years of driving in India have finally anaesthetized me.

But of course we make it. At Devaprayag, the soon-to-be neutered Bhagirathi merges with the Alaknanda flowing from Badrinath. Visually it's quite striking — Bhagirathi muddy brown because of all the construction silt from Tehri upstream, and Alaknanda smooth green. Anish explains that Bhagirathi is all fury because its gradient is much steeper than that of the Alaknanda just here. For two hundred meters the two colors (and rivers) run chastely side by side, no contact. Here, they overcome their shyness and mingle furiously.

Devaprayag itself forms a rocky *V* where the two rivers meet, although one pilgrim, Sunil Kumar, swears there is a third river, the always invisible Saraswati.[21] It joins them in another triveni[22] under the Raghunath temple that was established by the great ninth-century Hindu reformer Shankaracharya to mark the rock where Rama stood and performed tapasya after defeating Ravana at Lanka. Before the advent of the motorized yatra, this was the first place of worship on the char dham yatra.

Sunil is an electronics engineer from Mumbai who comes here every year to visit his parents. Our conversation is interrupted by the constant ringing of his cell phone — clients calling from Mumbai. "I'll get to it on Monday. I'm out of station right now," he says.

I routinely ask him my standard question about bathing in Ganga to wash away one's sins. He looks blank: "Sorry I couldn't get it." I

---

[21] I had always assumed the Saraswati was imaginary until I read frequent references to it in a very serious and sober account of scaling Nanda Devi in the 1930s. It flows into the Alaknanda and is very real, at least in the Himalayas. Cf Eric Shipton and H.W. Tilman's *Nanda Devi: Exploration and Ascent,* Baton Wicks, London 1999. References to Saraswati at the Sangam in Allahabad are a different matter entirely.

[22] A triveni is a meeting of three rivers.

repeat the question. "No, no, it's not like that. This is just tradition, not religion." Sunil returns to his cell phone. Hirilal Bhat, a purohit in his sixties and with Shaivite marks across his forehead, tells me in a rich, gravelly voice that he was born here and also spends part of the year in Badrinath where his family now lives.

When someone dies the soul can only go to heaven if the rituals are performed at Devaprayag (Vishnu's navel), Badrinath (Vishnu's forehead), or Gaya in Bihar (Vishnu's feet). "But the navel is the most worthy of worship," he says. It doesn't matter when you do the pooja — it can be ten, twenty years after the person has died, just in one of these three places. Not Allahabad or Varanasi or Haridwar, but here, in Badrinath or Gaya, none of them exactly easy to get to.

Another pilgrim, Gita, says she saw me at the opening of the temple in Gangotri. This is her first visit to Devaprayag. I tease her, "What took you so long?" Stupid question. "Till it calls you, you can't come," she tells me. Gita is holding on to the chains that prevent the current washing one away. She has none of Sunil Kumar's doubts. "I came here because I have been told that if I bathe here my sins are washed away. I'll drink Ganga jal and I'll take some back with me across the mountains to Jammu."

~

We drive on a bit more sedately to Rishikesh. I always assumed Rishikesh must have some rich religious significance. It is indeed where the journey to the four shrines of the char dham yatra — Yamnotri, Gangotri, Kedarnath and Badrinath — begins, but that's all. The name means "the hairs of the saint." Nidish can remember a time when only sadhus lived here. "There were ashrams all over, especially on the other side. Rishikesh was then a small, small village."

Today, the site is well-known as a backpacker magnet; young Westerners are drawn to its numerous, well-endowed ashrams, which are built into thickly wooded mountainsides. The river here is broad and moves swiftly, full of mahseer fish and sparkling in the sun. It's become very fashionable to whitewater raft down to Rishikesh from beaches a few kilometers upstream.

Rishikesh was also the source of the first landmark Indian Supreme Court decision in the mid-1980s to close down toxic chemical emissions from a photographic plant that was polluting Ganga. A young Delhi lawyer, M.C. Mehta, brought a suit against the company and won. The Supreme Court subsequently extended the ban on industrial pollution to cover the entire Ganga. This jump-started an environmental legislation movement to clean up the river that would result in the 1986 Ganga Action Plan (GAP).

Today, Rishikesh is a fashionable place to retire to — good climate, nice scenery, walks in the mountains. It's especially suitable if you are religious. It's also openly commercial. God is big business. Officially, a night at any ashram is free; you leave a donation plus one rupee. In return you can expect a private room with hot shower, telephone, and television. Now you're expected to leave a donation of several hundred rupees.

We'd arranged to meet Swami Chidenand at the Parmath Niketan ashram. The swami has a slogan "Clean, Green, Serene" and calls the huge donations he brings in premiums to his "Divine Insurance Company."

My interest in the swami is simple. If the Ganga cleanup is ever to become a reality it probably has to be through men whom ordinary Indians — aad aadmi — can trust and follow. Who are better placed than religious leaders? But while the swami is a charming and articulate man, his answers are too formulaic and glib for my tastes. Cleaning the banks of the river, building latrines in villages to prevent people defecating directly into Ganga, instituting an evening aarti ceremony that really is one of the most professional and musical in the entire length of Ganga. Why do I still feel something is missing?

It's not the discrepancies between the swami's slogans and what actually happens on the ground. The man is a salesman, on the go round the clock. I can't really blame him if practical details are passed over. And how can you criticize a man who is trying to increase awareness about daily mistreatment of the river?

No, it's what's left out that bothers me. Nowhere in all the religious discourse is there any acknowledgment of the deeper danger, the real reason Ganga can die. Indians are simply taking too much water out of her. It's like a hospital that needs more and more blood transfusions for its operations. Their surgeries get more and more complicated and wonderful and costly in terms of blood. One day there are no more donors. Then what do you do? India's insatiable thirst for electricity and irrigation is normal. But it surely has to be met by other means than just Ganga.

Haridwar

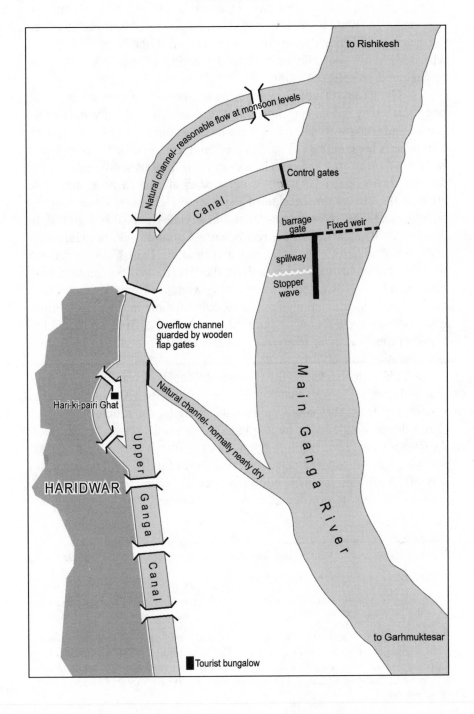

The dilemma is obvious in even starker terms at Haridwar. The Ganga breaks out of the Himalayas and enters the plains at Haridwar,[23] which literally means the "gateway of the gods." Haridwar is of supreme importance in Hindu mythology and culture. It is one of four places where the gods spilled amrit when they were churning the oceans. It's also where Vishnu's foot allegedly pierced the skin of the Milky Way by mistake and so released Ganga.[24]

Ganga at Haridwar resembles an anaemic version of the same river just thirty kilometers north at Rishikesh. It's already noticeably slower and shallower. Here and there large sandbanks cut it into several channels. A huge barrage[25] has allowed engineers to divert a lot of water sideways towards the bathing ghats to satisfy religious sentiments. At the famous Hari-ki-pairi Ghat the water rushes at such a pace that most cling to the chains on the side of the concrete channel. Once past the bathing ghat, the river calms down and divides: part flowing straight down in the Ganga Canal, the rest heading left and back into Ganga.

It was here, over 150 years ago, that the British committed the first massive environmental assault on the river, albeit for humanitarian reasons. They constructed an engineering wonder of the world — a four hundred mile-long canal to alleviate repeated famine in the Doab region. It's working even today — built of local bricks, fired at such high temperatures that even today they allow almost no water to penetrate, and operating entirely by gravity.[26]

The British pacified the Hindu priests at Haridwar by cutting a six foot-wide slit in the weir that controls the flow of the river into the canal system. This way, they could maintain the mythological article of faith that Ganga flows unimpeded by human agency down to the sea. In the monsoon the Ganga Canal diverts a tiny fraction of the river's flow into the canal, but in the lean season it can take the entire flow of the river. The irrigation network eradicated famines, but it has been so successful that it has now spawned an entire region of water-thirsty sugarcane farms. The prosperous

---

[23] Followers of the god Vishnu spell it as Haridwar; devotees of Shiva Haridvar.

[24] Yet another version of the origin of the river.

[25] A barrage is another name for a weir. For the differences between a barrage and a dam, see Chapter 7, pp. 188.

[26] Rajpal Singh, the former chief engineer of the canal, told me Kipling wrote about the actual construction of the canal in his story "The Bridge Builders." It's a fine story but I wonder — that story is about a railway bridge that gets swept away in the monsoon. It's found in Rudyard Kipling's *Collected Stories*, Everyman Library, London, 1906, pp.439-476.

farmers are a major electoral vote bank courted by politicians of all stripes. The Doab has indeed been saved, but at what price to Ganga?

Ironically, it's democracy (of all things) that is responsible for the de-watering[27] of Ganga. Everywhere in the thirsty northern plains dams have been built and farmers encouraged to draw down the water of the Ganga for commercial agricultural use. But so little water is left that pollution is exacerbated for large parts of the year. Only the monsoon finally washes it away.

Everywhere in the pristine Himalayas there are huge pressures on a finite stream of water as India gallops towards modernization and there is a constant demand for ever more electricity. Can India ever generate enough? Without its being diverted illegally and ingeniously for the have-nots and the greedy? But that is another story entirely.

Nothing better epitomizes the physical and moral dilemmas facing Ganga than the Ganga Canal. It was designed to carry six thousand cusecs.[28] This doesn't sound like very much, but in the dry season before the monsoon that's just about all the water there is in the entire river. No problem, of course, once the monsoon breaks, because the amount of water increases a hundredfold. The former chief engineer of the canal, Rajpal Singh welcomes the Tehri dam because he says it will smooth out peaks and troughs and regulate year-round flow of Ganga.

Neither the British nor their Indian successors at the canal are evil exploiters of a natural resource. In the first instance famine was averted; in the second farmers are asking for the water and it brings prosperity to rural India. One can argue that irrigation water goes to the wrong sort of farmers and the wrong sort of crops. But would Ganga really be nursed back to health if sugarcane, rice, or eucalyptus were pulled up? To be replaced by what?

How many Indians were there when the Ganga Canal was built? Maybe two hundred million? And today? One billion and counting. How many Indians lived in cities and towns, whose inhabitants consume ten times as much water as villagers? Who would dare tell ordinary Indians that development and modernization has to stop because it's straining natural resources? Economists will argue that the market will push entrepreneurs to find ways to produce water artificially and store it until needed. Great in science fiction. But in reality? In a democracy it is the people who decide, and if they decide to suck Ganga dry, can one prevent them?

---

[27] De-watering is the term geographers use to describe taking more water out of a river than flows in through aquifers and tributaries.

[28] Cubic feet per second.

~

That evening we attend the obligatory aarti at Hari-ki-pairi. We turn up a bit early and walk across the pedestrian bridges built for the Kumbh Mela here in 2004[29] to the auspicious ghat. Pandas are sitting under awnings waiting for business. There appears to be little happening, so I stop and talk to Harish Ajnish Kumar, who is sitting cross-legged on a wooden daybed, sheltered from rain by a bamboo and plastic awning, bundled in the obligatory brown woollen sweater that most Indians seem to put on as soon as the weather starts to turn cooler. I've always been fascinated about what a panda actually does.

Harish corrects me: "Panda is slang. The proper word is purohit. You find us only at tirthas.[30] Our job is to pray on behalf of our customers because we know all the mantras. So people come here for christening ceremony, a barsi [a ceremony one year after someone has died], a havan mundan [a head shaving ceremony] or a pind daan [offering of the ashes and bones], then we do the prayers for them."

His family have been doing this for five generations for anyone living from Rajasthan or Delhi. But Harish Ajnish is pessimistic. His children are not interested in following in his footsteps. They want white-collar financial security in an office. His youngest is interested in computers.

Other things are changing too. Earlier his clientele were uniquely from within India. But now people come from all over the world, and not just NRIs, but non-Hindus from Europe, North America, especially South Africa. "Many of them have adopted the Hindu religion," which goes to show how out-of-touch I am. I had no idea. To become a panda he took a BA in Hindu religious studies at university; 'but there were no practicals so I came to a special purohit school here in Haridwar where I learnt all the mantras and shastras from acharyas and Vedic scholars, and how to perform particular ceremonies. You have so many different ceremonies — for a dead person or a newborn. The school is called Karam Kand Siksha Samiti (Rites and Rituals Teaching Society)."

Business has been slow today. Just two customers who wanted him to perform the pind daan pooja "for their ancestors. They brought the asthi to be immersed after the prayers." I mention that the ashes of

---

[29] The last Ardh Kumbh Mela was held in Haridwar between February and April 2004. See the glossary for further details.

[30] See Chapter 4.

Indu and Vijay's fathers and grandfathers[31] were all brought up here to be immersed. Since they come from Rajasthan they could have well come to him. Indu told me he has a book that records all their family history going back many generations. Is that true? Can I see it?

His assistant asks Harish Ajnish if he should fetch the book? "Yes, let them see it." The "book" is like no other. Long narrow sheets folded back on one another like the automatic towels you used to find in public wash rooms, all bound with cloth and string and maybe two-feet-thick. To open you unfold and peel back. Everything is there, recorded meticulously in longhand. "These are the records for New Delhi and Rajasthan. There are over twenty-five hundred pandas here at Haridwar and we each have a different area, even a different district, and a different caste. These go back three, four hundred years."

"This is a new bahi [register]. Which one did you get? Wrong one." He sends the assistant off for a really venerable register. He triumphantly returns with another one for Samvat 1861. "This is about 170 years old, but we have some that go back seven hundred years." Harish Ajnish peers and reads out an entry written in Hindi: "I can't read this name. You see each person has different handwriting." He looks at it more closely: "It is written here, Jwala Das, son of Kanhaiya Lal, grandson of Shiv Shankar Dayal. Names of the brothers, father, and grandfather. This is a record from a certain village, from a certain family. On such and such a date this person came and I did a prayer for him."

Nidish wants to know what Samvat 1861 translates into in terms of the Roman calendar. Do you subtract 104 from the Roman calendar? Harish Ajnish becomes impatient. "Oh no, I will do the calculations myself. You have to subtract 143, not 104." This gets tortuous. The Hindu Vikram Samvat Calendar at any given point of time is fifty seven years ahead of the Roman Gregorian calendar. So Samvat 1861 will be 1804 AD. Or is it? They continue to get tied up in knots subtracting and adding.

This is getting us nowhere. I change the subject: "Why is Haridwar so important in Hinduism?" That's simple. It's because of the Brahmakund. I'm uncertain what he's referring to: "What's the Brahma Kund?" Harish Ajnish points to his right: "Brahma Kund is a little pond just over there, by the Hari-ki-pairi Ghat."

Tell me more. "It is a very old story," he says. (A new story would be something unusual in India.) "It is like this. In our India, the

---

[31] Indu and Vijay Agarwal, originally from Rajasthan, now live in Mumbai.

ocean was churned between the devils and gods. And this produced a kumbh or pot, which was kept in four places — Nasik, Ujjain, Allahabad, and Haridwar, here at the Brahmakund, which is also where Lord Brahma created the world. He performed a yagya [sacrifice] right here so this place is called Brahmakund. This is the reason why Haridwar is considered a holy city. Because we feel that the formation of the universe started from here. Come, I'll show you."

"I thought Vishnu's footstep was also here?" I ask. "No problem. I'll show you that too. It's inside the temple next to the Brahmakund."

The panda moves very swiftly down the stone ghat, up steps, down steps. Both Nidish and I struggle to keep him in sight. Just when we're sure we've lost him, he pops up. "This is the Brahmakund, from here up to the temple, which is very old, it is from the seventeenth century. It is a temple of the time of Akbar. Lord Vishnu's feet are in there. I will show you. I will be back in a minute."

And he disappears, never to return! Luckily Balram Gairola Shastri, priest of the Shri Hari Charan mandir, comes to the rescue and shows me the footprint.

"Vishnuji stood right here." But what he shows me is just a modern plaster cast. My skepticism shows. "Where are the real feet?" He lifts a stone slab to reveal dainty size ten footprints set into marble. I am underwhelmed.

The priest laments. His children will not be taking over when he retires. One is in Dubai, the other studying for his B.A. in communications He then proceeds to give me yet another version of how Ganga came down to earth, this time from the sweat of Vishnu's toe when he became over-excited, watching a beautiful young woman dance.

Dusk is fast approaching and we want to leave soon to get back over the other side of the water and watch the evening aarti. I ask a final question, which I think innocuous and fairly innocent. Wrong!

"If I bathe in the river what will happen to me?" I ask. I have pressed the wrong button! "Please don't call this a river. She is Ganga ji."

"Yes, but what will happen to me?" I ask. "All the sins in the body that have been there for many lives will finally come to an end," he replies, continuing "*Yada yada yanti nirop jahanvi, rudandti papani vadanti cha priya. Are, kritghna, nirattam naradhama.* All the sins in our body — physical, mental, verbal."

"And if I drink the water of Ganga?" Wrong choice of word again!

"This is not water, this is amrit [nectar]. The diseases in our body are removed. This is a medicine," he replies.

"When I drank this amrit at Gomukh I was told that I would live for a hundred years." I say. "Correct," he replies. "It is written *'Jeeviyeshah shardah shatam.'* You can live for more than one hundred years."

*****

Ganga from Haridwar to Varanasi[1]

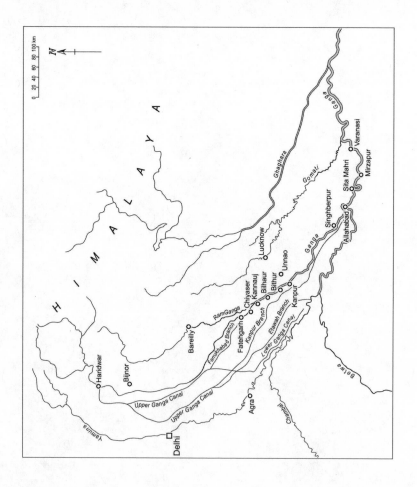

CHAPTER 2

Travels with *Basanti*

The reach of Ganga between Haridwar and Kanpur is less than four hundred kilometers. But it's a Ganga that few ever visit. There's no major town, no crossing by rail, only a handful by road. Ganga here is trimmer than at Rishikesh or Haridwar, muddy brown, not particularly deep — four meters after the monsoon, often less than three feet deep in the dry season (February through May).

Ever since Haridwar, Ganga has taken on a dual role - as goddess and a river whose waters are vital to farmers for irrigation. The issue of water flow becomes central here to understanding the environmental problems plaguing the river downstream. There is simply too much demand and not enough supply of fresh water. But rural India is unconcerned with the future; it lives in the present and the past.

For me it's a chance to see India from its own backyard. Four hundred kilometers to Kanpur, four hundred to Delhi. It might as well be four hundred years away. Previous travelers have been confronted with the nightmare of trying to take a boat down from Haridwar to Kanpur. It really cannot be done, certainly not with any substantial equipment and luggage.

Eric Newby and his wife spent half their book on the frustrating struggle to make more than a few kilometers progress a day without either getting lost or being forced to carry their boats on their backs until they found deeper water. And if that isn't enough, this part of the river is dotted with yet more dams at Bijnor and Naora, impounding the river to generate yet more electricity.

Haridwar signals not just a change in our method of travel but also a new cast of characters. For twenty years Bijoy Tivari has driven us everywhere in India in his Ambassador. Bijoy is slow, obstinate, but utterly reliable and loyal. He is more than a driver; he's a member of the family. For years, Bijoy used to inflict cassettes of my radio programmes on unsuspecting passengers. In turn, he expected me to make an effort to like Anup Jalota. He's from a village an hour north of Allahabad, where his wife still lives. He has four brothers — all of whom I've met at some stage — and four children — three girls and a boy.

Bijoy has been with us in Kolkata, all over West Bengal, to northern Bihar, to Kanpur for three months to record the monsoon, and now Ganga. He's good for my ego: he laughs at my jokes and calls me "chief." He is "little chief" and Martine is "madame." For this yatra though it's been modified to "sister."

Because Bijoy will have to spend so much time alone on land while we're on the river, we've asked Raja Chatterjee to come along to help Tivari and act as an extra interpreter, especially in Bihar and West Bengal. I could go on and on about Raja — how he's unreliable, lazy, has very few practical skills, if any. But others might say the same about me, so let's just leave it at this. Raja can be very exasperating to the point you're ready to brain him, but in the end would probably give his life for me or Martine (or so we'd like to believe).

Nidish is the only element of continuity. He's agreed to come down as far as Kanpur. Then he has to get back to Dehra Dun and the mountains. But we want his professionalism and common sense to rub off on Bijoy and Raja.

Oh, and one other element of continuity, the most important — Martine. She says she's there just to keep me satisfied. I know better. She will run this ship and all its crew, leaving me free to concentrate on making radio.

~

Thoma Gokhale has built us a tiny twelve-foot long boat — *Basanti* — in his boatyard in Kanpur. Thoma and his comrade under sail Captain (Retired) Sudhir Subhedar had surveyed this stretch of Ganga many years ago: they still have the official Topo maps (scale 1:50,000), along with their notes on where to land, where to avoid, where to camp.

Our Indian colleagues are worried about our security, especially above Farrukhabad. One of our scientific advisors, Dr. R.K. Sinha from Patna University, has told us a lurid cautionary tale of a German couple murdered ten years previously in precisely this stretch of the river. I have no idea if the dacoits were ever caught, but Sinha strongly hints they took a fancy to the blond, long-limbed German woman. The husband tried to intervene. Result: both were killed.

So we decide to drive down past Bijnor and Naora, then travel by boat the reach where Thoma and Sudhir have contacts. We take *Basanti* upstream in a Tata truck and put it into the river at Chiyaser just south of Farrukhabad and on the banks of Ganga.

The temple itself is maybe a kilometer from Ganga and the priest Avadh Bihari Das Ayodhyavasi Swamaji claims that Chyavan rishi, who is famous for Chyavanprash strengthening tonic, meditated here for fifty thousand years, before he met Sukanya, daughter of the king.

Sukanya seems to have had confused emotions about the rishi because she poked his eyes out with a stick for fun. Her father therefore banished her to serve the blinded sage. But his eyesight was restored thanks to the Ashwini Kumars, twins who were physicians to the gods and are supposed to have given the ayurvedic system to ancient India. The Ashwini Kumars also made the rishi twenty years young again, so the couple married and lived and loved happily ever after.

Chiyaser is a pretty village, maybe five kilometers off the GT (Grand Trunk) Road. It is surprisingly wooded. I'm so used to forests in India being reduced to isolated clumps that it comes as a shock, a pleasant shock.

The second surprise is how narrow Ganga appears, no more than a hundred meters across, and on the other side just sand and tall Ganga grass. Maps can't help me here. Is the land opposite an island, with the main channel of Ganga flowing in majesty on the far side? Impossible to rely on the official Archaeological Survey of India topographical maps because even they are out-of-date as soon as they're published; that's how much and how fast Ganga can change her course in twelve months.

Chiyaser is also a village still waiting for electricity. Concrete pylons lay scattered across fields and in the yard of the Gopinath Adar Vidyali Chiyaser school, where the principal, Hari Babu Agnihotri, offers us the school compound to pitch our tents and cook our evening meal in security once school is over for the day.

However, before any of this we need to go down to Ganga and see where we can launch our boat, and find some boatmen. At the last moment Chhunar, a boatman I've worked with for several years near Kanpur, failed to report for duty with his mates. Urgent calls on the mobile: he's holding out for more money. Thoma says forget him.

"Go up to Chiyaser and pick up a couple of local boatmen who also know the area. They'll cost you a fraction of what you'd pay Chhunar." And with that parting advice we set out from Kanpur with *Basanti*, two oars and no crew.

At the river in Chiyaser, a small ferry is returning with six bicycles and their riders lined port to starboard across its mid-section in perfect symmetry like a squad of soldiers. When it arrives, I ask if we can go across next trip, so we pay five rupees a head, sit down and wait while the boat fills up.

The travelers are mostly returning to their villages on the other side — Dehliya, Jivanpurva, Nikamanpur. The furthest of these is ten kilometres away, so the other bank isn't an island and there isn't another main channel. This *is* Ganga. Most have come over this morning to work or go to market at Kannauj. Now they're going home. Most, but not all. A confident voice says: "Some people are from Chiyaser and they are coming for the ride only because of you."

Everyone's on board now so we set sail. In no time we're over, the villagers have disembarked and the waiting passengers are clambering on board. That confident voice, a young man called Bimal, offers us his tiffin. "Have food?"

I politely decline. I eat too much anyway and the last thing I should be doing is taking precious food away from these villagers.

Raja doesn't share my scruples: "What is the food? How is it?" Bimal shows him: sabji, aloo, and roti. Raja thinks long and hard and then senses it's better to decline. Bimal dips a metal cup over the side of the ferry, scoops it full of water.

"Do you drink Ganga jal every day?" Routine question.

"Of course. The water is good. It keeps. It never gets worms." It doesn't look very clean to me. I can't even see the bottom of the cup. Bimal concedes, "During the rains it is somewhat dirty. We don't drink it during the rains."

A traveling salesman lifts his bicycle on to the ferry. Tied to the carrier is a small pile of cotton shirts and dresses. His name is Hasruddin. He lives near Chiyaser, and had taken the ferry over to the villages on the north bank early this morning.

"How many pieces have you sold?" Raja asks. "It's a loss. I only sold four pieces, just twenty rupees." Hasruddin proffers that anyway during the monsoon it's hard to get across to do any business.

In no time at all we're back at Chiyaser. Everyone gets off, bikes are wheeled down a plank on to the mud and then the travellers straggle up the path next to a banyan tree and on to the network of dirt roads that lead to yet more paths along fields, and to home.

Before we get down I ask the ferryman, Mandrisharan, a tall young man in a check shirt, how business is. He explains he's been doing it for five years now. His family has done it for as long as he can remember, and his children will probably follow in his footsteps. He started at seven this morning. The last ferry is at eight o'clock. He worships Ganga because it gives him his livelihood.

"But I have to pay forty-five thousand rupees a year to the government in Lucknow for this ferry concession." Forty-five thousand is a lot (equivalent to a thousand U.S. dollars).

"So how much did you make last month?" I ask. "In September I made five thousand rupees." The only consolation is that he does own the boat. But even allowing for lucrative months from say October until early June, that's still only eight months a year of steady income, and all the while the government is waiting for its cut. If he can't pay there will be plenty of others who will. A motorboat would drive them all out of business. "I've thought about it. But it won't happen. Not enough passengers willing to pay that much," Mandrisharan replies. I hope he's right.

Before we leave, Bimal agrees to row us down to Kanpur over the next few days for a quarter of the price Chhunar in Bithur wanted. He will bring along an assistant and his own food and bedding. "Meet you here at eight o'clock tomorrow morning."

Back at the Gopinath Adar Vidyali Chiyaser school, Nidish and Bijoy have been chopping vegetables and preparing dinner. As always, night falls very quickly everywhere in India. In the dusk I look for some Bisleri water, find a bottle, take a swig, splutter, spit, and swear at my own stupidity. This is the cooking oil bottle. In the dark they looked and felt similar. The others think this is hilarious. Bijoy's still laughing about it four months later.

The headmaster, Hari Babu Agnihotri, has been waiting behind to talk with me. Brahmin, pandit, school principal, Hari Babu, of course, begins his day with a dip in Ganga before coming to school. Its full Sanskrit name is *Lomahish Sanskrit Mahavidyalaya, Uncha Goshahi, Kannauj. Lomas Rishi Sanskrit Vidyalaya, Unchha Gorshai, Gun Kannauj*, which he then proceeds to rattle off at a rate of knots.

Nidish is a bit taken aback. "Sanskrit Mahavidyalaya will be ok, my friend."

Hari Babu opened the school because the nearest government school was more than three kilometers away. There are presently five hundred pupils, ages five to fourteen who will have to go on to high school elsewhere. But Hari Babu hopes his school will soon be able to offer the final two years of education so students can do all their education at his school. Although this is a government-accredited school, Hari Babu gets no subsidy; the younger pupils pay five rupees a month, the older ones in classes six to eight pay ten rupees.

We hold the obligatory conversation about Ganga, how she was brought down to earth, purifies the soul of sin and so on. But the good pandit is not going to let this opportunity pass. He launches into a stream of Sanskrit: *Ganga yaa darshanaat mukti* (when you see Ganga it liberates your soul).

I try out my wit on Hari Babu: "Your soul may go straight to heaven but if the Ganga is flooding in the monsoon it also may take your home to heaven." Hari Babu luckily finds this hilarious. "That is correct. Something that profits us can also harm us. We lose crops and land, and it's hard to get around during monsoon."

"So you still think that this is a sacred river." Maybe one day I'll get a totally unexpected answer, but not from Hari Babu. He talks of holy dips at full and no moon days, and the powers of Ganga jal every day: "Otherwise we are not purified." And of course he never gets sick. "Just saying Ganga, Ganga removes all illness." To reassure himself he recites the sloka at top speed:

"*Ganga, ganga, ti yovruyat, yojananaam shatairathi. Munchhate sarv papanaam, paap jaat rasaatalam.*"

He then thoughtfully offers his own English translation: "By saying the words *ganga ganga, yojananaam shatairapi*, the sins run away for thousands of miles, merely upon hearing the name of the Ganga. Total satisfaction of the soul and prosperity for all my family."

"And your staff here at the school?" I ask.

"Even they have faith in Bhagwati Bhagirathi. Everyone has faith. The people in the area all have affection for her." He sets off again on another Sanskrit sloka:

"*Ganga paapam, shashi taapam, dainihm kalpataru satah. Paapam taapam cha hi dainihm, hansa jansamanama,*" he declaims.

"See, when we get up in the morning, *Bhagwati tav teere, neer matra sanoham, vigat vishaya trishna Krishna maradayami, sakal kalush bhange, swarga sopaan sange, taral tal tarange, devi gange prasiddhah* is the sloka we recite," he tells me, then reverts to slokas.

"*Namaami gange stavpaad pankajam, susaasure bhitim bhukti muktim; bhuktim cha muktim cha dadaati nityam, bhaavaanusaren na yathaa naraasani.*"

Nidish doesn't know whether to laugh or to cry. "Today is very difficult for me. I've never learnt Sanskrit in my life. I am sorry about that."[2]

Our first night under canvas. We unfold sleeping bags, put out the fire, take our plastic mugs and go to perform our respective ablutions in the field outside the school compound, and settle down to a cacophony of bhajans and howling dogs. One of them, growling, sniffs by my head in the tent. I hold my breath. He lopes away and I go off to sleep.

---

[2] Hari Babu says that only two or three people in the village actually speak Sanskrit, and they are all members of the same family.

~

Next morning we set out on the river on time. Of course, half the village (so it seems) is there to wave us off. Bimal reports for duty with his assistant Bipin, a slight young man of twenty, who seems to do most of the work while Bimal exercises his management skills — alternately eating or sleeping. Because *Basanti* is so small we carry the minimum of supplies to last us till we make land each evening. Martine looks at ease on the water; Nidish and I are obvious landlubbers. You can see it in our eyes. We pose in our boat. The village kids gawk, make rude and ribald comments under their breaths. And then we're off.

Progress is slow. The oars, like the boat, are toy-like. We manage on an average of thirty kilometers a day. The river has extravagant meanders. Often we can see a landmark but it takes forever to reach it. Everywhere the "put-put" of pumps lifting the precious water as local farmers tap the river to irrigate their fields.

This gets me wondering: these farmers are prosperous thanks to Ganga because their crops are highly water-dependent. But what happens to the run off from the other ingredient in their success? Fertilizers and pesticides? C.K. Jain, one of the few Indian scientists who has studied this form of pollution (called non-point source pollution), warns that India may be storing up giant environmental problems in the long run because the emerging evidence suggests farmers are unwittingly poisoning the ground water. As they draw down the water table oxygen fills the vacuum; otherwise-harmless metals such as arsenic get transformed by the addition of the oxygen into potentially lethal compounds.

Unfazed by this potential silent spring,[3] villagers everywhere here engage with their river in customs and rituals light years removed from urban, modern India and its frenetic pursuit of Lakshmi or wealth. The month — any month — is delineated by two dates, the full moon and no moon.

Everywhere along the river banks villagers are celebrating the anticipated purnima or full moon with bathing and head-shaving ceremonies. Multiple pennants mark individual villages which have come to the river for the day, for their dip. At some places where the land slopes gradually into Ganga, orange flames and healthy black smoke mark where funeral pyres burn fiercely.

---

[3] Rachel Carson's book *Silent Spring* has become shorthand for environmental poisoning no one notices until the damage has been done.

In small villages that slope down to the river, children and adults lovingly wash buffaloes, soaping their backs with shampoo. Everywhere there's a feeling of festivity, but also of being in a lonely quarter of northern India. It is of course anything but empty here, yet one gets a very real sense of the fact that these are areas which are forgotten by the breathless electronic headlines about terrorism and political shenanigans in Lucknow or New Delhi.

We are witnesses here to unforgettable images, without which India would not be India — a huge flat-bottomed ferry transporting a solitary buffalo across the river, another boat almost invisible under a mountain of fodder that slowly topples over into the water before our gaze, like the lorries that capsize the length of the GT road.

Graceful white herons pick their way along newly-formed sandbanks like so many slender fashion models on the runway in Mumbai. And then, far off in the haze, another oddity: a Hero bike parked on the water, no rider in sight. Close up, it turns out to be an optical illusion. It's standing on a sandbar while the owner goes off to cut Ganga grass to take back to his village that evening. A bloated animal carcass floats past little *Basanti*. Farmers pull their tractors up to the river's edge; armies of villagers disgorge themselves, bathe, eat, and chat in the warmth of a late October midday.

Bimal let slip this morning that his grandfather used to regularly row fifty quintals of Dusheri mangoes down to Kanpur in summer, presumably when the river was in flood, once the monsoon had broken. The current would fairly hum then, so it used to take him two or three days; of course the boat was probably bigger than *Basanti*.

"Wasn't that dangerous? Going to Kanpur in the rains?" I've seen Ganga in late July and it didn't strike me as a picnic. Plus that boat that we just saw capsize was quite large.

"No, it was not dangerous because we know our water." Bimal admits he's never personally taken mangoes down-river. He ferries people from place to place, but he used to be a teacher at Hari Babu's school in Chiyaser. So why did he quit for what would seem, on the face of things, to be the not so lucrative job of boatman? To cut a long story short, Bimal matriculated, in fact has an MA (acharya)[4] and then applied to study for a Bachelor of Education, necessary if you want to be a schoolteacher. As usual there was a catch.

---

[4] See Glossary.

"I didn't have the one lakh twenty thousand rupees they demanded to bribe my admission." Three times he applied, three times he was rejected. Bimal says things are alright: "I can earn enough as a boatman and also as a middleman for selling boats." He has a house, wife, and daughters. But he regrets he couldn't follow his first love.

We are making very slow progress, maybe because only Bipin is rowing while Bimal talks. Bimal assures me we'll make Kannauj before the end of the afternoon. Martine has been lulled fast asleep by the rhythms of the oars and the afternoon heat.

On the bank a large boat is being dragged up against the current. Bimal says they once dragged a big boat back to Chiyaser from Kannauj, six of them. It took two days, one dragging, the others steering and rowing. A mile further on we hear bhajans from what appears to be a celebration of some sort. Nidish asks Bimal if it's a wedding.

"Eh what? No, it's somebody's havan mundan (head shaving ceremony)."

"So what is the age for a mundan here?" Nidish asks.

"Here we shave their heads usually when they're a year old. But that one looks to be nearer five."

We're tempted to move nearer the bank but Bimal advises us to stay out in the midstream, not because the current is stronger but to avoid getting stopped by any goondas. A few miles back the Kali flowed in from the south. Now we come abreast of the Ramganga. The latter drains the Shivalik hills and is a substantial river.

Bipin shouts, "Susuwa, Susawa. Over there!" Where? By the time I've swivelled round whatever it is has disappeared. Does he mean a Susu — a Gangetic dolphin? I've only ever read about them and this seems very far north to sight one. Bimal's excited: "Susawa is big, maybe one hundred kilos. Like a buffalo under water. Just keep looking over there. It is somewhere here. See, there it is." Once again Nidish and I turn our heads, too late. I remember similar frustrations in the Sundarbans looking to see crocodiles. Everyone else spotted them except me.

Two months later, in Patna, R.K. Sinha, a leading authority on the Gangetic dolphin, explains why we sighted them so far north. Where two or more rivers meet the currents churn up the mud and the small fish that the dolphins feed on.

It is just our luck to camp the first night in the grounds of an ashram on the eve of the purnima. In the middle of the night we are awakened by sounds of a violent attack. The fate of that murdered German couple flashes across my mind.

At breakfast, Nidish casually asks if anybody's sleep has been disturbed during the night. Tivari says nothing but smiles. He knows the answer to the question because he was part of the ruckus last night. At four o'clock early this morning, two truckloads of noisy male bathers arrived in our field to take their dip at the auspicious hour and Tivari had joined them in their boisterous revelry. Raja snored right through it all.

At eight o'clock, everywhere near the ashram people are taking their holy dip with much laughter and joy. Once clear of Kannauj, however, human presence falls off markedly, with the exception of solitary men encountered undressing or getting redressed, the ubiquitous bike parked alongside on the bank. I'm immediately struck by how little human activity there actually is on the river. We scarcely see anyone that or any other day, and when we do see one we reel him in as tenaciously as a fisherman who's unexpectedly got a bite on his line.

The poor unfortunate is one Gangaram. He's crouched on one end of his boat, blue bandana wound loosely round his head, in white undershirt and blue shorts, punting his craft with a long oar against the current. He's obviously unhappy we've rowed over to talk with him, and answers Nidish's questions in monosyllables.

Q: "What do you catch here?" A: "Fish." Q: "What type of fish?" A: "We catch fish in a net." But once Nidish convinces him we're not river police, he at least expands to multiple sentences: "[We catch] Krauchi, Chhilkaari, Digharia. I have cast my net many times but not got anything today. Look, there's nothing in the bottom of the boat."

Gangaram says he hasn't seen many fish in Ganga this year. I know that almost all fishermen all over the world will always tell you fish catches are down because of weather or misguided politicians; they somehow manage to make a living and rarely admit that over fishing or other human misdeeds could be responsible for reduced catches.

On cue, Gangaram reads from the script. "Yes, there were more fish earlier. We don't know what has happened." Martine plays devil's advocate. "Do you think anyone is maybe putting stuff in the water [i.e., chemical and other toxic pollutants] that could kill the fish?"

Gangaram doesn't think so. It can't be pollution because "we find plenty of young fish and we can tell if they're diseased. They wouldn't lay their eggs if the river was polluted. Anyway, what you call dirt is the very food fish eat." Gangaram blames reduced flow in the river, an interesting observation.

If he had anything worth eating we'd have bought it off him but his boat really is bare. Gangaram tells us when he does catch fish he sells them in the local bazaar in Kannauj or in his village.

Very little fishing, no transporting crops or goods up and down. The only boats on the river are wooden ferries crossing laterally. The life of a ferryman must therefore be quite lucrative. Bimal confirms what Mandrisharan told us back in Chiyaser — lucrative for the government, not the ferryman. The government auctions off the right to make a living from ferrying people across. Why such a huge river and nobody working it? Bimal's answer is fatalistic: "What can we do with this river?"

I counter that in most civilizations rivers have been the catalyst for a variety of industries — grinding corn, saw mills, any number of occupations central to an economy making the transition from agricultural to industrial, from rural to urban. Bimal looks blank. All he knows is how to ferry people across from one bank to another.

Nidish adds: "We cannot produce the power on our own, that's one thing. That is illegal. Another thing is, we cannot collect the sand to sell it in the market. All these sand beaches, they are auctioned by the government every year and then only the contractors who have that contract, they are allowed to sell that sand. Which means that again it is the role of a middleman who is there, who is making money and these people, off and on they get work as labourers. And they earn seventy rupees, sixty rupees, fifty rupees that's all."

In other words, no private initiative on the river — quite extraordinary.

We've accosted Gangaram at the beginning of a length of steep cliffs. They're pockmarked with holes half way up. I ask Bimal to move closer. A whole new world comes into focus. At the entrance to each hole sits a green parrot guarding the entrance to a nest. Doves, kingfishers, and humming birds are watching us from their ringside seats far above. And owls. Bimal says they're serpent eagles.

The "owl" takes off, dives down into the water and swoops back up, a snake wriggling in its beak. Seeing a serpent eagle take wing is one of the wonders of the natural world — huge wingspan, sand and brown markings, and when it lands it transforms itself back into a beady-eyed owl, watching and waiting. At the base of the cliff tiny turtles take fright at our approach and plop down into the water from mud clumps.

The river appears in rude health in this "empty quarter." Which is more than can be said for us this afternoon. We come to a broad stretch of river with at least four channels. In the haze and with a flat horizon there's no way of telling which ones are blind alleys, which will lead us out into an open river. In despair we hail Chhotelal, a fisherman who actually has caught four bacchuaas that morning. He points out the correct channel (the longest) and we get back on track.

That evening we camp at Nanamou Ghat in Bilhaur, in another ashram, this one sandy and shaded by mango trees. Thoma and Sudhir had recommended, wherever possible, camping in ashrams because they offer security off the beaten track.

After just two days there's a general consensus emerging that we've already reached and gone beyond the limits of Nidish's cooking. I know Bijoy is a better consumer of food than preparer and Raja can't even boil an egg. My vegetarian cuisine is very limited and I wouldn't eat it unless desperate, so we ask Nidish and Tivari to go into the town, find a dhaba (as a driver Tivari will always find the best one) and bring back dinner. While they're gone I phone up Kalayani, Nidish's wife, back in Dehra Dun.

"Does Nidish cook at home?" I ask her.

"He told you he could cook?" she replies, shocked. "In his imagination!"

The subject is never again discussed. In future, by unspoken mutual agreement, Nidish's cooking will limit itself to making tea and dispensing high altitude medicine.

Raja has shuffled off to see the swami of the ashram — a young wild-haired man called Rameshwar Das. For what seems like hours Raja sits at the swami's feet, nodding and talking. Eventually, Raja shuffles back up to our camp site.

"Chief [meaning me], swami has very interesting things to tell us about Ganga. I think you should come and talk with him." Raja usually does come up trumps, just when you despair he can ever be useful. Many years ago, in Kolkata, we wanted to record the chants and sounds of a cremation. Raja asked Martine for fifty rupees and went off all morning. After lunch he came back for another fifty rupees. At the end of the day he returned yet again and handed back all the money. Why? What had he been up to all day?

"You said you wanted to record a cremation, so I went round all the hospitals to see if I could buy a dead body we could take to Ganga. Nobody would sell me one." Thank God!

Rameshwar Das' short name is Ramesh Das, full name Shri Mahant Baba Rameshwar Das. He looks very Das — Bengali, thin, glasses, high forehead — the sort of person Raja would share a table with at a coffee house in College Street back in Kolkata. I need to find out what they've actually been discussing.

"Raja has been telling me that you have a theory about why Ganga jal is so pure," I say.

"It's quite simple really," he explains. "All her length you find gandhak — sulphur — and that is why the water does not have any germs, bacteria, that pollute. Ganga was born in the kamandal [the gourd water pot] of God, and then Bhagirathji brought it down. It's all in the texts."

The sulphur would be in the bed, the water acting as a catalyst all the way from the Himalaya to the Bay of Bengal. The obvious question is why no scientists ever mentioned this? Ignorance? Or is it because the theory just doesn't hold up. After all, you can smell sulphur, and while it would disinfect bacteria it might also kill a lot more desirable substances in the water. Where did the swami discover the presence of sulphur? By sampling water here at the ashram?

"No, it is written in the Puranas and the Vedas, when they talk of how Ganga came down to earth. The Hindu texts say gandhak is in Ganga. If you fill a bottle with Ganga jal and keep it for many days there will be no germs. That is the difference between the water of other rivers and the water of Gangaji. All waters are different. Each has its own specific qualities. Some have elements which nourish our body, some water has elements that are harmful. Ganga jal is amrit [nectar]."

So the answer has been there all along. Ramesh Das maintains the ancient texts really do offer a valid alternative to purely scientific explanations of the natural world. He — like most Indian holy men — doesn't belittle science. But science isn't the only explanation of the universe, is it?

"The scientists give one explanation for the eclipse of the moon. But my Vedic texts or geography say something else. They are both right."[5]

I suggest that if his sulphur theory pans out he will become famous as the man who solved what I call "the Mysterious Factor X."

Ramesh Das giggles coyly. "If I'm becoming a famous person it's due to the Vedas. It's nothing that I discovered."

~

The wind literally in our sails, we break camp and row on, past more spectacular cliffs full of parrots, kingfishers, and serpent eagles, down to Bithur — center of the universe. Talking to ordinary Indians and swamis I get slightly differing accounts of how the universe was actually

---

[5] See Chapter 5, pp. 133–140 for the equally interesting views of Indian scientists.

created, but there seems to be general agreement that Lord Brahma left a wooden sandal here on the bank, and all that remains, lovingly guarded in the little shrine at the river's edge is the nail that holds a chappal between the big and other toes.

Bithur has at least one other claim to fame and two to notoriety. It is said that Valmiki wrote the Ramayana here in Bithur, although I have been solemnly assured he in fact lived on the other side of Ganga.

The claims to notoriety both go back to the First War of Independence (or Indian Mutiny) of 1857. The first concerns the Rani of Jhansi, one of the leaders of the war. Reportedly, when the Rani was defeated in Avadh, the United Provinces, she fled back across Ganga here and back to Jhansi through a secret tunnel entered in those cliffs. Nobody has ever found an entrance and Jhansi is far, very far, even as the crow flies. But who knows?

The other piece of notoriety concerns why Sudhir Subhedar[6] has a house overlooking Ganga in Bithur in the first place. The family actually comes from Pune in Maharashtra. What are they doing up here? Well, they fought on the wrong side in 1857, so the British rounded 123 of the ringleaders in Pune and deported them. Where did they want to go into internal exile? They opted for Bithur, where they could at least be next to Ganga.

So they came, built houses and settled down. Sudhir's house commands a magnificent view over a dried-up river bed directly below the walled garden. A quarter of a mile the other side of a sandbar covered with tall Ganga grass runs the present course of the river. Come the monsoon it will doubtless all be one again. Sudhir says only a score of the original 123 families are left. Now Bithur is dotted with new swanky farmhouses, a weekend getaway for the rich of Kanpur.

Bithur is always in a state of chronic disrepair and has a healthy population of pandas, temples, and ghats. I wonder if the Pune families who chose the place of their internal exile picked Bithur because, like Devaprayag, Gangotri, or Haridwar, it is a tirtha — a sacred place where mortals can cross to the world of the gods, and vice versa? A place to bathe away your sins and say last farewells to souls of the dead? I hadn't

---

[6] Sudhir Subhedar, together with Thoma Gokhale — the dredger skipper in Kanpur — built *Basanti* for our trip. He supplied us with Topo maps and a list of recommended camping sites on this reach, and lives in Bithur, where he has invited us to camp in his garden.

thought about it much till now, as we carefully pick our way along the crumbling ghats from the center of the universe.

Then Bijoy suddenly strips and plunges into the river like a buffalo, scattering the throng of mahseer fish that waits for handouts from pilgrims and the curious. For Bijoy, our journey is the chance of a lifetime — to make an entire tirtha yatra or pilgrimage of sacred bathing places — and in the holy month of kartik, no less. But I have yet to understand where this will lead. That evening, I fall asleep to the sounds of exotic birds and temples chanting bhajans.

~

Next morning we walk down and across the sandbar to find Bimal and Bipin ready for the final leg to Rani Ghat in Kanpur. We have received instructions to take a channel that leads off the main river down to the ghats in Kanpur.

There our Tata driver R.C. Kesharwani and his son will be waiting for us with Raja and Bijoy to lift *Basanti* out of the water, into their truck and back to Thoma Gokhale's boatyard in town. Bimal and Bipin will then take a bus back to Chiyaser. They both want to row down with us to Allahabad to see the Sangam. But first we have two weeks of work on land in Kanpur.

This is perhaps the last occasion I have to talk in peace with Bimal while we're on this leg of the yatra. Most of what he tells me about the river and its origins is standard stuff. He's sure that living next to the river means he will attain heaven which demonstrates once again the depth of mythology's hold on the popular imagination.

Bimal says his grandfather's ashes were not thrown into the river. His uncle took them by train to Gaya in Bihar. But Bimal wants *his* remains to be thrown into Ganga here.

Bimal actually has a more immediate concern. He has four daughters and his parents are pressuring him to try one last time for a son, to carry on the family name and ensure his property stays within the family. But more importantly because only a son can light the funeral pyre and ensure the soul will be released on its next journey.

Bimal admits boys are encouraged to get a better education than girls, but swears if he doesn't get a son he will educate his girls beyond high school and into college. I'm very skeptical. When the time comes social pressures will probably force him to seek the usual way out — marry off his girls. But who knows how rural India will have changed a decade from now?

The river here is cloudy with silt, its normal condition. But as we approach Kanpur signs of pollution — oil, plastic — become all-too-visible. From Kanpur down the real problems of Ganga in her middle reach begin.

"Bimal, do you think Ganga is polluted?" I ask him.

"It is dirty,"[7] he replies.

This apparently innocuous exchange is pregnant with misunderstandings that tell as much about Nidish as about Bimal. Nidish's question to Bimal is in Hindi. Part of Nidish is Westernized, but part very Indian. One day in the mountains Nidish had assured me he believed literally in Ganga's descent to earth through Shiva's locks. Because I know Nidish is sincere I believed him. But I did not understand him. That only came much later.

Bimal does not suffer from Nidish's cultural schizophrenia. He knows little of the world beyond this stretch of northern India. He has no need to. He understands that the tanneries are dirtying the river. But he can't understand this concept of "pollution." It's beyond him. What he does know is that Ganga can always purify herself.

"Then all the talk about cleaning up Ganga is just so much hot air?" I ask.

"It's not bunkum. A mother can say anything to her son and the son can say anything to the mother, yet the relation is always there. But it is certainly not acceptable if the child shits in its mother's lap. It is not acceptable. So same thing here, we should not shit next to the Ganga because then we are polluting our mother. We should not do this. We must always respect our mother."

The Brahmapurana dates back at least two thousand years. It lists thirteen unhygienic acts you should not commit near a river. These are in the form of taboos and have rules for treating water bodies and even water sources in the house.

For instance, washing your hands three times before touching the water pots in the house. When you eat with your hand you should not

---

[7] There is a important distinction between dirty (gandagi/asvaccha) and pollution/impurity (apavitrta/assudhata) although most Indians I have met use the word pollution when they actually probably mean dirty. Ganga can be dirtied but never polluted in the eyes of most Indians. "Dirtied" is on the surface — throwing plastic bags, flowers from temples, but pollution means to defile. It has tremendous unspoken religious overtones. If Ganga is polluted it means the river had been defiled, has lost its status as a goddess, and has to be cleansed by appeasing the gods in poojas.

touch anything else with that hand. You do not eat in public or out in the open. When you shit in the open fields you always pour sand on the faeces. You do not spit while walking around.

Bimal, like many others, cannot explain pollution except in terms of dos and dont's. These taboos are nowadays being ignored and broken, yet you can still see them in some form or the other in traditional families. Most industry was established by the British and since they didn't have any taboos, they set up systems for draining the industrial and sewage wastes into the river. On one level this was to be welcomed. But on another, once taboos have been broken can they ever be reclaimed?

Nidish has to take the night train from Lucknow back to Dehra Dun. But he has been sickened by what he's seen of the river in the plains. For Nidish there's an interesting analogy between the cow and Ganga:

"In the mountains we say Ganges is the holy river and cow is the holy animal. We do poojas to the cow as our mother. We do not eat her meat. It is a holy thing. But if you go in the plains the cow is left all by itself. It is eating paper, plastic, anything and nobody seems to treat the cow as a holy animal. People's interests down in the plains are entirely different.

"Same thing with the river. Down to Rishikesh people pay their respects to both mothers — Ganga and the cow. One ashram — Parmath Niketan — has even built a gaushala to give stray cows food and shelter. But down here in the plains people treat cows with no respect. Same thing with Ganga. Downstream of Rishikesh all the dirt from the factories is going into the Ganges, in some places even raw sewage is going into the river.

"When Tehri Dam is finally completed, then I think the importance of river Ganges will remain only up to Tehri, no further, because once water starts going inside those tunnels and turbines and everything — I think the holiness will finish then and there. So Ganges and our holy cow, both of them they are sailing in the same boat. Up in the mountains everyone has got respect but down in the plains people pretend. Maybe some people will not like what I have said but it is what I truly feel."

~

Ganga has swung away from the river front in Kanpur in recent years. So they've dredged a channel in an attempt to keep Ganga flowing past the various bathing ghats. Entrance is indicated by a dredger beached on a sandbank in the shape of a traffic rotary. Thoma has told us to look out for a narrow channel at this sandbank.

"Enter it and it'll bring you to Rani Ghat. I'll be waiting for you there."

We find it and row down towards Kanpur. The channel is little more than a barge canal, punctuated by yet more dredgers which, when actually working, threw sand back onto the bank, not over it, so that come next monsoon it will be washed back down again. It seems a waste of time and money.

Eventually we see the tall tops of radio masts and temples: we've reached Rani Ghat where Bijoy, Raja, and R.C. Kesharwani and his son are waiting to haul little *Basanti* out of the water.

~

A year later, Thoma takes me out at six in the morning to the same area. "The maps you've just had drawn are completely out of date. Come and I'll show you the new barrage and what they've done to the old channel."

I don't recognize it. A vast embankment has been built clear across the river, effectively changing its course.

Just upstream of the little channel we'd rowed down, engineers have diverted the entire river so it now flows directly through a brand new six hundred meter-wide barrage, down to Rani Ghat and Bhairon Ghat, the traditional city cremation ghats, and then caresses Kanpur's entire waterfront. Very impressive.

"But Thoma, why do they need a barrage if they've already stopped the river with the embankment?"

Thoma's a dredging skipper. He understands this river and its hydrology better than almost anyone else.

"It's completely unnecessary. The water's just as muddy as it was before. They say it's needed for the new water treatment plant they've built next to it. Maybe. But it's a hell of a lot of money to spend just to divert water to the plant."

Worse, who knows what effect it'll have on the river? Anytime you tamper with the behavior of this river it takes its revenge in ways they've never even thought of.

At Farakka in West Bengal the barrage has provoked the entire river upstream to destroy villages and farmland because its behavior has been altered. I ask Thoma if it could do the same here?

Thoma's answer is not reassuring at all: "Naturally. It could break through the embankment and continue like it did before they diverted it down to this barrage. Or it could go off in an entirely new direction. You see a river like Ganga has many old courses. Stop it up one way and it may decide to flow in an old and different water course entirely. But these people don't study the past. They sit at their drawing boards in Delhi or Lucknow and design these ideas on paper. They never come to see for themselves."

~

He's right. Great on paper, in the abstract. In reality, perhaps another disaster in the making? Kanpur is full of such good intentions. But for Indians, its name is now synonymous with manmade pollution and environmental failure.

* * * * *

Greater Kanpur

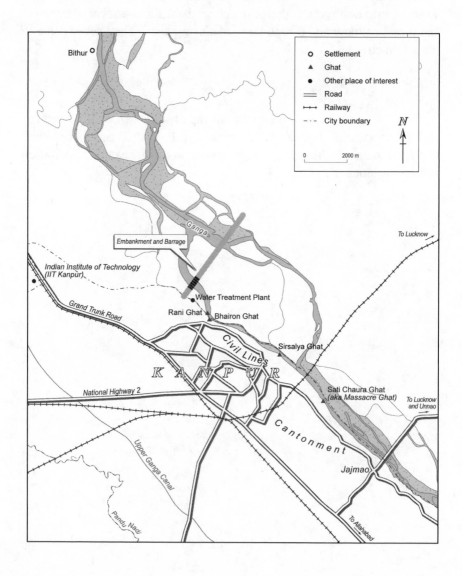

Bithur

Settlement
Ghat
Other place of interest
Road
Railway
City boundary

N

0   2000 m

Ganga

Embankment and Barrage

Indian Institute of Technology
(IIT Kanpur)

To Lucknow

Grand Trunk Road

Water Treatment Plant

Rani Ghat   Bhairon Ghat

Civil Lines

Sirsalya Ghat

K A N P U R

National Highway 2

Sati Chaura Ghat
(aka Massacre Ghat)

To Lucknow
and Unnao

Cantonment

Upper Ganga Canal

Jajmao

Pandu Nadi

To Allahabad

CHAPTER 3

The Rape of Ganga

Ganga at Kanpur is dirty, unappetizing and synonymous with pollution in everyone's eyes, including those of most of Kanpur's own citizens. Environmentalists love to cite Kanpur as proof of the failure of the government's still ongoing massive programme to clean up the river. Not all the criticism is either accurate or fair. Kanpur is too convenient a whipping boy for the sins and omissions of others, both upstream and downstream.

Kanpur is on the road to nowhere. Lucknow, just fifty kilometers away across the Ganga, has the airport, history, architecture, and the culture. Kanpur has factories, money and pollution and a strictly functional relationship with Ganga. Established in 1801 by the British to supply uniforms, boots, saddles and ordnance for their army in India, Kanpur is the largest city in Uttar Pradesh[1] and sits on the higher, southern bank of the river. On the other side Unnao and other typical one-story UP towns — honking car horns and black and yellow three-wheeler water buffaloes masquerading as taxis. Kanpur is an anomaly, an industrial city which accidentally happens to lie on the banks of a river that almost everyone else round here thinks of as a goddess.

~

Not many people go out on the river in Kanpur. But we find Bhagwan at Sati Chaura Ghat,[2] and he agrees to row us as far as possible upstream towards Rani Ghat where we'd disembarked from *Basanti* a few days previously.

---

[1] Three and a half million residents approximately.

[2] Often called Massacre Ghat because it is the site where a hundred and sixty seven British women and children were killed after they'd been promised safe passage from the doomed and ruined Residency of Cawnpur (the British name for Kanpur) in 1857.

The first thing I notice is how shallow the river is in Kanpur. The culprit is, of course, lack of adequate flow. It's so shallow Bhagwan has to take off his trousers, clamber overboard and walk the boat upstream till the arches of the railway bridge. But we only ever make it a little beyond halfway, to Sirsalya Ghat. Then the river becomes too narrow and shallow to go any further.

"Is this Ganga or a nullah of the same name?" Raja is quite serious. He's never been to Kanpur.

In recent years, Ganga has swung away from the city and only returns just below Sirsalya Ghat. The tiny channel we traveled down in *Basanti* is the only source of water for the top half of the town, and it's a pretty fetid nullah that washes the city between Sirsalya and Bhairon Ghats. The whole waterfront is a mixture of broken concrete, untapped drains and piles of garbage tossed over garden walls.

Between the main river and the nullah that calls itself Ganga are substantial sandbanks. A small group of men are bathing on the far side. Surendra Kumar Yadav, who works for a local jeweller, has just finished bathing.

"Only this side [he points north to the main channel] is good to bathe in." He and his friends have been going to this bank for thirty years because he says the Kanpur bank is so dirty. "It comes from the drains and it also has tannery water. Nobody bathes in this nullah."[3]

Surendra blames the tanneries for anything and everything that causes pollution in Kanpur. He believes if the river is filthy it must be because of the tanneries. Unfortunately the tanneries are all located several kilometers downstream, which means the pollution up here cannot be caused by the tanneries. Surendra brushes aside my logic. "It must be the government's fault. If the government had banned the discharge of raw sewage then the water would have remained clean. Brother, if any man uses Ganga as a drain, you should stop him right there and then. The problem would be solved."

Always blame it on government. But then Surendra adds a little remark that goes beyond the usual platitudes: "The biggest contribution to spreading this dirt is we, the public. If we stop polluting Ganga by throwing our plastic bags into the river then automatically the river would be cleaner."

In theory fairly easy to regulate: ban people from disposing of their plastic bags (trash) in the river. But of course it's anything but. A

---

[3] The city's Jal Nigam admits many of the city's nullahs are still untapped, though having seen at first hand what they mean by tapped, I wonder if that would really make much difference anyway.

local environmental group called Eco-Friends has been promoting just such a program here, but with only moderate success. The river's just too convenient a dumping ground. Besides, there's an entire economic subculture that lives from producing or recycling these gossamer-thin plastic bags. The Indian government can ban sale of ultra-light plastic bags, but how many lives will be sacrificed as a consequence? And if they ban plastic bags ten millimeters thick then tomorrow factories will start producing plastic nine millimeters thick.

Plastic bags are the easy part anyway. Surendra is a jeweller. Jewelery manufacturing uses many metals and chemicals to separate and refine its product. It's not a major polluter like the tanneries. But it isn't blameless either. Surendra's both a good man and intelligent, yet he doesn't see a connection between his profession and pollution of Ganga. He just harps on about how it's the government's job to make the public aware and tell them what they must do to prevent it:

"Gangaji is our heritage; they say that this Ganga jal is nectar. If you drink and bathe in it, all the sins of previous births can be washed away. So the river should be kept as clean as possible. The people must cooperate fully with the government, but first the government should tell us what to do." This reminds me of the lamentations of affluent young couples in Karachi, Pakistan, who used to tell me how they wanted to become good Muslims, give up sin and pleasure, all in the name of Islam — but only if the government first ordered them.

Another of Surendra's group — Dashkaran Lal — is a bona fide pandit. So I ask him, "If Ganga can purify your soul, therefore she can purify herself. Yet she is polluted. You see all this plastic and garbage. What argument can the government make to convince you personally to not throw plastic bags into the Ganga?"

Dashkaran Lal replies that Ganga can absorb much of the dead bodies, flowers, and plastic bags. He says this religious belief in Ganga's ability to purify herself of pollution has some validity — but only to a certain extent. It isn't carte blanche to continue dumping indiscriminately. This is an interesting answer because there is solid scientific evidence[4] that the river can indeed absorb a surprising amount of organic waste. Not inorganic waste from the tanneries at the southern end of the city. Nobody can figure out how to do that yet.

~

---

[4] See Chapter 5.

Those tanneries have been an integral part of the city since the British established Kanpur as a manufacturing centre of boots, saddles, and all other forms of useful military equipment two hundred years ago. They've presumably also been polluting Ganga for most of that time. Many people in India have therefore been aware for a long time that something has to be done to clean up Ganga at Kanpur. In 1986, the Indian government launched a massive campaign with huge amounts of foreign aid to clean up not just Kanpur but also the holy city of Varanasi (and a host of lesser cities), precisely because they were such eyesores.

Rajiv Gandhi's launch of the Ganga Action Plan in fact took place at the other end of this four hundred kilometer stretch of Ganga, at Dasasvamedha Ghat in Varanasi on June 14, 1986. It's a fine speech[5] though I've heard it criticized by academics for using Western concepts of pollution that they — the critics — maintain are alien to Hindu culture.[6] That may be true. But then how many Indians ever read the speech?

The speech probably does make more sense to a Westernized mind. But the basis was and remains sound: intercept and treat pollution *before* it's discharged into Ganga. This would be achieved through sewage treatment plants, "low cost" sanitation (whatever that means), electronic crematoria and river front development. Twenty-five Class 1 cities (including Kanpur and Varanasi) received the full range of these schemes in Phase One that lasted till 1995, at a cost of seven hundred crore rupees (150 million dollars at 2002 rates). A second phase extended the Ganga Action Plan to an additional fifty-nine towns and cities along the river. This second phase is still ongoing.

In 1995, New Delhi claimed that Phase 1 had "improved the river by seventy percent." But what did this mean? Seventy percent of what? To be honest no serious scientist would give much credibility to the way the government measures the health of the river. Figures are rarely made public, and when they are there's little or no attempt at either consistency or scientific credibility.

Everything I've heard or read suggests the Ganga Action Plan was implemented in a rush. The ideas were fine but the execution anything

---

[5] The text and the audiovisual record of the speech is in *Rajiv Gandhi Selected Speeches and Wrings 1986,* Ministry of Information & Broadcasting, Government of India, New Delhi, 1992, pp 170-175. Both were kindly made available to me by Mr. Krishna Rao (media advisor) and Ms Jyoti Kumari (archivist), Rajiv Gandhi Foundation.

[6] Cf. pp 36-37 in Kelly D. Alley's *On the Banks of the Ganga: When Wastewater Meets a Sacred River.* University of Michigan Press, Ann Arbor, Michigan, 2003.

but. Politics, not science, ran the show.

There was frequently a lack of coordination. In the largest cities sewage treatment plants were built to great fanfare but to handle the amount of sewage generated in 1986. No one seems to have thought ahead, ten, twenty, even thirty years. Result? They were already inadequate in 1986, and the problem has only got worse since then. The untreated sewage is often simply poured directly back into the river.

But the original intentions were sound: many of the men and women charged with implementing the Ganga Action Plan are highly competent. Even the institutions they work for are generally honorable. But everything that could go wrong has gone wrong. There's little deliberate malfeasance or evil intent. It's incremental: a decision is made, a direction taken, without fully anticipating the possible consequences. It's never anybody's fault.

I also wonder about the choice of criteria to measure the success of the cleanup. The Central Ganga Authority opted for two standard measurements that had been used in rivers in the West — Dissolved Oxygen and Biological Oxygen Demand — but were no longer.[7] They appear to be commonsensical. But are they apt criteria?

"They are basically irrelevant to the health of Ganga," declares Vinod Tare. Tare is a professor of Environmental Engineering at the Indian Institute of Technology in Kanpur. "We never had a DO problem here before 1986." But aren't the BOD levels extremely high? "Yes, but above Kanpur, on precisely that section of the river you've just come down."

I'm mystified. Surely organic waste — sewage — is BOD? So why would the BOD level be higher upstream, where there are no cities, no factories, than down here in Kanpur? Tare explains that "the BOD is from farmers' fields upstream of Kanpur, it's from the fertilizers and pesticides washed out of those fields into the river."

That's why the BOD level above Kanpur is in fact far higher

---

[7] Biological Oxygen Demand (BOD) is fairly easy to grasp: it's the amount of oxygen needed to break down organic material — human and animal sewage, leaves, food, anything organic — in water. Dissolved Oxygen (DO) is more complex. It measures the amount of oxygen available in the river to handle the organic load of BOD. So with a heavy BOD you'd expect to find lower DO because it's been consumed in breaking down the organic load. Dissolved oxygen is a good demonstration of how so many disparate elements are inter-related. The sun causes photosynthesis in plants on the river bed (carbon dioxide or CO_2) which fixes carbon and releases oxygen, which in turn helps other organic matter decompose.

than the BOD from sewage here in the city. "So if there wasn't a BOD problem inside the city in the first place why did we need to improve DO here? Upstream yes! That's why I think these really are totally inappropriate [Western] parameters."

Today, many Western scientists also question the choice of Dissolved Oxygen, because it's such a tricky thing to measure. The World Health Organization no longer even lists it as one of its criteria.[8]

But what few Indians seem to know is that someone in the government — The Ganga Action Committee? The Central Pollution Control Board? — back in the 1980s set the permissible standards of DO and BOD at artificially low rates that met no known international standards. So not only did they choose largely meaningless criteria, but they then passed them off as "internationally accepted standards."

An Indian environment engineer who evaluates projects for the Indian government inadvertently let the cat out of the bag. I'll call him Ajay Gupta. (For obvious reasons that's not his real name, but his credentials check out.)

Ajay meets me in Kolkata, several months later. He brings with him a bunch of books on some of the environmental hot spots along the river. These are places where he'd been asked to make objective evaluations of the state of the river and its cleanup.

I ask to see one of the volumes: "Can I buy a copy?"

"It's not on sale to the public. Too sensitive. It's a private study, government property. You'll have to get written permission."

"See, if the Indian public reads these figures they will get very agitated. So we are protecting them."

"Why would they get agitated?"

"Because these are true figures."

Ajay mentions arsenic. The World Health Organization recommends a maximum permissible limit in water of 1 milligram per thousand litres.

---

[8] A farmer ten kilometers away from the river applies fertilizers on his fields to increase yields. Come the monsoon and the remains of the fertilizer get washed down and eventually into the river. After the monsoon has spent its fury the hot Indian sun stimulates the growth of far more algae than the resources of the river can ever absorb. Algae bloom, especially if they feast on untreated sewage from nullahs. Algae are not usually considered beneficial: they suffocate rivers, prevent the sun's ultra-violet rays acting on plants under water. But before they start to decompose and consume the available oxygen they photosynthesize and so raise dissolved oxygen levels in the water. Is this healthy? Can't be sure but it can skewer readings. So how can anyone totally trust DO readings? You therefore have to know a great deal about the local physical condition of the river to use DO as a measure.

"Our limit is five milligrams. We cannot adopt WHO limits. They are for developed countries. India is a developing country. So we've set limits that work here!"

The door is open. I plunge in: "The limits for Dissolved Oxygen and Biological Oxygen Demand that were adopted for the Ganga Action Plan, are they WHO limits or Indian limits?"

"Obviously they are Indian limits. We are a poor country. We cannot reach your standards yet. It will take many years."

"Ajay, the figures you publish, not just for Westerners but for Indians themselves, you could use a euphemism and call them misleading. But some would call them lies. What do you think is going to happen when the Indian public discovers they've been duped?"

"You tell me, sir."

~

Vinod Tare in Kanpur says no one can precisely say why these criteria were chosen because in India the workings of the government will remain secret until the end of civilization. No one can even lay hands on a copy of the Ganga Action Plan. This is a cultural phenomenon specific to very old civilizations such as China or India. Indian governments, whatever the level — central, state, or local — simply do not publish information. Period. Information belongs to the state, and should only be divulged if absolutely necessary. If I ever hear that the Indian government is proposing to actually enforce the Freedom of Information Act I shall probably choke with laughter.

Vinod and I both suspect the Indian government chose these criteria on the advice of the official consultants to the original project — the Thames Valley Water Authority. Why were they chosen in the first place to design the parameters for the cleanup of the Ganga — a tropical not a temperate river? Common sense suggests they were the only outfit at the time with a proven track record of river cleanups. Rajiv Gandhi, then the prime minister, was an Anglophile and the mindset in Delhi and most of India was, and probably still is, West is Best, though in the twenty-first century the locus of West has probably shifted from London to Washington DC.

So much money has been wasted because of this flaw. Plants and systems have been designed which are particularly ill-suited to Indian conditions because of a second flaw — they all rely on a constant supply of electricity, the one thing no one can guarantee in northern India.

The original Ganga Action Plan (GAP) to intercept, divert, and treat raw sewage[9] is also admirable as far as it goes. But in Kanpur there's yet another basic design failure — the Dutch sold them the wrong technology.

Soon after the launch of the Ganga Action Plan, the Dutch government funded a ten year project to implement parts of the GAP in Kanpur. They offered to build three sewage treatment plants[10] in Jajmao at the southern end of the city, just below the tanneries. Two of these plants treat wastewater in a traditional manner, using sedimentation after aerobic treatment and anaerobic[11] stabilization.[12] Together they have a capacity of 135 mld,[13] which seems large until you realize that Kanpur today generates almost 400 mld.[14]

Another smaller treatment plant in the same complex, with a capacity of 36 mld, incorporates a proprietary Dutch technology known as "Up flow Anaerobic Sludge Blanket" (UASB). This plant was built as a pilot project to evaluate the effectiveness of the new technology in India. UASB makes use of anaerobic bacteria to decompose the waste material, and requires some amount of post-treatment. It quickly became all the rage because it's cheap to operate but it's not quite as effective at reducing BOD levels as the traditional method. This plant was also slated

---

[9] This includes household sewage, industrial waste (often toxic), animal and human bodies, and ashes from cremation and flowers from pooja ceremonies.

[10] In environmental jargon these are often referred to as STPs. In Kanpur there is a main STP complex at Jajmao on the southern end of the city, called a CETP. This is the acronym for Combined Effluent Treatment Plant.

[11] Aerobic uses oxygen to decompose organic waste. Anaerobic uses micro-organisms (bacteria) to decompose wastes and does not require what is known as free oxygen. Aerobic treatment generates considerable heat — think of a compost heap in your garden. This may or not hold true for anaerobic treatment.

[12] A sewage treatment plant treats sewage at three different levels. Primary treatment removes most solids in settling ponds — the solids sink to the bottom and are then removed. In secondary treatment the wastewater is oxygenated and most bacteria are thereby removed. The final tertiary level further purifies the wastewater so that it can be re-used as drinking water.

[13] Million liters per day.

[14] Kanpur plans for a massive new treatment plant south of the city on the Pandu river.

to receive effluent from the tanneries. The idea was that the chromium[15] and other heavy metals from this wastewater would be removed ("recovered" in technical jargon) and recycled at the tanneries before being sent to the treatment plant.

So far so good. But everything happened the wrong way around. The Indian Supreme Court ordered the tanneries of Kanpur to get rid of their most toxic by-product, which is the chromium used to tan animal hides. You don't want this substance in your soil, air, or water, and certainly not in industrial sewage going to a treatment plant. It's highly toxic. The large tanneries were therefore ordered to install their own chrome recovery plants by 1996. The smaller tanneries were asked to pool their money and build a joint recovery plant they could all use.

Both large and small tanneries took their time. The UASB plant was built and up-and-running before any of them even began to comply. So for the first few years the waste coming to be treated contained the very substance, hexavalent chromium, which would sabotage the entire treatment process. Everything had been done the wrong way around.

Today, ten years later, most of the large tanneries do indeed have these plants. But these again require that scarce commodity, electricity to run. If they get it, they can more than pay for themselves. Chromium does not come cheap. What is "recovered" can be reused. After one year the recovery plant has paid for itself: you can actually start making money. One large tannery owner estimates a recovery plant would have a life span of maybe twenty years.[16]

The small tanneries are a different story. They claim they were promised large amounts of aid to set up a combined plant. It never happened. In any case, they claim they were assured they could send all their chrome waste along to the new plant. It could handle it. But any scientist worth his salt must have known failure to remove Cr(VI) would sabotage the whole process. Someone was asleep at the wheel. Result: the experimental plant doesn't work.

Vinod Tare thinks the Dutch probably acted in good faith, but without thinking things through. Anaerobic treatment was what they knew about and it had worked well in the Netherlands. But Holland doesn't have toxic chromium waste from tanneries. The Dutch UASB technology

---

[15] The tanneries in Kanpur use trivalent chromium Cr(III). There is debate whether or not this is toxic. When this is oxidized in the tanning process it becomes hexavalent chromium, which is highly toxic. The chemical symbol for hexavalent chromium is Cr(VI).

[16] Interview with Imran Siddiqui of Super Tannery, November 2, 2004.

breaks down organic waste in an anaerobic process. But if toxic chemicals have not been previously removed, and are therefore still present in the raw sewage coming into the plant, that entire anaerobic process will be aborted. No biochemical process will now take place.[17] The solids will be removed but the toxins suspended in the waste water will remain untreated and highly active. Hexavalent chromium also kills the oxygen the anaerobic process needs to do its job. As for tertiary treatment, which restores waste water to a drinkable state — forget it. It can't remove toxins. So they will be still present in any waste water that is released for use by the public.

~

Varanasi, just four hundred kilometers downstream, is the other city everyone thinks of whenever the Ganga Action Plan is mentioned. This is after all where Rajiv Gandhi launched the plan in 1986. Varanasi is Kashi - the holiest of holies - and a tourist magnet. This was the one place, Rajiv said, where Ganga must be visibly clean. The ghats should be restored, open sewers pouring raw sewage into the river must be tapped and diverted to sewage treatment plants far from the gaze of tourists. The actual river should be free of muck and debris. In short, a cosmetic makeover.

On the face of things Varanasi should therefore have little in common with Kanpur, the gritty industrial city. But both are obsessed with the condition of Ganga through their city. Each has a major environmental group led by a charismatic leader. And in each city political, institutional, and administrative breakdowns have aborted much of their efforts to clean up Ganga. This is where the obvious similarities end. No one bathes at Kanpur. But it seems that's all anyone ever does in Varanasi.

As a rule of thumb, if you want to get a good first impression of the health of Ganga get out on a boat and take a look for yourself. In Varanasi everything seems superbly organized on the ghats. Boatmen are to be found everywhere — they'll take you up from Asi Ghat to Panchganga Ghat, or even beyond the railway bridge to Adi Kesava Ghat and down again. The younger and fitter boatmen will row; the lazy ones have fitted little diesel engines to the sterns of their boats. The ghats are clean, full of bathers, and pandas, sitting under extravagant umbrellas of Ganga grass, waiting for the faithful and the curious.

---

[17] This has been confirmed to me in conversation by several scientists in both Varanasi and Kanpur. See also the report at www.ecofriends.org/gal/default.htm.

The river front is by and large pretty clean, especially now the Asi river has been diverted so it no longer flows into the river right next to the eponymous ghat. A few years ago, before the Asi nullah was diverted upstream, it leaked its fetid slime into the mud next to the actual stone steps. In 2001, I remember seeing one man sitting in the muck lathering his entire body with this toxic ooze. At the time I was told this showed the religious faith of the devotee in the healing powers of even Ganga mud. Now I'm not so sure: he may simply have been using the ooze as liquid thermal insulation against early morning air, much like the naked Nagas one meets at Allahabad or any great mela. What happens up the other end where the Varuna river flows into Ganga — out of the gaze of the devout — is sadly a different matter.

So Ganga is central to Varanasi's identity. It's a vital part of its raison d'être. But the implementation of the GAP in Varanasi had an equally obvious flaw. When they'd designed their sewage treatment plants in 1986, it was to handle 105 mld of raw sewage. But the city was already producing 140 mld. In 2005, that figure is up to 300 mld.[18] So where does 195 mld go? Straight back into the river, untreated. Government officials simply shrug it off.

In both Kanpur and Varanasi the sewage treatment plants (and all the intermediary pumping stations) rely heavily on regular electricity supply to operate. Unfortunately, the Western design engineers overlooked two basic realities of life in northern India. The monsoon that floods factories and generators; and regular load-shedding (or brown-outs) when electrical plants simply give up the ghost and shut down. For four months of the year, during the monsoon, there is often no electricity at all. So pumps cannot pump and *all* this raw untreated sewage is poured straight back into the river.

I've been told Thames Valley consultants in fact anticipated this and proposed the plants should generate much of their own electricity through a mixture of methane and outside electricity. But no one has yet succeeded in producing methane from biogas on such a large and regular scale.

You can see the practical effects of regular cuts in electricity ("load-shedding") at the Konia pumping station, a few hundred yards beyond the bridge that carries the railway down to Kolkata. Konia pumps

---

[18] Both Varanasi and Kanpur have now woken up and are planning to meet sewage needs projected out to 2040. In Varanasi new sewage treatment plants are planned at Sarnath and Bhagwanpur, in Kanpur on the Pandu river. But will they get adequate regular supplies of electricity?

up raw sewage[19] which then flows to the Dinapur sewage treatment plant a few kilometers away. The morning I rowed up past it a trickle of water poured absentmindedly down a spillway into Ganga.[20] But at ten o'clock precisely, the electricity stopped and all the raw sewage from the entire city poured down that spillway and back into Ganga. The only consolation is that it is at least downstream from the bathing ghats.

~

The Pollution Control Board in Kanpur admits candidly that Uttar Pradesh simply cannot produce enough electricity on a consistent basis, so there is daily rationing. A city like Kanpur gets cut anyway because it doesn't have the money to even pay the electric bill. In theory UP[21] could buy in electricity from a state with a surplus. Only in theory, because UP is broke too. Which means they need either expensive emergency generators to keep the whole elaborate system of pumps and treatment plants going or just letting everything revert to where it was before 1986.

Later that afternoon I head across Kanpur to meet Mr. Sinha, manager of the city's Jal Nigam.[22] A lot of staff are milling around outside. Inside, engineers sit and try to keep cool next to open windows, computer screens blank. Mr. Sinha is reading a report with the help of a flashlight. "See, we have no electricity. We cannot work!"

"Hey, please tell them to be quiet." The crowd outside Mr. Sinha's office are getting a bit boisterous. "And get the bench removed from there. Here we are talking, doing something, and they are sitting and gossiping." Question: how many days have been like this in the past week? Answer: two days so far. Today is Thursday. What a routine: report to work, fire up the computer, and just when the hardware is ready it all dies — load-shedding.

---

[19] Unfortunately, it already has one strike against it. Even when it operates it can only handle forty percent of the total town sewage.

[20] For the technically-minded the pumping station uses three screw pumps to lift the water up into a main pipe that will carry it to the sewage treatment plant at Dinapur. The pumps obviously run on electricity, large quantities of it.

[21] For the rest of this chapter I have used the initials UP for Uttar Pradesh. Most Indians use it as a figure of everyday speech anyway.

[22] Water Authority.

There are alternatives, and they rely on what India has in abundance — sun and time. Vinod Tare proposes settling ponds located on a decentralized pattern throughout Kanpur. "No need to centralize everything in Jajmao," he says.

These settling ponds would remove forty percent of the organic load in just three hours, reducing the total amount of sewage that needs to be pumped to sewage treatment plants, saving the need for costly electricity and mechanization throughout the city. The solids simply sink to the bottom. That's a pretty effective alternative.

In Varanasi, Sankat Mochan has been proposing something along the same lines — stabilization ponds — or to give them their full name Advanced Integrated Wastewater Pond Systems (AIWPS). They sound very similar to settling ponds but are in fact much more sophisticated. They treat the sewage in a carefully engineered series of natural algae ponds. Each pond breaks down the organic wastes differently using algae and photosynthesis. The end result is a harvest of algae that can be fed to livestock, and wastewater clean enough to be used for irrigation. But the water does have to be moved between the ponds through gravity and paddle wheels.

It's an elaborate but sound system that has been working in California.[23] USAID[24] funded a feasibility study in Varanasi that demonstrated the system could work and cost far less than the present elaborate mechanized monster under the Ganga Action Plan. A site was selected at Sola on an island downstream. In 1998 the Nagar Nigam — the municipal government in Varanasi — endorsed it.

The Varanasi system does have some weaknesses. Vinod Tare says getting the waste to the ponds requires complex hydraulics because all the waste has to be pumped out of the city to the ponds, located twenty kilometers outside the actual city. The problem, according to Vinod, is that Varanasi is significantly lower than Kanpur, so there's a risk that the pipes can get flooded during the monsoon.

"But they will probably work and cost far less than the present scheme," Vinod concedes.

Veer Badre Mishra at the Sankat Mochan Foundation says the Varanasi Nagar Nigam approved it unanimously and forwarded it for

---

[23] In Alexander Stille's fine profile of Veer Badre Mishra, its founder William Oswald, a retired professor at Berkeley, explains how the AIWPS works in California. See "The Ganges' Next Life," *The New Yorker,* January 19, 1998, pp 58-67.

[24] United States Agency for International Development.

approval and funding to the state government in Lucknow. But Delhi nixed the idea and Lucknow went along with the central government.[25] Neither Delhi nor Lucknow gave convincing reasons for their refusal. Mishra told me Delhi had rejected his plan because it proposed treating just 200mld, a bad joke when you remember they built a treatment plant that could only handle 102mld. Mishra told them: "Fine. Then we will expand it to treat 300mld." That's where matters stand today.

~

One Sunday morning, Rakesh Jaiswal asks me to come and take a look at Kanpur's sewage system in the raw. Rakesh has been militating in Kanpur for fifteen years to try and increase public awareness about the need to do something to clean up Ganga. Earlier this week, Rakesh made an alarming discovery.

So we pile into the Scorpio and head for Dapkah Nullah, just beyond the golf course where my friend Chutku plays religiously at 5:30 every morning. We bump down an earthen track towards the river and park near a small Shiva temple at the edge of Ganga. It's a beautiful scene — a whitewashed temple in an oasis of calm inside the bustling city.

Beyond it is a nullah — a stream flowing into Ganga. We follow the nullah back up fifty yards. I hear a dull roar. We clamber up the bank: the roar suddenly becomes reality — a waterfall tumbles out of the shattered brickwork of the Kanpur municipal main trunk sewer, five feet in diameter. It's severed almost in two: the whole city's raw sewage is cascading down into the nullah twenty feet below.

"Rakesh, how long has this been broken? Why doesn't the municipality repair it? Does the city know?"

"I got to know of this only on Thursday. The water authorities have no idea. But I think it has been broken for some weeks."

We climb down to what remains of the brick pipe. Rakesh explains: "This is the main trunk sewer for the whole city. All the sewage from the city is carried through this to the Sewage Treatment Plant. It has completely failed and now raw sewage is going to the river directly." He repeats those last words with huge contempt: "Raw sewage."

The main aorta of the city's sewage system has burst. Its heart — the Sewage Treatment Plant at Jajmao — can't be getting much blood at all. There's still some liquid flowing in the unbroken bottom of the massive pipe. But no more than a quarter of what should be in the pipe.

---

[25] This decision makes a bit of mockery of the recent seventy-fourth amendment to the Indian constitution that mandates decentralizing decision-making to the local level.

Rakesh has pleaded with Jal Nigam to carry out regular maintenance. But Jal Nigam simply throw up their hands and say they're starved for funds. Lucknow in turn says it doesn't have the cash for maintenance. Everyone, from the Pollution Control board to Jal Nigam to the Mayor of Kanpur, sings from the same song book. The end result: a smelly mix pouring directly into the river.

We walk back up to the Scorpio. Down at the Shiva temple a gaggle of geese are inspecting the Ganga lapping against the beach. On the sand are discarded clay idols. The water in the nullah is oily and black from the waterfall fifty yards above. It's pouring out into the river. But oil and water don't mix. There are in fact two distinct rivers, visible even to the unobservant eye — a black Ganga flowing out of the nullah into the milk chocolate Ganga, side by side as far as the eye can see. Visually, it reminds me of Devaprayag, except it's not the (fairly) pristine mountain torrents of the Alaknanda and the Bhaghirathi, but raw sewage and a sluggish, muddy river.

Even the geese wandering round the shrine sense something is not quite right: they waddle down to the water's edge, but then think better of it. They don't want to swim in this muck. With much vociferous protest they waddle away from the water, heading downstream in search of something rather more appetizing.

Bijoy Tivari is visibly shaken: a few days before he'd filled plastic bottles with Ganga jal, presumably for drinking. He now goes back to the Scorpio, takes them out, goes down to the river and pours them mournfully back into the river.

"Tivari chalo chalo. I want you to look at mother Ganga. Would you take a dip in this?"

Tivari looks insulted I'd even ask the question. "No, no, not here. It is very dirty water right here. I won't take a dip."

"Why not? Remember this is a holy river. It can clean itself."

He won't bite. "Yes, what you say is right. The river has the purifying capacity but here it's very much obvious and visible that it's raw sewage. It's not the Ganges water. Maybe a few kilometers in the downstream when all these pollutants will get diluted then I can think of having a dip."

If this isn't bad enough, a hundred yards away on the cliff overlooking Ganga another huge pipe is pouring a dark oily liquid directly into the river below. How come? It can't be raw sewage because the trunk sewer that would feed it is broken.

"This is directly from the tanneries. See how blue it is. This is untreated chromium." Rakesh looks angry. This site visit confirms an unwelcome truth he's probably suspected for some time. Many tanneries can't be treating their chromium waste, as they endlessly tell the outside world. Otherwise, this would be fairly clear water.[26]

Rakesh is by now very angry. His hunch is, that it's pure, raw effluent going directly into the river. But just yesterday R.K. Sinha at the Jal Nigam had assured me the opposite.

Rakesh is contemptuous: "A total lie. I will show you other drains which are also carrying toxic tannery effluent and contaminating the Ganges water."

We've parked near one of four Shiva temples in Kanpur. Rakesh jokes: "I don't know how Shiva would be feeling about this stench. He has to watch the discharge of raw and toxic sewage directly into Ganga which he brought down from Heaven through his hair." Varanasi also has its share of untapped nullahs, but though the main trunk sewer dates back to the British, when its population was maybe a tenth of what it is today, there have been no catastrophic ruptures of main aortas as here in Kanpur.

~

The Ganga Action Plan mandated electric crematoria in many cities. A friend tells me that in Delhi two thirds of cremations actually take place in these electric crematoria. At Nimtala Ghat in Kolkata the ratio is also roughly one is to three in favour of electric crematoria. In Varanasi the electric crematorium next to Harishchandra Ghat seems largely idle, while fifty yards away the traditional funeral pyres are in regular use.

There are two official cremation areas in Kanpur — Bhairon Ghat and this one at Jajmao, where the local dhoms, called dhanuks in Kanpur, perform the needful on the beach. Rakesh has worked with them before, when his group led a campaign to fish out dead bodies and clean up Ganga.

Disposing of dead bodies in Ganga sounds lazy. But there are several obvious reasons why someone would want to avoid having to pay even a modest fee of several hundred rupees. Poverty (it costs a minimum of five hundred rupees in wood) or simple practicality (you need to dispose of a body on the quiet), for example. Of course there are also accidents

---

[26] There are more than 350 tanneries in Jajmao. Under the Ganga Action Plan the idea was to collect raw tannery effluent through four pumping stations which receive the effluent from the tanneries of Kanpur. These intermediate pumping stations then send it to the CETP. Rakesh has long suspected that the intermediate pumping stations are not working and raw effluent is going directly into the river without treatment. As he says: "This is how Ganga is being polluted by leather industries of Kanpur."

(you drown or accidentally fall in) — and dead bodies can also include cows and other large animals which fall into the river and drown.

On the beach in Jajmao a dhanuk called Munar explains that they now bury the ashes of those they have burned. Near the waterline are three fresh mounds — bodies they have fished out of the river this morning, proof that someone is listening to Rakesh's campaign to clean up Ganga.

Munar admits that the condition of the river is now so foul that rituals themselves have to change. When families bring bodies for cremation they often bring their own water with them to wash the body. They've seen the condition of Ganga, even in mid-channel. The relations and friends of the deceased are also supposed to take a dip when they bring a body for cremation. They now go back home and take a shower instead. Much like using a few drops of Ganga jal in various everyday rituals. I can see why purists feel it's the thin edge of the wedge.

Martine has wandered off meanwhile, and finds a mother and two children scooping bluish sludge on to a cart to make into mud-bricks. Seems enterprising, but Rakesh and Martine gesture to me to come see. This is solid waste from the tannery; the bluish colored clay is chrome mixed in with the other waste. In plain language, a toxic brick. It may get even worse. Diwali is next week and the women are going to paint the walls of their houses with this toxic mud-wash for the festival.

Jajmao is a poor area. People here often have little alternative but to wash, cook, and drink the water from either the river or the various nullahs that flow down to Ganga, often in pristine lined canals. None of the four intermediate pumping stations built to receive tannery waste water here in Jajmao are working, presumably because of load-shedding, so raw tannery effluent is reaching Ganga directly instead of going to the Sewage Treatment Plant less than a mile away. Needless to say the groundwater is contaminated with hexavalent chromium. Surveys have been done, reports published, and nothing gets done. And meanwhile the inhabitants suffer.

Sunderlal, a tannery worker, says, "The water here is not good. It's yellow and brackish." But there's no alternative for washing or cooking. They're too poor to buy water so they have to travel to find a pump with clean drinking water. He lifts up his shirt. He has a rash that looks like prickly heat, and white blotches. His kids have worms. I know instinctively he is the rule, not the exception.

A truck bumps down the paved road to the beach, followed by several cars. Men of all ages bundle out and carry a light stretcher covering a dead body down to the edge of the river. Normally, they would push it out so that the river could wash the body. Definitely not here today.

R.K. Awasthi says he won't be taking a dip in Ganga, even though he's supposed to. "It's pucca, dirty water. We are supposed to take a bath here, but I will take it back home. This is dirty, very dirty water."

What about the traditional washing of the body in Ganga? A real dilemma: "We have to avoid all this, but we are bound. What to do?"

The solution: "I take the water from either hand pump or we bring the water from the house and that way we are giving bath to the dead body."

"But then you're not performing the ritual correctly," I point out.

"You are very right, I mean one hundred percent. But we are bound."

His voice trails off. Change the subject please! Rakesh asks him why he isn't up in arms against this pollution of Ganga.

A delicate subject. "If we protest there will be a riot."

The tanneries cause the pollution, but who works and lives in the tanneries? Muslims. Accusing the tanneries of pollution is therefore code for a not so indirect attack on the so-called minority community. The main political parties jump in and the whole thing quickly becomes a public mess. His friend K.P. Chauhan sees this in very personal terms:

"We are small people, if we complain they will kill us and throw our bodies in this Gangaji."

Some of these problems — the toxic waste from the tanneries and the very real political repercussions — are not present up at Bhairon Ghat at the other end of town. This is very different from Jajmao. It's a much older cremation ghat, added on over the years with a paved road, a parking lot, marble, and stone floors, two raised slabs on which bodies are washed with groundwater, a large central covered area for the actual burning of the body. But the rituals, the problems, and above all the adaptations are similar to Jajmao. Until Ganga was diverted in 2005 through the new barrage, the only water Bhairon Ghat received regularly was from the already-deficient channel and highly dubious discharge from an untapped drain from a local tuberculosis clinic.

The gates open and a Tata pickup delivers a load of fresh wood. I'm curious so I go up to Shivkumar Tewari — the head pandit:

"How long does it take to burn a body? Any idea?"

"Three hours, if it's thin and skinny. Longer if it's got some fat to burn." he replies.

Bodies are washed on the two shining white marble slabs, then burned in the covered area. A family is sifting through the ashes of an earlier cremation, looking for phool, or the ash and unburned bit of bones, euphemistically called flowers. These are then collected in an urn or pot. They are the mortal remains of a person that will be carried to the edge of Ganga for the last rituals. Mr. Tewari chants slokas so that the souls of both the dead person and the family will attain peace.

One family member tells me he will take a dip here in Ganga after the ceremony. "The river is dirty yes, polluted no.[27] How can she be polluted? She is Gangaji, she is holy to us. This is our mother. We don't think that mother can ever be polluted."

Next door is the imposing electric crematorium, gates padlocked. No one answers the bell. Shivkumar Tewari says they don't turn up until after lunch anyway. Is it competition for him? "No way. Only the reformist Hindus such as the Arya Samaj use it."

Muluk Goel, the head of police in Kanpur, complains it doesn't really make any economic sense to use the electric crematoria: "It costs us two thousand rupees to cremate a body we've fished out of the river and the government only gives us five hundred rupees. Plus the crematorium doesn't work." Well, actually it does, but not regularly.

Shivkumar Tewari isn't complaining. His traditional crematorium still averages ten bodies a day. "Many people prefer that certain rituals be performed before cremation," he says. "So, traditionally people like to cremate their dead on a wooden pyre." He adds, mischievously: "People don't like the electric. I think a lot of the bodies burned there are basically unclaimed anyway."

I'm curious about the economics of cremation. How much does it actually cost?

"A conventional cremation at this ghat costs around six to seven hundred rupees, including wood. That's the single most expensive item and the one in shortest supply. It takes four to five quintals of wood to burn a body. At today's rates that's five hundred rupees — and we're not talking sandalwood but ordinary wood. Of course, the softer the wood the more you'll need because it will burn quicker."

The electric crematorium used to be a lot cheaper — twenty-five rupees a body. But the Allahabad High Court ordered the city to raise the

---

[27] In 1986 in Varanasi, Rajiv Gandhi said the purity of Ganga was not in question. But the river had been adversely impacted by dirt and wastes and made unclean (ganda). "If it is to be made clean again we have to stop throwing so much waste into it. We have to clean it up." Cf. Alley, op. cit. p. 37.

fee for the electric crematoria from twenty-five rupees a cremation to five hundred rupees. While even the poorest of the poor could afford the former, those fees were totally inadequate to pay for the actual costs of running the electric crematorium. As a consequence the building was more or less closed for twenty years. Even today the gates are more often padlocked than open. The price differential has almost vanished: it now costs virtually the same, however you cremate the body. And the traditional method doesn't involve load-shedding.

"No one over there," Shivkumar jerks his head towards to the electric crematorium, "of course, ever performs the sanatana dharma.[28] We're much more adapted to the modern world than they are. My elder brother has even conducted rituals with a family in the USA, using a landline phone. Before mobiles! Part of the family here, part over there, and he saying the slokas into the phone."

~

, A few days later, Rakesh and I drive down to the Combined Effluent Treatment Plant complex at Jajmao. When I'd visited it a few years previously I'd been quite impressed by its working efficiency. Today, the place appears shut down. The only visible sign of activity are a few workers playing cricket on the lawns. They tell me they've not been paid for four months by the state. So they've gone on strike in the autumn sunshine on a "glorified time pass."[29]

All three treatment plants have stopped functioning. The Jal Nigam say they haven't received any funds from Lucknow so they can't pay any salaries, even their own. I would feel more sympathy if it wasn't for a large clean vacant administrative building at the entrance of the complex marked Administrative Building UP Jal Nigam. This was constructed with Ganga Action Plan funds but now the UP Jal Nigam office is right at the other end of the city, nowhere near the river they are supposed to regulate.

Meanwhile they pay heavy rent for a vacant building, where they could be on top of things. They'd see firsthand how little wastewater is actually coming into the plant since that main trunk sewer is broken. They'd also surely notice that tannery waste containing hexavalent

---

[28] Literally the "eternal truth" or "eternal religion."

[29] A few weeks later, when I visit the Dinapur sewage treatment plant in Varanasi, the strike is still unresolved. The Jal Nigam workers there are also on strike.

chromium is going directly into the river because no plants are working. They'd also see that the machinery inside the sewage treatment plant is visibly rusting. If the strike continues much longer, those machines will start to resemble an animal skeleton, picked clean by predators and bleached white by the sun.

One thing is working though. Jal Nigam have eighteen malis tending the grounds. They're impeccable.

I think all this has come as a terrible shock to Rakesh. He just wanders round, shaking his head, muttering a mantra of despair. If only the Jal Nigam had kept their office manned here in Jajmao. But nobody in government seem aware that the whole plant has been idle for months. They know about the strike, but profess total ignorance about its effect on the plant.[30] Anyway, to a man they (the Pollution Control Board, the Jal Nigam) all throw up their hands and lament impotently:

"It's not my responsibility!"

Or as the wily Mayor Akhil Kumar Sharma suavely puts it: "This is the state government's responsibility. It does not depend on me, so I can't comment."

Time and again I meet the same refrain. "It is someone else's responsibility!" And when in doubt blame Delhi for not giving them enough money.[31]

"The rates for taxes on sewers and water supply were set in the nineteenth century — fourteen percent on water and four percent for sewers." F.U. Rehman tells me over biscuits and chai, even though it's Ramadan and he's fasting.

Rehman is head of the grandiloquently named Project Planning & Coordination Unit, Ganga Action Plan Support Project, which means his unit measures progress (or the lack of it) of the Indo-Dutch part of the Ganga Action Plan here in Kanpur.

---

[30] In 2005 they moved even that office from Kanpur to Lucknow, ninety kilometers away from Ganga.

[31] In theory, India has a utopian constitution and a beautiful institutional pyramid. There are now three layers of government — federal, state, and local, with powers and resources devolved to each level. In practice, democracy is the proverbial spanner in the works. The rates haven't changed much since 1880. But raising taxes requires approval by the state assembly in Lucknow. And since when did anybody get elected by advocating raising taxes on voters? So, while Indians are visibly getting wealthier by the day — acquiring the trappings of a modern consumer society — their infrastructure crumbles because politicians invariably choose the easy way out.

"At that time sewerage meant open drains. Now we have underground sewers, we have pumping stations, we have treatment plants, yet the rates have stayed the same."

Something obviously has to give, new taxes need to be levied. Progress is slow, very slow, but at least the city has managed to broaden the local tax base. Twenty years ago only seventy-two thousand households paid any tax at all. Now it's up to two hundred thousand households. It's a start. But the target is 350 thousand.

"After all, if people want better services they have to be prepared to pay for them." says Rehman. In the meantime, until both the state and the municipal assemblies vote new taxes for sewers and water, Kanpur needs subsidies to run the entire sewer and water infrastructure. In between biscuits I remark:

"You always use the future tense, I notice."

Rehman agrees: "Unfortunately, that is the reality. We have a democratic system where things are not done in a very harsh way. They have to be done in a very smooth manner." A polite euphemism surely for saying few politicians ever get elected for raising taxes. In a democracy that's usually messy and takes time.

As Mr. Sinha of the Jal Nigam says forlornly in his darkened office: "If the local body says no, revenue stays the same. The asset [his jargon for a proposed new sewage treatment plant in south Kanpur on the Pandu river] will be just a beautiful white elephant."

All is not entirely lost, however. The Mayor Mr. Sharma says the sewage treatment plants will be handed over to the municipal Jal Sansthan[32] in 2006: "We will look at the need for raising taxes to operate the sewage treatment plants. Jal Sansthan is an autonomous body. It can set rates independently."

But Mr. Sharma dashes the cup before it even reaches my lips: "All hypothetical, of course."

"Why?" I ask.

"Let Jal Sansthan have this baby then they will see how to feed it, what to feed it, how to make the baby healthy. But since baby's not here yet, no point in speculating."[33]

The same dilemma is doubtless present in Varanasi, though they have bigger fish to fry — getting the state and the central governments to endorse their choice of the Sankat Mochan's stabilization ponds. I presume

---

[32] Municipal government.

[33] Mr. Sharma *is* indeed standing again but the election has been delayed. If he's reelected, will he do the needful and raise the rates?

that if power is really devolved in Varanasi the municipal Jal Sansthan there will also acquire the autonomy to raise rates. At least that should start to pay for the running and maintenance of their system.

Corruption never seems to be rigorously documented but all Kanpurites are convinced it's rampant and the reason why Ganga is still dirty. Many assure me that the State Water Board is selling off the diesel it needs to run the treatment plant at Jajmao. If this is true then the actual corruption has to be taking place in the state capital in Lucknow.

"We don't have enough money to even buy diesel fuel for our office generators. So how can we be selling it off?" Mr Sinha, the head of the Jal Nigam, shrugs as I lend him my torch to find a phone number in his darkened offices.

For Rakesh Jaiswal, though, public apathy is the real culprit. He simply cannot understand why the citizens of Kanpur don't rise up against all the public institutions that are responsible for cleaning and maintaining the river: "Why don't they demand accountability, raise water taxes, stop throwing their garbage directly into the river?"

I've heard this echoed up and down the entire Ganga. Activists have not yet come to terms with the reality of a deafening absence of public anger.

In Varanasi Pandit Satyindra Mishra of Dasasvamedha Ghat dreams of mobilizing devotees. MC Mehta, the lawyer in Delhi who single-handedly has been responsible for getting industry to make a nominal start at cleaning up its act, wants to create an independent foundation to clean up Ganga. Rakesh Jaiswal wants Indians to rise up in an andolan.[34]

Rakesh's group Eco Friends have succeeded in making some people aware of pollution; they've got the mayor to spend money beautifying the river bank (though I've yet to see how and where) and they have mobilized high school students and at least made them enthusiastic and alarmingly articulate "Ganga ambassadors."

But apathy and just plain ignorance rule.

~

One day on the river I stop and talk with Tanga Lal who is performing his pooja at Bhagwandas Ghat. He's been coming here every morning for most of his sixty-eight years. He says all the right things: things like "Those who pollute are sinners," while pouring milk from a

---

[34] Mass movement.

plastic bag into Ganga "to feed her." When the bag's empty he casually throws it too into the river.

"Why do you just do that, if you know you are sinning?"

Tanga Lal is immediately contrite.

"I will stop as of today. Ganga is my mother. I worship her for peace of mind. You are right, Sir. I will no longer pollute my mother."

Somehow I doubt it. Tanga Lal can't help himself or change the habits of a lifetime. And he really doesn't understand why pouring milk into Ganga is a form of pollution. For him it is showing respect for his mother.

Raja exhorts Tanga Lal to spread the word. I think it would be in vain. Tanga Lal admits as much:

"I will tell them, tell them sir. But the public here, does not agree sir." Raja sternly admonishes him: "We have to make them agree."

Tanga Lal repeats his simple statement: "The public here does not agree."

A little bit further downstream we pull in to chat with some dhobis rhythmically beating the hell out of someone's clothes on flat stones propped up at the river's edge. Washing powder contains phosphates. Everyone knows that. Most people in the West also know phosphates and caustic soda are harmful. They've been banned from all laundry detergents not least because they stimulate the wrong sort of algae blooms. But word hasn't reached the dhobis on Ghola Ghat. Mithai Lal is proud that his family have been washing clothes for as long as he can remember.

"Yes, of course we use detergent powder. It is good."

"You don't think it's harmful to Ganga?"

The conversation takes on a surrealistic tone: "It is good because it cleans Ganga. It kills all the germs and small insects. It bleaches the water. See the dirty water coming from the nullah. This is sewage, shit. This is what is killing the water. But we are *cleaning* Ganga, with these detergents and caustic sodas and acids."

Of course Ganga is pure and yes, in case you doubted, Mitha Lal does indeed drink Ganga jal daily and never gets sick.

We pull up back in to Sati Chaura Ghat and are drinking chai, gazing out at the river, talking with our boatman Bhagwan about the on-going campaign to prevent people using the river as a dumping ground for their plastic bags. A young Gurkha soldier from the nearby cantonment strides up to the ghat, throws a ball of flowers and plastic bags as far out into the river as he can, turns round and marches briskly off back to the barracks.

~

It's equally hard to put all the blame for the pollution of the river on the tanneries. The bigger plants solemnly swear they have indeed complied with court orders. They claim to have installed recovery plants in their factories to remove toxic chromium used in the tanning process to soften animal hides. But it's also true that many of these plants are often idle.

Quite why is unclear. Imran Siddiqui, owner of Super Tannery, one of the largest in Kanpur, assures me it's in the tanneries' own economic interests to recover the chromium. The recovery plants can pay for themselves within five years. He's probably right. So why don't they run them all the time and get their money back?

Most of my discussions with tannery owners, great and small, are like conversations with politicians. We fence around the issues, the owners carefully avoiding saying anything on tape that could come back to haunt them later. The one thing that emerges clearly is that they feel they've got both a raw deal and bad press, so why make things worse by admitting any guilt? But that still doesn't explain why they don't use the recovery plants. If recovering chrome actually makes such good economic sense, why would they try to save electricity by not running their recovery plants?

Mr. Siddiqui does make some interesting (and probably misleading) points: the tanneries produce trivalent chromium that only becomes toxic hexavalent chromium when it is oxidized. He suggests the agent could therefore be something else entirely, say latex or cyanide from the electro-plating industries in city, or even, perish the heresy, oxidisation taking place in the anaerobic treatment phase itself. Are the large tanneries indeed the only culprits? I go down the lane to a small tannery. Small tanneries are not required to remove their own chromium at their plants. So could they be the real sinners?

Akhtar Hussain, owner of a traditional vegetable tannery unit, says their process takes three months instead of the two days tanneries need if they use chromium, so he's not guilty of pollution. Using crushed bark and various seeds sounds so simple, how can anyone actually make money? The answer is probably that it is not just a simple matter of crushing a few seeds and soaking the leather in it. These units, though small, would have a dedicated clientele too, and that is why they are able to withstand the faster processing competition. Proof surely is that Akhtar Hussain says he makes a good living and has married off all three daughters.

But he's tired of always getting blamed for the inadequacies of the Jal Nigam. I ask him if it's true that some tannery owners bribe the agencies to look the other way. He won't go there and dances round all my attempts to pin him down. He signals his agreement with a nod of his head, but nothing on tape.

He suggests I talk with Hafiz ur-Rahman, aka Babu Bai, president of the Small Tanneries Association, who makes it clear the small tanneries have been duped by the Indian government. He confirms they are paying almost two crore of rupees[35] in maintenance fees for the treatment plant at Jajmao. If it isn't working he feels gypped. Doubly so because "the government assured us that the Dutch treatment plant at Jajmao can remove hexavalent chromium. So why do we need to band together and set up our own chromium removal plant? Now you tell us chromium is the reason anaerobic treatment doesn't work?"

"OK. I admit there is a problem, but I will still send my waste directly to Jajmao." He literally throws up his hands: "It's all the government's responsibility. We have to stay globally competitive. We cannot afford a removal plant. It's all a plot by the large tanneries to drive us out of business."

Babu Rai mutters he doesn't feel very well. His skin is indeed an unhealthy dull grey. Martine whispers to me, "I bet he's got chromium poisoning."[36]

A final question: "What do you feel about all the accusations in the press that the tanneries are the cause of all the pollution?"

"Do you know the analogy of the goat and the lion? Here in India the lion is called the king of animals. And the goat is very small and that's why in any religious sacrifice, the goat is sacrificed. Never the lion."

"Are you the goat?" I ask.

"We are such easy prey."

~

Just when you thought it couldn't get any worse, we're invited to Motipur village a few kilometers inland from Jajmao. The plants in both Varanasi and Kanpur have been sending treated waste water through canals to irrigate the fields in local villages, and charging for it. In Varanasi, the local pollution board has sided with villagers near the main sewage treatment plant at Dinapur, who complain their fields are getting contaminated by irrigation water from the plant, and demand action be

---

[35] The actual figure is Rs 1.75 crores.

[36] Thank goodness only I heard it, or we might have been lynched on the spot. In Hindu culture, it's the equivalent of putting a curse on the man.

taken. Villagers are having trouble finding brides for their sons. No one wants to come and live in smelly Dinapur. But to date nothing has been done.

In Motipur and the surrounding villages in Jajmao there are similar problems but on a far more serious scale.

Mohammad Owais, one of Rakesh Jaiswal's assistants and himself the son of a small tannery owner, explains that the irrigation water used to be 50:50 Ganga river water and raw sewage. Now it's one hundred percent sewage, including the supposedly chromium-free treated effluent. In theory this should be okay, because anything harmful will have been removed at the sewage treatment plant.

But not if hexavalent chromium is still flowing from the tanneries to the plant, and out again into the irrigation water. The plants can't remove hexavalent chromium, so the new "improved" irrigation water will be toxic and lethal. The old irrigation water was just plain dirty and smelly. Not much of an improvement.

In 2002, the National Botanical Research Institute in Lucknow found Cr(VI) in the groundwater and soil in the villages around Jajmao. More recently, the Facility for Ecological and Analytical Testing at IIT-Kanpur carried out more detailed testing, and it's bad, very bad.[37] Hexavalent chromium and a whole host of other heavy metals — cadmium, mercury — are now in the food chain. The villages all rely on that irrigation water from the plant for their fields and animals and, to add insult to injury, Jal Nigam had the gall to charge them for it. Past tense because now they've at least had the decency to suspend payments.

Motipur is probably the worst-affected being nearest to the main irrigation canal. Walk down the main road in Motipur village and all you'll see are buffaloes. Motipur supplies much of the milk for Kanpur.

We go to the clinic of the village doctor Parshuram Yadav. He also covers all the surrounding villages. The total affected population is forty thousand. Of those he says three thousand are sick because of the irrigation water. Sickness means the usual skin diseases, eczema, stomach worms. But in Motipur things are worse. The ground water is now contaminated down to a depth of forty feet. They have to sink deep bore tube wells to a depth of twelve hundred feet to find pure drinking water,

---

[37] You can see the results at www.ecofriends.org. Click on Reports and scroll down to the bottom of the page to *Report of the Public Hearing on the Issue of Supply of Toxic Sewage Irrigation water to the Farmlands at Jajmao and its Disastrous Impact on Drinking Water, Agriculture, Health and Livelihoods.* RK Sinha of Patna University has also discovered alarmingly high levels of Cr (VI) and eight other toxic heavy metals in the groundwater at Varanasi. But nobody has taken any action.

and at their own expense. They could go after the Jal Nigam or the Dutch. But people are understandably reluctant to go to court because the effort could take a lifetime.

He's treating ten new patients a day with symptoms of Cr(VI) poisoning. We tramp down Motipur's main street. Dr. Yadav points out a two-year-old buffalo that is so weak and thin it can't even stand. Others have mottled skin. A third of them have aborted. For any farmer the loss of unborn livestock is equivalent to an uninsured bank collapsing, taking with it all your savings. A female buffalo costs at least twenty thousand rupees. You can expect it to give twelve litres of fresh milk a day. The buffaloes in Motipur are now giving half that yield.

Dr. Yadav calls out a healthy young boy, asks him to turn round, pulls aside his thick dark hair: underneath, the scalp is completely bald. While we've been walking, a middle-aged woman called Ramkali has been summoned and now comes in from her fields. Ramkali pulls back her left sleeve. Her entire hand is deformed by leprosy: she'd contracted it five years ago. Dr. Yadav has sent her for tests at the Medical College: they say it comes from washing in the contaminated irrigation water.

A young farmer, one-eyed Sunil, asks me to follow him: he wants to show me his fields. They look the picture of health. In the center of one field is a small pile of threshed wheat. Sunil picks up an ear; crumbles it in his hand. The husks are empty. An entire standing crop is in effect dead on arrival.In a healthy harvest this field should yield one thousand kilos of wheat. This year twenty-five kilos, fit only for fodder.

All the correct things have been done. The courts have told the state government to clean up the contaminated land, and pay the medical costs of the villagers. The state government does nothing. So the court issues contempt notices, which are equally casually ignored.

Martine in disgust calls what has happened here "a crime against humanity." Certainly these are crimes against their own kith and kin. The state pollution control board and the Jal Nigam do not see themselves as evil. They are flawed human beings in a system that makes it hard to stand up for basic moral standards. But if children and adults in Kanpur start getting sick, even dying from drinking milk contaminated with toxic metals, then maybe Martine isn't exaggerating: it will be a crime against humanity. But who to bring to justice?

When I described what I had seen at Motipur to Babu Rai, the ailing president of the Small Tanneries Association, he denied even the . smallest smidgin of responsibility.

"All these villages are lying. Look at them, their fields are green, not brown. It's all a plot to avoid taxes."

I explain the reality of that paddy and show him photos. He changes tack.

"We only send 7 mld a day of waste to Jajmao anyway. The rest of Kanpur sends 160 mld. So everyone else is far more guilty than us. Why do you always blame the tanneries?"

He changes direction yet again: "It's all caused by nuclear radiation. The large tanneries want to drive us out of business. So they're spreading this false propaganda that it's all our fault."

He sighs, like a man nearing death. "We are so helpless."

~

Rakesh Jaiswal feels all his life's work has been wasted.

"Total waste of funds. Ganga Action Plan is a complete failure. It's neither Ganga-friendly, nor people-friendly."

Others — Veer Badre Mishra or Vinod Tare — agree, although those who are inside the GAP, of course, see things differently.

Mr. Sachin, manager of the UP Pollution Control Board says, "Well, pressures on Ganga, just like India's population have doubled. But DO and BOD levels are roughly the same. That is real progress. Imagine what they would be without Ganga Action Plan?"

I can cite a dozen officials and other apologists who have made that or similar statements to me. But let's take them at their word. Imagine if there had been no Ganga Action Plan? What would have happened then?

Maybe Vinod Tare's settling ponds and Veer Badre Mishra's stabilization ponds would have won favor. But then again maybe not. They would have both meant government's surrendering power to local solutions. Similarly, MC Mehta's proposal for an independent people's trust to control Ganga might have led to deadlock as various groups fought it out as to who should have the ultimate say.

It's always tempting to try and turn the clock back to a simpler, more innocent age. But history does not go backwards. The Ganga Action Plan is still a good idea but it has been mis-managed from day one. Ineffective and (possibly) inappropriate criteria were selected. The whole operation was run badly from the start and maintenance was scandalously neglected.

Everyone today in Kanpur feels powerless. They know it. They have no money to do the needful. At the same time as the Indian economy is growing by leaps and bounds there are still staggering inefficiencies, bordering on criminal incompetence.

Kanpur is the scene of this tragedy. Ironically, it's also the doorway to India's most sacred heartland, where millions of Indians (among them our driver Bijoy Tivari) come to worship Ganga as *the* goddess.

But even though he's visibly disturbed by what he has seen here in Kanpur, Bijoy Tivari's faith remains unshaken:

"It has not lessened. I have seen this pollution and I will tell people how much it is polluted. She will become pure and clean again when she reaches Allahabad and beyond. This is her greatness, how she purifies this much dirt. I do not believe Ganga will ever really dry up, even if she has much less water."

*****

Allahabad

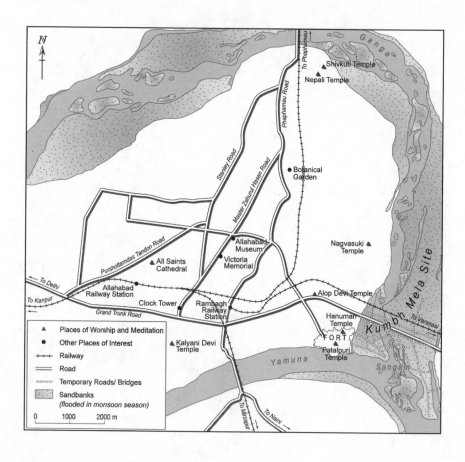

CHAPTER 4

Sacred Heartland

How can this poisoned river limping out of Kanpur ever survive? Yet, within less than twenty kilometers, it has somehow recovered.[1] It's still frighteningly emaciated because too much water is being pumped out for irrigation, yet all vital signs are now positive.

The devout claim this is simply proof of the powers of the goddess to purify herself of man's pollution. The skeptical scientist might draw a more frightening conclusion: out of sight, out of mind. He would argue that all the highly toxic heavy metals that have been dumped unconscionably in Ganga have not been purified at all. They have simply sunk to the river bed where they now lie, still highly poisonous but dormant.

And then, who knows? This is uncharted territory. Will they enter the groundwater, then the food chain and so into the human bloodstream? And when? In a few years, several lifetimes? Nobody really knows. They just sit and wait, a toxic time bomb waiting to explode, while people forget and go on living their lives.

Two hundred kilometers downstream at Allahabad, Himalayan Ganga will finally be rescued and rejuvenated by a massive transfusion of fresh water from the Yamuna, and will then flow down to Varanasi. In terms of volume, Yamuna becomes the senior partner. By rights the river should now be called Yamuna Ganga. But nobody does because while Yamuna is sacred,[2] she is not considered a goddess. Just as in the

---

[1] Measurements show repeatedly that all Ganga's vital signs (DO, BOD) are back to normal less than twenty kilometers downstream.

[2] There are seven sacred rivers in Indian mythology: Ganga, Yamuna, Narmada, Krishna, Godavari, Sindhu, Indus, Kaveri, and Saraswati, although other rivers, notably the Krishna, are also considered sacred.

Himalayas Bhagirathi alone carries the "divine gene," so here in these northern plains, Ganga, and her alone, is a goddess.

This awareness is physically concentrated at innumerable tirthas up and down the river. There are some tirthas in the eastern half of Ganga, Jahngira Island in Bihar is an obvious one, but the vast concentration is found in the Himalayas and in Uttar Pradesh (UP), especially between Allahabad and Varanasi. Ganga here is a benign presence — Ganga ma (Mother Ganga) — who bestows only blessings on human beings. She is mythology in liquid form, whose waters irrigate the fields, cleanse the soul of sins, and carry the ashes of the departed to heaven.

This four hundred kilometer stretch of river between Kanpur and Varanasi is doubly sacred because it's the setting for the great epic Ramayana. This is where its heroes — Rama, Sita, and Laxman — lived, loved, and experienced tragedy. The universal popular greeting here is Sita Rama. Sita has thus become synonymous with Ganga. Sites along the river associated with episodes in the Ramayana are highly auspicious. Time collapses. Events two thousand years old happened just yesterday.

This is the "sacred heartland" of Ganga, the goddess whom millions of ordinary Hindus believe can never die, whatever the level of pollution or physical overuse. The main attraction for millions of Hindus is the sangam at Allahabad, where three rivers — Ganga, Yamuna, and the mythical Saraswati[3] — merge. It is always especially auspicious to bathe wherever and whenever rivers meet in India.

There is also less urbanisation and few heavy industries in this reach. From downstream of Kanpur all the way, and including Varanasi, most pollution tends to be run-off from fields and human sewage. Hazardous to one's health, but not fatal. So the river gets a much-needed

---

[3] Most foreigners, especially scientists, assume Saraswati is a figment of mythological imagination. However, many distinguished Indian geologists believe it really did exist. They argue that the Saraswati river would have risen in the Himalayas and now flows into the Ghaggara in Pakistan. Various authors have speculated that Saraswati was the parent river of both Satluj and Yamuna. In the special volume cited below, many of the contributors are convinced it flowed into Rajasthan, through the Thar desert and out into the sea in Gujarat. Its disappearance would have been caused by earthquakes and seismic movements in the Himalayas. None of the authors makes the link to the Sarawasti of sangam fame, but that doesn't mean it couldn't have happened.

There are indeed important rivers — Karnali and Satluj — which rise on the north side of the Trans-Himalayas in Tibet, but flow through ancient, deep and narrow gorges down into the southern slopes of the drainage divide, against all apparent laws of geology. Cf: pp 329 of *Vedic Saraswati: Evolutionary History of a last Rover of NorthWestern India*, Ed. B.P. Radakrishna and S.S. Merh, Memoir 42 Geological Society of India, Bangalore, 2002.

second-wind. But the same lack of enough water in the river remains a major problem. Thoma Gokhale, the dredger captain in Kanpur, warned me that irrigation for agriculture takes off ever more water down to Allahabad: "I wouldn't go down to Allahabad by boat. You'll spend all your time walking with *Basanti* on the river bank."

~

So we follow his advice and travel from Kanpur to Varanasi by car, camping along the way. Our journey is leisurely, stopping at various tirthas, big and small, all chosen according to a master plan known only to Bijoy Tivari.

The first night we camp at the Hanuman Mandir run by a tall bearded swami called Siya Ram Das, on the south bank of the river at Palhana. Ram Das offers us fresh vegetables from his garden and milk from the cow whose byre we share. It's a wonderful spot, high on a bluff. But Ganga has already migrated several kilometers away, so Tivari suggests we drive through Allahabad and head out to Singhberpur near Lalgopalganj on the northern bank of Ganga, about thirty kilometers upstream of Allahabad. It doesn't figure on our road map. But it turns out to be an inspired choice.

The village is on the banks of Ganga and appears timeless and far removed from modern India. We pitch our tents in the grounds of the local Sanskrit school, whose great and proud claim is that Murli Manohar Joshi studied here. Mr. Joshi was Education Minister in the BJP[4] government and hell-bent on "saffronizing" the national curriculum. Not surprisingly, the school is a true-blue Hindi culture school. But it has a water pump and plenty of wood for cooking. And just outside its walls are rather nice ghats.

We soon discover the real reason why Tivari has brought us here. Singhberpur is a tirtha. A tirtha is indeed more than just a pilgrimage spot. It is a place where a human can cross into the world of the gods, and a god into the world of the humans. Ganga is dotted with such tirthas — some famous like Haridwar or the sangam at Allahabad, others small like Jahngira Island, Bithur or Singhberpur — known only to devout Hindus. Diana Eck, a Harvard professor much respected in Varanasi, calls them "sacred power points."

In Sanskrit, tirtha literally means to ford, to cross over to the other side. So, it's not surprising that some (though not all) tirthas are

---

[4] The Bharatiya Janata Party (BJP) headed a coalition that ruled India from 1999 to 2004.

along river banks where one could ford the river more easily. They were real physical fords.

There are thousands of tirthas in India, not necessarily specific to a river. They can be places where holy men — sages, sanyasis, and sahdus — congregate. Tirthas can therefore be formed by the sheer physical concentrated presence of such people. They can also be of the mind. There's a long passage in the *Mahabharata* which talks about tirthas of the heart, the qualities of love, generosity, truthfulness, and patience.

Tirthas never stay constant — there are new ones that appear and ones that have been important in centuries past that most people scarcely know about anymore. Some are purely local, others regional (say Bengal or Maharashtra); a few are known all over India. Tirthas can appear because a new goddess has become important, such as Vaishnodevi in Jammu in the last few hundred years. There are brand-new tirthas associated with contemporary religious leaders like Saibaba.

Singhberpur has an additional claim to fame because of its connection to the *Ramayana*.[5] This tirtha is where Rama, Sita, and Laxman, after being forced into an exile that would last fourteen years, crossed Ganga on their way south. A rishi who meditated right here gave them food and shelter.

The ferry on the far bank at Palhana, where we camped the previous night, marks the spot where they crossed, according to Bhagwat Prasad Misra, who is one of the purohits in Singhberpur. It is said Sita talked to Ganga here. Singhberpur is also a favoured place for women to come and pray for sons, interestingly not to Ganga or Sita but to the rishi's wife, Shanti Devi.

Bhagwat Misra tells me that at this January's Marg Mela the river turned red from the pollution of the tanneries in Kanpur, two hundred kilometers upstream. Misra laments, "There's nothing we can do about it. So we only use Ganga jal for religious purposes. We bathe here but we use tube well water for drinking." But red doesn't make much sense. Chromium is blue. I probe further. Misra then admits the water was probably stained red because of all the sheep slaughtered for Eid-al-Fitr by the predominantly Muslim community, who just happen to live in Jajmao, near the tanneries.

Tivari has been in a state of high excitement since we arrived. To please him I strip down and take my first-ever dip with him in the

---

[5] In Book 2 of Valmiki's *Ramayana* there is a lovely description of Ganga at Singhberpur. Cf p. 102, Ch 21 of the Ayodhyakanda's *The Ramayana of Valmiki*, translated by Makhan Lal Sen, Munshiram Manoharlal Publishers, New Delhi, 1976.

river. I've never really before thought about swimming in Ganga. The water is warm, quite clean to the eye and skin, altogether refreshing. Mine surely isn't a true "holy dip" because I'm not a Hindu and don't know the rituals, but it sends Tivari into paroxysms of happiness. "Chief has bathed in this holy tirtha with me. To take a dip here can only add to his virtue." If I'd only known it was this simple to make him so happy I'd have bathed in Ganga a lot sooner.

I really should have asked a lot sooner why we had abandoned Palhana for Singhberpur. Tivari's always been a huge believer in the Ramayana. He knows the entire epic down to the smallest details. He's overjoyed because Motilal Sukla, the headmaster of the Sanskrit school, has just told him that Radha and Krishna also visited Singhberpur. Mr. Sukla assures him that Radha is an avatar of the goddess Ganga.[6]

~

The *Ramayana* is as present to the villagers here as if it had unfolded within their own lifetimes. I've often wondered: how come?[7] For Tivari, it always seems that such and such event occurred literally yesterday, certainly within the lifetime of his grandfather, when we know it really took place (if at all) two or three thousand years ago. It is very real to him. But why?

Tivari looks mystified when I ask him, but later in Delhi my friend Sharada Nayak says it's simple. "In an oral culture, stories are repeated day after day till they become real. They may just as well have happened yesterday. Not that one always believes these stories actually occurred." The *Ramayana* or the *Mahabharata* therefore can unlock the door to understanding a very different sense of time. For someone raised in the Indian countryside (still the vast majority of Indians) what's most important is the actual experience.

---

[6] As far as I know she isn't, but belief is always in the mind of the believer, so if you want to believe that Radha is an avatar of Ganga, why not?

[7] For most Indians, time is naturally circular, an idea so basic to Indians they probably never stop to even think about it. But it's one that never seems to occur to non-Indians. Other non-Western civilizations (China, Islam) continue to function quite well with their own calendars. Amartya Sen has a very interesting analysis of the various calendars (Hindi, Bengali, Tamil, etc) in use in today's India in Chapter 7 of *The Argumentative Indian*. Western culture, on the other hand, has a linear concept of time, which is closely linked to a Western idea of progress. The present is better than the past, and the future will be by definition better than the present. My friend Indu Agarwal thinks this is just plain stupid. Time for her is circular, so human beings are fated to repeat the same mistakes, warts and all.

As Sharada explains, "If you tell me that such and such a thing happened, and you tell it well, it is immediately vivid. I believe it. It isn't important if it happened to you yesterday or it happened ten years ago. What's important is the very fact that it happened to you and affected you so deeply and that your narration conveys this to me. It's the event, the transformation, not when, that's important."

Sharada continues, "If you identify with the *Ramayana* myth or the *Mahabharata* myth so strongly, actual time (the date or the year) becomes unimportant. The fact that it happened is what is important. If it happened, it has implications for the entirety of human experience." Whole centuries, even millennia, are collapsed through oral folklore into the span of a single lifetime.

Great myths such as the *Ramayana* also help define a sense of the geography of India because, "Stories are the traditional ways of defining the shape and geography of the land. My great-grandmother was totally illiterate but she heard these stories so she knew all of India even though she'd never traveled beyond her village."

~

The villagers in Singhberpur ask me if I've visited the ruins of Gawuk's Fort. Mehendi Hassan, the official in charge from the Indian Archaeological Survey, isn't quite sure what to do with us: refuse us entry or go along and hope no one says anything. In the end he opts to show us around.

Mr. Hassan explains that this isn't a fort at all, but a partial excavation of an ingenious water harvesting and purification system. The tank is two thousand years old. Water from Ganga came in, was purified, stored, and then expelled out the other side into containers. The "fort" also had a clever use of jagged tiles to aid the grip of bathers. The villagers, of course, will always believe it is a site from the *Ramayana*.

When we get back to the school, Mr. Sukla has prepared a surprise. His students are going to recite part of the Ganga Lahiri in Sanskrit. Normally, I'd be very excited, but the recitation is unfortunately off-tune, and about as inspiring as warmed-over rotis. Even Tivari is unimpressed. He goes to dust down the Scorpio. That evening, before aarti on the village ghats, I ask Dr. Sukla out of curiosity if he speaks Sanskrit at home. "A little," he replies, "But it's really the language of the gods."

The aarti is a more pleasant experience because it is short and devoid of all the hoopla that surrounds aartis at the more obvious pilgrimage spots along Ganga. Much of it is slightly out-of-tune and unpolished, interrupted by chants of Ganga Jai and Sita Ram, assorted gongs, and blasts on the conch shell. The performance is impressive not least because of the extraordinary breath control displayed by the pradhan, Bhagawat Prasad Tripathi, who then recites Singhberpur's connection to Ramayana as told by Tulsidas in the *Ramcharitmanas* — the Awadhi dialect version of the *Ramayana*. After ten minutes, mercifully the other pandas hurry him along. They want to finish the ceremony, go off home, and eat.

At seven the next morning, Bhagwat Prasad Misra is circumambulating the temple chanting in praise of Shanti Devi. Far below men bathe and chat, a man hammers a charpoy back together. But our time is up.

Reluctantly we have to leave Rama, Sita and Shanti Devi for the legendary Sangam at Allahabad, where Ganga and Yamuna (and Saraswati) meet. In Hindu mythology Varanasi, Gaya in Bihar, and Allahabad are the three most holy places to bring the ashes of a departed family member.

In front of Allahabad University we pick up Manoj, one of Bijoy's five brothers. The family village near Sultanpur is a hundred kilometers north of Allahabad. I first met Manoj in 2001, in slightly unusual circumstances.

Bijoy had an Ambassador back then. We'd come from Haridwar en route to Varanasi. Mobile phones were still around the corner, but somehow Bijoy had arranged a time and place with his youngest brother. We came to a halt on the side of the main highway outside the High Court and a young man stepped forward. Bijoy got out, opened the boot of the Ambassador, took out the spare tire and lifted out a twenty five-kilo sack of basmati rice stored underneath. Little brother was being re-supplied by his elder sibling. Transaction completed, off we drove to Varanasi.

Three years later cell phones make such rendezvous commonplace. Manoj speaks Sanskrit and Awadhi, so Bijoy has picked him up as we drive through Allahabad.

In guide books for Allahabad, Ganga is often described as sweeping down from the north. Sweeping is too grand a word. Limping would be far more appropriate. Ganga staggers round, exhausted, from the north; Yamuna, green and pregnant with vitality, from the south. Ganga is no more than three feet deep, Yamuna twenty.[8] A boatman

---

[8] Yamuna, of course, rises at Yamnotri in the Garhwal Himalayas, just a few kilometres to the west of Ganga, and is roughly the same size when it leaves the mountains for the plains. It's virtually brain-dead at Delhi, because pollution has exhausted virtually all its supply of dissolved oxygen. And then it too miraculously recovers. And it swells in size, much of its new water coming from rivers flowing off the Deccan Plateau to its south, notably the Chambal and the Betwa. By the time it meets Ganga at Allahabad it's one and a half times as big as Ganga.

swore to me that Yamuna is a hundred feet and Ganga thirty feet deep at the Sangam. But I've walked in the latter so I know he's wrong.

Most visitors, pilgrims, or just the plain curious, camp at the sangam — the sandbars where the two rivers physically meet. Allahabad is called Tirth Raj Prayag, the king of tirthas. I can see why.

The actual sangam is marked by a line of country boats — little floating villages — moored in a very gentle crescent along part of the ridge where the two rivers meet. Yamuna — the more vigorous — flows into the muddy brown Ganga almost at right angles. For several hundred metres the two keep their formal distance — you can see the strict line of demarcation as they flow side by side. And then natural reserve breaks and they become less and less distinguishable until they are just one.[9] The sangam as the sun goes down is one of the most beautiful sights in the world.

Each of the hundred or so country boats displays a pennant to inform those who can't read where to find the purohit or pilgrimage priest for their district or state. A peasant coming from Madhya Pradesh or Rajasthan would immediately know where the panda with his family records could be found.

The kumbh camping grounds are huge, criss-crossed with roads. As we enter, youths leap on to the running-board of the Scorpio, offering protection and advice on where to go — in return for the usual bakshish. I've been warned about them.

"Manoj, we can't stay here," I tell him. "Those guys will strip the Scorpio as soon as we're asleep. Is there anywhere else?"

"I know somewhere quiet on the Naini road on the other side," Manoj replies.

Half an hour later we drive into the Sri Sachcha ashram complex on the southern side of Yamuna, directly opposite the camping grounds we had so recently fled. In the center is a sunken garden. Martine and I are of one mind: "We'll camp here."

---

[9] Devout Hindus, of course, believe a third river — the Saraswati — also joins with Ganga and Yamuna to form a triveni, a meeting of three rivers — the most auspicious of all. Most foreigners and quite a few Indians pooh-pooh this idea but reputable Indian geologists say it's not impossible. Indeed Saraswati exists. It flows into Alaknanda (and hence into Ganga) near Badrinath. Recent surveys using infra-red aerial technology have confirmed that it once flowed parallel to the Satluj and Indus to the sea in Gujarat. But earthquakes several thousand years ago probably blocked its overland course; instead it flowed into the Alaknanda. There is often more than a grain of truth about myths in India — they are usually worth exploring because they echo an actual physical catastrophe that once occurred. I would therefore never dismiss out of hand the story of the Saraswati at the sangam.

Manoj asks if I'd like to talk with Sachcha Baba Gopalji. "Yes, why not?" I say.

Sachcha Baba Gopalji is a vigorous seventy year-old sporting a long white beard. He is reclining on his roof terrace under a shade covered with Ganga grass, cell phone in hand.

"The mixing of Yamuna and Ganga here is the meeting of the Krishna and Rama cultures. Ayodhya and Vrindavan — different attributes. One is a place of wisdom, the other of love, devotion. Krishna is love; Rama is knowledge."

I've always associated Shiva with Ganga; his temples and statues dot the river bank from Gangotri on down. I just don't associate Krishna[10] with Ganga. Rama yes, because Ayodhya isn't that far north and this is believed to be the landscape in which much of the early parts of the *Ramayana* took place. But Gopalji makes it sound so obvious. He continues, "Not only different cultures but different colors. Yamuna is green and Ganga is white. While it is called Ganga until the sea, the color is that of Yamuna."

That's pure poetic license. Both above and below the sangam, Ganga remains its usual muddy brown because of the silt it's carrying. Not a trace of green anywhere all the way to the Bay of Bengal over thirteen hundred kilometers downstream. But in such a beautiful spot I too might give myself over to such flights of fancy. "What is the significance of sangam? Why do people come here to bathe?" I ask.

Gopalji is not to be rushed. He's had his lunch and is in an expansive mood. "Allahabad is a place where we venerate knowledge. People who believe come here from all over India, remain for a month and talk. Allahabad is the most hospitable place in the entire world. Here no one will disturb you in your ways. No one will say, 'You get out, you don't belong to my culture.' Here everyone has a place. You must have seen the statue of Lord Harshvardhan?"

"Actually, I haven't," I admit.

"Go and take a look at it. Harshvardhan was the emperor of India after Ashok. He used to gather all the intellectuals here. That tradition has continued. Once a year, lakhs of people come here for the Marg Mela. Every twelve years [for the Purna Kumbh Mela] millions of people come and stay here. There is no hostility." Gopalji goes on to the story of the Kumbh.

---

[10] Yamuna flows through Agra and Vrindavan and gets much of its new water from the south, so it might be accurate to call it the river of Krishna.

"The gods were fighting over amrita, just like you Americans are always fighting."

"I'm an Englishman!"

"Same thing. [Ouch!] Man always wants to be immortal."

An assistant comes up. Tomorrow Gopalji has to take the night train to Dwaraka in Gujarat. Which clothes to pack? "Those two dhotis I had taken out, the khadi ones. I'm missing one dhoti... Oh I remember, I gave it away."

Gopalji gestures to the fruit on the table between us.

"There are flies on this fruit. Nobody will eat it. These visitors are foreigners. If there is a fly they won't touch it. Get a thali and cover it up."

I'm anxious to get back to the story of the Kumbh before Gopalji loses the thread. But I needn't have worried.

"The Devatas and Danavas fought over the amrita. So the son of Indra stole the bucket and made his escape. On his way, four drops were spilled, at Allahabad, Haridwar, Nasik and Ujjain.[11] So that is why it's specially auspicious to bathe here."[12]

Gopalji sighs, "Modern man is so selfish. He pollutes Ganga without thinking of the consequences."

Swami Chidenand at Parmath Niketan in Rishikesh had also said all the right things about pollution. But when pressed had admitted his well-endowed ashram poured its raw sewage directly into his beloved Ganga ma. So is this ashram any different? Apparently. They dump their waste into the ground not the river. Baba shows me the pipes. He blames the government for the physical condition of the river, and more.

In 1912, Hindu priests had asked the British in Delhi to allow some part of the Bhagirathi to flow uninterrupted by human agency at Haridwar. The British had agreed. They cut a slit through the barrage to allow Ganga to continue its uninterrupted flow down to Sagar Island.

In 1990, Delhi stated that the waters of Ganga would be allocated in a ratio of 40:60 among farmers and the people of India. But the BJP government later reneged and changed the ratio rather drastically to 80:20 in favor of irrigation. So a compromise was suggested.

---

[11] Ujjain is on the Shipra river, Nasik on the Godavari.

[12] The full story is a bit more complex. Maybe Gopalji thought I had a short attention span. For fuller accounts try Ganesh Hebner and David Osborn's *Kumbh Mela: The World's Largest Act of Faith*, California, Entourage Publishing, 1990 or Tony Heiderer's article, "Sacred Space, India's Kumbh Mela" in *National Geographic*, May 1990.

Dr. Murli Manohar Joshi (alumnus of the Sanskrit school in Singhberpur) suggested a straight 50:50 — half to be impounded behind the dam for future release as irrigation to farmers, and the other half to everyone else (for cooking, washing, industrial use, etc). The government said it would only cost two hundred crore rupees. Of course, even this is theoretical because the dam has yet to start operating.

But Gopalji says, "The gods were angered. Vajpayee was swept from power precisely because he did not listen to us over the Tehri dam. He perpetrated a crime against Ganga, India, and humanity." According to Gopalji this is the real reason why the BJP lost the 2004 general elections.

I ask Gopalji if he thinks Ganga will ever die — literally dry up and go back to the heavens. He fulminates, "We have become too self-centred. But those who have faith will not permit the government to let Ganga dry up. No government can now go against the Ganga Action Plan and hurt the people. Ganga is not only a river, it is living humanity, living faith. We will not permit the goddess to die."

~

Our audience over, Martine and I go back down to our sunken garden, attracted by a group of students chanting Vedas on the grass for their teacher. I remember once attending a Vedic recitation class in Varanasi in 1986 and being amazed not just by their accuracy and melodic facility but by the teacher's insistence that Vedas can be transmitted orally over millennia without the slightest deviation. I've always had my doubts. Surely an inflection here or there, a difference in punctuation and rhythm? I simply cannot believe subtle changes don't creep in.

But for lack of evidence I am reluctantly forced to accept that when the teacher says "unchanged over three thousand years," he may well be right, and I wrong. In any case, the chanting is wonderfully natural, spontaneous and so joyful even the crows join in.

The next day at 10:00 A.M. Dassirat, the ashram boatman, rows us out across Yamuna to the sangam. Mixed in with the chanting of mantras are the squawking of squadrons of gulls. Basant, Gopalji's young PA who accompanies us, buys ten rupees worth of bird seed from a passing boat, and then proceeds to coo *"aao aao aao."* I find this very irritating, but later realize it's the north Indian way of calling "come." The gulls squawk and squabble with joy at so much food — "Oh, to be a sea gull at the sangam!"

We moor with everyone else at the line of tethered country boats along the ridge that marks the actual meeting of the two rivers. Men and women wade on the Ganga side. The water barely comes up to their knees. Tivari points at a man dunking himself in the shallow water, "He has come for visarjana, the submersion of ashes of departed relatives."

These boats belong to the pandas or purohits who intercede in the ritual prayers between the individual and Ganga. Next to us is a boat filled to the gunwales with families from Jharkhand and Chhattisgarh.

The Chhattisgarh family have come to throw the ashes of a dead aunt into this most auspicious of spots while the purohit chants the appropriate mantra. This way, the soul gets to heaven faster. The family from Jharkhand came overnight by the Chambal Express, and will leave again tonight. They have brought the asthi or ashes of their late sister: "So that her soul will be at peace. All this is written in the *Ramayana* and *Mahabharata*. We follow the rituals accordingly."

Their panda Abdesh Misra specializes in families from Orissa, Bihar, Jharkhand, and Assam.

"I get the travelers to do puja and make offerings for Gangaji. Then there are those who bring the ashes, the asthis, for the pinda daan [offerings for the soul]. We do all those things for them. Your next life will also be better if you bathe here."

I have a more immediate agenda: "I'm going to have a bath. Tivari will be very upset if I don't."

I undress and take my holy dip with Tivari. Martine merely hitches up her salwar and pronounces the water surprisingly clean. "Maybe this belief in miraculous powers has some validity. It really feels fresh," she says.

Tivari keeps repeating: "I am very happy, I am very happy, I am very happy, By bathing here my mind is now very calm. All my sins have been washed away."

He first came to the Marg Kumbh when he was eighteen, then a gap till he was thirty, and since then on and off: "Chief, Prayag Raj is the king of all tirthas."

I ask Raja if he's now going to take his bath.

"No!" he says. "Why not?" I ask him.

"I don't want to make my mind calm."

Raja has personal problems at home in Kolkata he cannot work out. Throughout our yatra his mood alternates between ecstasy and depression. Only when we are near or in West Bengal does the black cloud lift. Raja wonders if Martine is blessed because she didn't take a full bath. Tivari replies indignantly, "Memsahib? To get clean you only have to see Ganga. Memsahib had darshan of Ganga, she took photo of Ganga, even she went into this water half up to waist line. So it's ok."

A procession carrying a big red flag advances down the far bank, led by a raucous band. Tivari explains, "They are taking the flag for a holy dip. Then they go to the Hanuman temple, offer it to him, have it blessed, then return to their village. This is flag dipping ceremony."

In the boat next to us, a family from Lalitpur in Jhansi district in UP, south of Kanpur, explain they have come simply because "this is a holy river of our country; this is why we came to bathe here." Anticipating my question, he continues, "We offer a shriphal[13] after the puja. We believe that an offering of shriphal frees you of your sins."

The husband and wife have come once before. For their mother it's the first time: "We have managed to stay faithful to the shastras [holy books]. We feel good inside because we are going along with Hindu culture."

Why are they filling plastic bottles with Ganga jal? The husband says, "Scientifically the water of Gangaji is good. It says in the Veda shastras, that if somebody commits a sin then Gangaji's water absolves you from that sin. We will take it home, keep it in a sacred space. If somebody is dying then we put this Ganga jal in his mouth, so that he becomes pure, attains salvation."

His wife adds, "It is better than distilled water, it never gets insects. We also use it for puja and rituals. It is needed in our rituals. We mix a few drops with ordinary water."

Yes, but what about the pollution?

They acknowledge that everybody back in Jhansi knows how polluted the river is in Kanpur. The husband blames the Kanpur tanneries; then he expresses happiness with the new sewage treatment plants built under the Ganga Action Plan; finally he offers a third observation full of contradictions:

"This is all because of pollution and population. It is not as though the Indian government is not trying. They are building plants on such a large scale so that river will not become impure due to the pollution. In any case, how could it ever be polluted? Ganga rises in Gaumukh. But even here it's still fresh and very sacred. If you take this water and keep it for some time it will never get any insects or germs. So how can you call it polluted?"

The wife jumps in quick as a flash: "She is our mother, she can never be impure and our government will not let it become impure. Isn't it normal for kids to shit in their mother's lap? Oh, children will be

---

[13] Coconut.

naughty, but a mother is a mother. Mothers always clean their kids. We cannot pollute our mother. This river will never die, no matter how many times they dam it. It is our belief that nobody can finish this river, even this Tehri dam. Ganga is eternal."

How I would have loved Bimal, our boatman back in Chiyaser, to have heard their answer.

~

Dassirat is eager to get back and eat lunch. He started rowing in 1954, when Nehru was prime minister and Dr. Rajendra Prasad was president. Dassirat claims that members of his family have been boatmen for at least five generations.[14]

He says,"This is a great river, babu. When you bathe here you might be tired as anything. But then you bathe, and all your tiredness falls away."

For all that Dassirat agrees the river has become dirtier, and he's noticed the flow often decreases. "But soon there will be watermelons this big,"[15] and his arms encircle the sky.

Back at the ashram, I ask Basant another of the intellectual conundrums that still puzzle me: "Why do Hindus need to bathe so often if Ganga washes away all your sins?"

"Because we start sinning all over again as soon as we've washed away the last lot."

Tivari agrees with this statement. But it still doesn't really make sense. There's something missing. Could it be a Hindu has a different idea of sin? That sin is regarded as more commonplace because it's so easy to atone for? Just take a dip in Ganga, do so many fasts, make the rounds of all the tirthas, and you've wiped the slate clean.

Indu Agarwal, who will join us in two days in Varanasi, thinks too many Indians repeat rituals without any feeling or sensitivity to their context.

She says, "We take a dip and pee into the river at the same time. This is what happens when taboos are broken. Indians are fast jettisoning

---

[14] I don't think we should take this too literally. I suspect it goes back a good deal further than five generations. Generation has a less precise connotation in oral cultures than in the precision-minded West. Let's just say Dassirat's family members have been boatmen as long as he or anyone else can remember.

[15] I've seen many boatmen up and down this reach of the river double as part-time farmers and plant watermelons in the dried riverbanks and sandbars in Ganga (and other rivers) in the dry season (February-May) and then harvest them just before the monsoon breaks.

the beliefs and lifestyle of an earlier age, becoming mere consumers. A lot of people you find in holy places are now what I'd call religious tourists."

At the ashram's splendid evening aarti there's an old blind man sitting with the swamis. Even Sachcha Baba defers to him. Who is he? He's a retired judge from the Allahabad High Court called Swami Chandra Bahl Misra. The next morning word comes that he wants to meet us.

He unties, at a stroke, the major conundrum that has long been troubling me: how can millions of Hindus believe this same polluted river is a goddess who purifies human souls and leads them to the next world?

For Chandra Bahl the answer is simple: "Ganga has a dual identity. If you consider her as a river then she can be polluted and die. But if you consider her as goddess then she can never die. Pollution is in the eye of the beholder. If you believe, you cannot get sick and there is no pollution. There are no mass epidemics and Indians are not fools, so how does the West explain this? The West should ponder this."

For millions of Hindus, Ganga can therefore never be dirty in the Western sense of pollution. For them physical pollution and spiritual pollution are two entirely different creatures. Only the most intellectually sophisticated attempt to make a possible connection, to argue that severe physical pollution might affect the spiritual purity of the goddess.

In Kanpur rituals have been modified. But "modify" does not mean undermining the sanctity of the river as goddess. A mother might fall on hard times but she will still be a mother; you don't disown her. A woman can still be a queen even if she is in rags and physically filthy. She retains her underlying grace. Similarly with a river.

As the judge says: "The river is simply the goddess in liquid form. No matter how much the physical river is abused she still retains her sanctity. All the evidence suggests she will always be revered. This is the feeling these people have for Ganga."

~

We reluctantly leave for Sitamahri, midway between Allahabad and Varanasi — another tirtha known primarily to Tivari. Sitamahri celebrates the place where Sita voluntarily allowed herself to be swallowed up by the earth rather than continue to suffer the doubts and suspicions of her husband Rama, who accused her more or less openly of being unfaithful with the demon Ravana all the years she was held captive in Lanka.

Many years ago, we'd stayed in Jitvapur, a village near Madhubani in northern Bihar. The villagers there also swore Sita returned to the earth nearby. But does it actually matter where it took place? Surely the important thing is why she wanted out. Women in many rural areas in northern India identify with Sita precisely because of all the tribulations she went through as a woman.

Hotel operators can make a fast buck — Sitamahri's the nearest equivalent to rural Disneyland I've yet to find in northern India. It has a Sita motel and a giant fifty-foot statue of Hanuman on an artfully sculptured backwater of Ganga.

We retreat in haste to the actual banks of the river, where we find a splendid refuge in the half-completed courtyard of yet another ashram, which Martine will never forget because the swami offered her a pickle to die for, made of green papaya.

The next morning, out on the bluffs overlooking the river, I notice the river being used for commerce for the first time. Boats bring down sand from upstream, unload it into wicker baskets that camels then gracefully carry up the bank to waiting lorries to be driven away to area building sites.

Indu arrives in Varanasi tomorrow and the day after is Kartik Purnima — the full moon day in the sacred month of Kartik — possibly the most auspicious day of all for bathing. And surely nowhere is more auspicious than Varanasi.

~

Varanasi, also known as Banaras, Benares, or Kashi,[16] is situated on the left bank of Ganga, where the river flows north. In Hindu culture this signifies a daughter returning to her father's house, a most auspicious event. This is probably why it is the holiest of all stops along Ganga, more so than the sangam or any of the other major tirthas.

Varanasi is loaded down with myths, not the least of which is the common conception of how old it really is. It is often called the world's oldest continuously inhabited city.[17] While it is technically true that people

---

[16] Kashi means "light of the world" in Sanskrit. Rana B. Singh of Benares Hindu University (BHU) says Benares is an amalgam of two words — bena (ready) and ras (to serve); literally, ready to serve the juice of life. Varanasi is a Hindi construction from the names of the rivers Varuna and Asi, which form the city's northern and southern boundaries.

[17] In his journey through India, Mark Twain made this famous quip: "Benares is older than history, older than tradition, older even than legend, and looks twice as old as all of them put together!" Mark Twain, *Following the Equator, A Journey Round the World*, p. 480, The American Publishing Company, Hartford, CT, 1898.

have lived on or near this spot for many thousands of years, it still strikes me as intellectually lazy because it is taken too much on unquestioned trust.

Some local historians, notably Rana B. Singh, date it as much more modern.[18] Rana claims that much of Varanasi, certainly the famous arc of eighty-four ghats, only date from the seventeenth century.[19] Other historians politely but firmly disagree.[20] No matter what its age, there is no doubt this is India's holiest city, because it is believed to be the city of Shiva on earth, and because it flows north.[21]

The ghats and narrow streets of the old city embody all the traditions, myths and images that go to make up Hinduism. Diana Eck writes that "this is a tradition of pilgrimage to sacred places, bathing in sacred waters, and honoring sacred images ... in which all the senses are employed in the apprehension of the divine ... a tradition that has imagined and imaged God in a thousand ways ... a religious tradition that understands life and death as an integrated whole.'[22] The old city literally breathes the presence of the divine everywhere.

---

[18] Rana B. Singh argues that the idea that Varanasi-Benares-Kashi is at least five thousand years old and the world's oldest inhabited city is suspect. There's no mention of the city in either the *Ramayana* or *Mahabharata*, except for a single line in the former that refers to kasha (grass), not Kashi (cosmic light). He doesn't deny the mythology but maintains Varanasi as we see it today is very much a modern creation that dates from only the seventeeth century, "I'm not an archaeologist but I haven't found any sites that show traces of continuous settlement. The legend is fine, but the reality is quite different. How many buildings can you find from the seventeenth century? Two or three at most."

[19] Historically, the word ghat only dates from the twelfth century. Rana claims that "nowhere in the ancient texts do you find a description of eighty-four ghats." The earliest reference to something like the modern-day ghat is to a jal teertha. Once the modern tradition is developed Rana says there are constant textual references to ninety six ghats. He claims it was he Rana who invented the number of eighty-four.

[20] Notably Diana Eck at Harvard. She does admit it's difficult to pinpoint events. The Buddha (sixth to fifth century BC) taught in the deer park at Sarnath, which today is on the outskirts of the city, and "eventually Varanasi became known as one of those sacred places where people come to die and bring the ashes of their beloved dead."

Rana B. Singh doesn't dispute there were sacred forests, a handful of ashrams, sages meditating: "But on nothing like the scale claimed." My suggestion is to read both Diana Eck and Rana B. Singh for a balanced historical picture.

[21] See Sharada Nayak's explanation in Chapter 1 — that the river is here paying obeisance to Mount Kailash, which is near Lake Mansarovar in Tibet.

[22] Eck, Diana. *Banaras City of Light*, p. 6, Princeton University Press, Princeton, NJ, 1982, 1999.

Varanasi

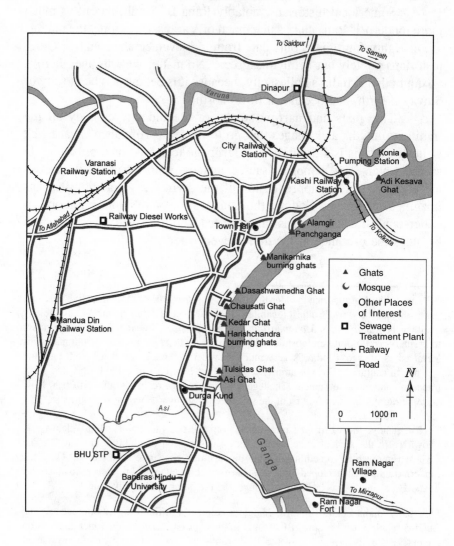

Map legend:
- ▲ Ghats
- ☽ Mosque
- ● Other Places of Interest
- ☐ Sewage Treatment Plant
- +++ Railway
- ═ Road

N

0   1000 m

Labels on map:
To Saidpur
To Samath
Varuna
Dinapur
City Railway Station
Konia Pumping Station
Varanasi Railway Station
Kashi Railway Station
Adi Kesava Ghat
Railway Diesel Works
Town Hall
Alamgir
Panchganga
To Kolkata
Manikarnika burning ghats
Dasashwamedha Ghat
Chausatti Ghat
Kedar Ghat
Mandua Din Railway Station
Harishchandra burning ghats
Tulsidas Ghat
Asi Ghat
Durga Kund
Asi
To Allahabad
Ganga
BHU STP
Banaras Hindu University
Ram Nagar Village
To Mirzapur
Ram Nagar Fort

Kashi is considered by the devout to be a microcosm of the entire world. All the gods live here, attracted by the brilliance of the shaft of pure light that meets the earth.[23] Everything auspicious and powerful is concentrated on this one place. Here are all the tirthas along Ganga rolled into one.

Is this why people come to die at Varanasi? If so, what's so special about death here at Varanasi?

Death in Varanasi is moksha, liberation. If one dies here, Lord Shiva himself will whisper the Tarika mantra, the boat mantra, the mantra that will take you across the ford to the far shore. That is Shiva's promise, that everyone who dies in Varanasi will be liberated from the endless round of birth and death that makes up the cycle of life. Sounds like a good reason to me.

So people come from all over India to die here because one can bypass the hell of endless reincarnation. Devaprayag, Haridwar, Allahabad, Gaya, Ujjain, Nasik, Ganga Sagar, and others are all very important in purifying the human soul of sin and conveying one's remains to the next world. But at Varanasi-Banaras-Kashi you can cut out all the waiting and go directly.

~

A trip one early morning on a country boat with Anil and Rinku, our boatmen, shows why Varanasi makes such a huge impression. Start from the ghat I am most familiar with — Asi Ghat. People are performing their religious ablutions, others are simply scrubbing down with soap and shampoo. For at least the last three hundred years visitors have found scenes of mourning and bathing along the river Ganga visually and emotionally arresting. It's the sheer size of the ghats at Varanasi — a gentle arc of three miles on tall bluffs. Can a Western visitor ever really understand this mixture of the sacred and profane, of life and death that is the essence of life in this very public, and very Indian arena called Varanasi?

Along the ridge are a bewildering confusion of massive and picturesque masonry, "stone platforms, soaring stairways, sculptured temples, majestic palace, softening away into the distances."[24] And everywhere human life in noisy motion.

---

[23] Kashi is therefore where light bisects the earth.

[24] Cf. Twain op. cit., p. 496. His descriptions are so succinct I don't think they have been bettered in more than a century.

Long flights of stone ghats lead down to the river, crammed with thousands upon thousands of Hindus going about their morning prayers waist deep in the river. Hands cupped, eyes closed, they pray to Ganga, Surya,[25] to Shiva, Vishnu, and many more besides, letting the water of Ganga dribble through the palms of their hands. The bather then turns seven times clockwise and dunks him or herself thrice in the river. The ritual completed, he dries himself, gets, dressed, and chats with his neighbors before mounting back up the ghats and to home, breakfast, and the day ahead. Most Westerners simply have never seen anything like this: massive morning prayer along the river Ganga.[26]

Everything about Hinduism is a head-on challenge to Western notions of religion and God. How many times have Westerners (and Muslims) poked fun at the notion of thirty or three hundred million gods? Fixation on a precise number misses the point. Hindus are expressing the idea that God is infinite, that whatever they mean by God cannot be captured by any one idea, name or form. Thirty or three hundred or three million is merely another way of saying you can't count the ways in which God can be present. For Christians, Muslims, or Jews, brought up to regard all forms of idolatry as heresy, this public display of bathing, faith, and jubilation is therefore profoundly unsettling.

Same problem at Harishchandra and Manikarnika Ghats, the two cremation grounds, smack dab in the middle of the huge crescent of ghats, in full public view. This is something quite frankly that most people who have grown up in European and American cultures have simply never seen, where death is carefully hidden away in professional crematoriums and mortuaries. Indians, on the other hand, make a very public display of death. They bring their newly dead, wrapped in cloth, strung between bamboo litters carried through the crowded streets to the edge of the water. A cremation pyre is built, the body bathed in Ganga, and then for several hours it will burn while relatives and priests chant and perform the prescribed rituals. In Varanasi death is the essence of

---

[25] The sun god.

[26] Most of today's images of India (and Indians) are determined by television and video. But it's very hard to film on Ganga in Bihar, or in the Himalayas or anywhere much off the beaten track, for basic logistical reasons. So the images Indians and the rest of the world has of India and Ganga are of the same small handful of places — Varanasi, Gaumukh, Kanpur, and Sagar Island. If these are the only images of Ganga, it's small wonder if distortion, ignorance, and stereotype are the norm.

Rana B. Singh suggests that the images the world sees of Varanasi (and that Varanasi itself probably now believes in) are therefore quite recent and reinforced and narrowed down by modern technology.

the public life of the city. That is what makes it powerful. This is also what makes it often incomprehensible to people seeing the city for the first time.

In between are the ghats where most people come to bathe — Dashashwamedh, Manikarnika, and Panchganga. They mark the mid-point in the crescent. On one of our boat rides up and down the ghats Rana B. Singh points out a tiny building near Panchganga Ghat: "This is Man Mandir, built about 1710. One of the three oldest buildings in the city. Only three hundred years old!" The oldest building — the Yogashram — dates from Akbar's time. It is said that scholars came, sat under its pillars, and had learned discussions. Next to it stood the Bindu Madhav, a famous twelfth-century temple which was demolished in 1669 by the order of the Mughal King Aurangzeb and converted into a mosque.

A little further on we come to a much photographed Shiva temple called Ratneshwar, which appears to have collapsed into the river since the beginnings of time. Rana says it actually collapsed two hundred years ago, around 1810, as the result of an earthquake that disturbed its pilings. But a whole modern mythology has grown up around it, another example of how "history" is both constructed and recent.

"The local belief is that a devotee of Hanumanji used to worship there." Rana says. "People said that if he had so much power he could jump over it. So they gathered to watch. The river was in flood. He went out in a boat, jumped over it, claimed it for Hanuman. But when he jumped over it, the entire temple sank! The crowds were in shock that one man could have such power. The man then also promptly jumped into Ganga and drowned."

~

On Kartik Purnima itself,[27] everybody has been bathing at every conceivable ghat, starting well before dawn. I can hardly hear myself think, let alone speak because of the distorted music blaring at some incredible decibel count from loudspeakers rigged up all along the ghats.

It's so noisy Anil and Rinku — our boatmen — row across the river to the largely deserted south bank, which isn't sacred. Rama Kanth Katheria is bathing there with his entire family, all ten of them.

---

[27] On Kartik Purnima Vishnu finally opens his eyes and blesses people. He had in fact woken a few days earlier and met his wife Brinda on November 13 that particular year (2004).

Rama Kanth is voluble. He explains that few people ever cross to bathe on this Maghar bank: "It has not been blessed by the gods. But we come here anyway because it is quiet and clean. Today is Diwali of the gods and for the gods. Yes, our sins are washed away, but we have so many that are invisible, from previous lives. Today I have taken a sankalp [vow] to give up some vices and bad friends. "

The entire day is very long, full of noise and kitsch, ending up with an interminable Bollywood-style aarti at Dashaswamedh Ghat. The guests of honor, seated on a giant floating stage, are Amar Singh and Jaya Bachchan.

A priest warms up the restive crowd with a few bars of Om Jai Gange Mata, the unofficial Ganga anthem set to the tune and words of the more familiar Om Jai Jagdish Hare. Then the guests arrive, a few more chants and responses, culminating in hosannas to the river: "Ganga Mata Jai" (Hail to Ganga), followed by interminable speeches and finally the actual aarti. It begins promisingly, if in slow motion, with amplified violin, tabla, and chorus.

Overhead spectacular fireworks light up the sky. On the ghat in three rows sit twenty-one young pandas, each on his individual throne. Behind each row a chorus line of nubile young women holding palm fronds in each hand.

At a signal from the podium the pandas take out gleaming ivory-coloured conch shells and blow them. Then other young men start ringing large copper bells to a crescendo of tablas. This is the cue for the female acolytes to sway from side to side, always in slow motion, waving their palm fronds like semaphore flags. Then the violin starts a new tune and the whole cycle begins all over again.

The entire spectacle lasts two hours and is only made bearable by the mass of church bells, which make the occasion sound like Easter Sunday in the Russian Orthodox church. As far as I'm concerned Kartik Purnima is a bust. But Tivari has a ball, in and out of the water like a child. He pronounces the water "very fine," himself "very happy" because he has cleansed himself of sins. None of the rest of us attempt to bathe.

~

Next morning, Rana meets me on Asi Ghat. He has a rendezvous here with a panda called Uma Shankar Gupta to discuss this week's yatra within Varanasi. Mr. Gupta heads an informal organization called Revival of the Pilgrimage System. Rana explains there are five important pilgrimages, but one of them is now rarely done. The most important is the Visheswara yatra in which the pilgrim goes round seventy-two shrines within the city, most of them Shiva temples, to be purified. Every third year the Hindu lunar calendar adds a thirteenth month — mull maas — and about sixty-thousand people come to make the Panchkrosi Yatra.

The entire route is eighty six kilometers in length and it usually takes five or six days. "I have done it eight times," says Rana. This yatra is an abbreviated version of a twenty eight day walk — now rarely performed — which obviously lasted the full lunar month. "I followed the textual tradition and stopped at each shrine, said a prayer and moved on." Finally, there's a small yatra — Panchatirtha — that pilgrims performed yesterday on Kartik Purnima where they bathe at five different ghats, starting at Asi and ending at Panchganga Ghat.

"It's a family affair. A particular family or neighborhood goes to a panda, makes a sankalp, and goes to bathe at each of the five ghats. We should ask a panda to explain this for you." As if on cue, Rana introduces me to his family purohit or panda, Devendra Nath Tripathi, sitting less than five yards away. Tripathi intones mantras for his customers at his stand here at the head of Asi Ghat. He gives them tulsi leaves, which he has blessed: they hand him coins, fruits, and vegetables in return. Tripathi explains: "Many women come here to make offerings before bathing. They make a sankalp and set their goals for the day. In return I bless them with a mantra."

The first couple has come to seek his blessing for the nitya pooja — the daily bathing ritual. They hand him fresh fruit and a few coins. Tripathi begins the mantra. It starts off listing time and place in descending order — Cosmos, India, Varanasi, Asi Ghat, month, day, name of the family — then purpose (take a daily bath in Ganga). Next, an appeal to Mother Ganga, then one to Vishnu to help one get through the day. The devotees give a symbolic offering of fruit as proof of their good faith and Tripathi in return takes tulsi leaves, while they touch Tripathi's feet. This is the proof that they have performed the initiation rite. Tripathi blesses them: "With the blessings of God you may now perform the rite."

The whole thing has taken barely three minutes from start to finish. The women may stop off on their way back home at a temple, but essentially this is it, the simplest of all daily rituals.

Two women come by and offer Tripathi fresh radishes, symbols of the link between heaven and earth. They need to get some details of upcoming poojas from Tripathi:

"If Panchami is on Wednesday, will Ganesh chauth be on Tuesday?"

Tripathi has the answer: "It will begin on Monday night."

Reassured, they turn to gossip about the health of family

members. "My sister-in-law is too bedridden to do all this. She has trouble even shitting and pissing."

Her friend commiserates: "I get afraid when I think of her, she should be released from her suffering now."

"Yes," says the first woman. "When I think she used to run around all of Benaras! Poor thing, she used to be so active, and now she is in this state. She used to go to Panchganga. Ganga mother, bestow your blessing on the sick. Listen Muni to my bhakti."

Her friend becomes philosophical, "It's terrible to get physical troubles in old age. It's the influence of Kali Yuga. I feel it."

From physical to cosmic infirmity in the same sentence!

"It has to be Kali Yuga. It's screwing up the whole dharma. Three legs have been broken, only one leg remains.[28] As long as I can walk then I can give alms. Now that I have come here, I will give a handful. If I don't even come out of the house then how will I give a handful?"

"You're right."

The first woman adds a colorful simile: "Kali Yuga has caught hold of Dharma's feet." Her friend sighs: "The only one he fears is Hanumanji, no one else."

And then they directly address Tripathi again: "Sir, the Kali Yuga is under the influence of the god Shani who has cursed us. It is because of Kali Yuga we have forgotten God. We remember our family, our children, we remember worldly things but we do not remember God."

And still muttering they head down to the river to bathe. When the women have bathed they will return to seek more blessings from Tripathi, because without them the dip is incomplete. Again, they will give offerings to the gods — Rama, Krishna, Vishnu — offer water to Tripathi's basil plant and make another sankalp for the day ahead.

A few days later, I stop by again to see Tripathi. It's been a busy morning: "Today is Sundari dwij [second day of the new month]. Mother Sita is worshipped today. All the women came for that. So today has been far better. It's been a good day for me."

"It strikes me that there's no single day when there's nothing going on," I reply.

Tripathi launches into a litany: "Yes, there's something virtually

---

[28] The allusion is presumably to the four ages of time. Three have passed — Satya Yuga, Dwapara Yuga, and Treta Yuga. The Kali Yuga is the final and present age, where everything that can go wrong will go wrong. The Kali Yuga will last forty thousand years. We're at the beginning of the Kali Yuga and Shani is the ruling planet influencing the Kali Yuga, so we have a long way to go.

every day. Of course, every day is Kartik. But today we have started a new month, Margshirsh. Today is this dwij pooja when everybody is doing the Sita pooja. Today they also start worshipping the kadamb tree. You tie threads round the kadamb tree and that pooja finishes in the fifth, on the panchami day. Next day you start Laxmi worship. That goes on for fifteen days, it ends with the worship of Annapurna and on day after that you donate dhan, rice husks, and whole rice grains."

Tripathi says the ears of new rice are given to devotees as prasad in the temple. They in turn take it home and store it with their own rice. The belief is these blessed ears will make the existing rice multiply so a home will never lack for rice. Annapurna Laxmi pooja is a symbol of prosperity, of plenty.

I am curious how Tripathi learnt the craft of purohit or panda. "My father was a pandit and he used to take people on yatras like the Panchkrosi yatra and things like that. But after he passed away I learnt it all from Narayan Choube, the pandit who is coming down the steps right now. Do you want me to call him?"

Narayan Choube arrives as if on cue in dhoti and black sleeveless jacket and utters the immortal line: "Everyone is a guru in Kashi." Where did he get his knowledge? Learnt it from Pandit Jagannath Tripathi, another guru. And so it goes down through the generations. "Kashi has a guru tradition and the gurus teach us everything."

I always thought gurus were very old with long flowing beards. But both Choube and Tripathi are clean-shaven, youngish, slim, and vigorous. Choube laughs away my stereotypes: "If you have knowledge to impart, age is not a bar. Anybody can be a guru." Choube takes his leave. He has a meeting to attend at the Durga Kund nearby.

Down at the river bank, a wedding party is preparing to clamber into a boat. The newly-married couple have come to ask for Ganga's blessings, so they are offering a garland to Ganga. The party will do a little pooja on the far bank and then come back. As one of them explains: "Ganga is our mother so we ask for her blessing, for their good married life." Before she climbs in the boat, Renuka ties a garland of flowers to the prow of the boat. "This is the maala [garland]. We'll leave it over there after the pooja."

Next to the boat, women at the water's edge are offering sarees to Ganga for her blessing. "We are offering sarees to Ganga and the saree has come from my brothers' house. We can do it any time. It's not any specific day but we all decided to come here today and do the pooja."

Why don't they bury their flower offerings instead of throwing them into the river? "No, all that doesn't work for us. We have this way of doing the ritual and that's it." Another couple of women are bottling

Ganga jal to take home for the ceremonial first bricks in the family's new home. They'll mix some drops in with the cement.

In so many ways Ganga is a patron saint who watches over every aspect of daily life. For all these people the idea of the pollution of the river is regrettable but it is only a physical blemish that cannot diminish the overall powers of the goddess. They see no need to make a connection between the physical and the metaphysical.

~

A few days later, Anil and Rinku row us up to Chausatti Ghat where we meet with Panda Ramakhand Shukla. We find him sitting cross-legged under an umbrella on a stone jetty high above the water. He reassures us: "Of course, Ganga isn't polluted. How can she be?" For fifteen rupees he agrees to recite the Ganga Pooja for Indu while she performs the actual pooja in the boat.

On our way back we stop at Kedar Ghat. It's full of south Indians washing dishes and bathing in preparation for their Kartik Purnima, which is fifteen days later than the one we have just celebrated.[29] Kusima is saying her mantra first to the gods, then to the different worlds,[30] and finally to Ganga. Kusima says she's come here from Hyderabad with her mother, sister-in-law, and brother. This is probably the greatest moment in their lives. And the proximity of the Harishchandra cremation ghat next door has inspired her: she now wishes to be cremated here. Bijoy Tivari turns up his nose at mention of Harishchandra Ghat: "People who come to cremate bodies go more to Manikarnika. Here less people come."

Kusima is unabashed: "We have seen God, we got a glimpse of the Lord and bathed in Ganga. Ganga is the ultimate event in my life. We attain salvation because we have bathed here in Ganga. No other river will do. Cauvery and Godavari are holy, but Ganga is divine. Only Ganga comes from heaven."

Others in the Tamil community are also in ecstasy: "For three generations no one in my family has had the opportunity. So this visit is very important." Literally, the opportunity of a lifetime.

Anil unloads us at Tulsidas Ghat, a hundred yards upstream of Asi Ghat where we are also staying. Tulsidas Ghat is also the home of Veer Badre Mishra,[31] the mahant or hereditary priest of the Sankat Mochan temple at Tulsidas Ghat. He's spent the past thirty years trying to alert

---

[29] Tamils follow a solar as opposed to a lunar calendar, hence the discrepancy.

[30] The worlds of the gods, of humans, of animals, etc.

[31] Like many I usually refer to Mishra by his initials, VBM.

people to the threats to Ganga here at Varanasi.

VBM has encountered a great deal of jealousy, even outright opposition to his ideas for solving Varanasi's sewage treatment right here in Varanasi. Rana, for one, is not a fan: "He's not a descendant of Tulsi Das at all. He's really a beggar who "captured" the temple; he sits on crores of rupees of foreign aid and won't tolerate anybody else's plans for cleaning Ganga at Varanasi but his own."

Veer Badre Mishra and I have met several times over the years. He's in his late sixties, tall, thin with charismatic eyes and voice — women swoon when they meet him. For a long time, VBM was also a professor of hydrology at the nearby Benaras Hindu University. His Sankat Mochan Foundation is internationally synonymous with Ganga. It has highlighted extraordinarily high levels of E.coli in the river: he tells Indians and the world that this makes it totally unsafe for bathing.[32]

VBM recently lost a son in a car accident. He has been in poor health. The Ganga clean-up has not been exactly a roaring success. It would be normal if VBM felt somewhat discouraged.

But it's worse than that.

"I am very sad. I can't express in words but I suffer inside because of my commitment to the river." He knows what has to be done to save the river, and it's simply not happening.

And then he brightens up: "But I am an optimist. We are not going to just stop. One day something will happen and we will be successful, though clouds are bound to return. There are times when man has to struggle. This whole situation is not good. It hurts me personally, but we have to undergo this. We are peaceful people, we have teachers and religious persons. We are not careerists. We're not part of the market-driven forces."

But doesn't VBM feel hurt by criticisms like Rana's from within Varanasi?

"Not really. We laugh at some of the things that are said. They are so wrong. I have been a public figure for so many years I know what it is to be criticized. I know people in the town discuss our work, that they associate Ganga and Mahantji. But I have never sought fame."

"If Ganga dies I too will die. It is normal and healthy that people criticize us. But if their only aim is to destroy us then I am sad because the goal is to save Ganga not Veer Badre Mishra."

I may not always agree with the emphasis of the Sankat Mochan Foundation's efforts to clean up Ganga, but I have to take my hat off to VBM. Even in hard times the man is wonderfully gracious, even to his

---

[32] I am still unconvinced, for reasons explained in Chapter 5.

most waspish critics.

But there's a puzzle. How can VBM spend so much time criticizing the government for its failure to clean up Ganga at Varanasi And yet bathe in the river every morning, all the while knowing as a scientist it's polluted? How does he reconcile the two?

Isn't there a contradiction? I'd expect the mahant to remind me that a river can be dirty[33] yet can clean human souls. And the professor of Hydrology at BHU to tell me there is some scientific evidence that Ganga has self-purifying capacities. VBM's initial answers surprises me.

"As a scientist I don't find anything which can prove that Ganga has self purifying capacity more than any other water mass."

But he then makes the same distinction as the blind judge in Allahabad. The metaphysical and the physical worlds are entirely different.[34] Yes, the river can be poisoned and make people sick. On a purely religious level it is nectar.

"But can't poison and nectar mix?"

"No, the two are entirely separate. I am committed to both Gangas. As a scientifically-trained mind I want to protect the river. But my heart has an entirely different relationship to Ganga. The physical world and the world beyond the limits of our senses are two entirely different worlds."

So can faith make polluted water clean?

"Let practicing Hindus believe. Let them live the way they want to live. For me they are jewels who have preserved this culture for thousands of years. But they are also human beings and it is a proven fact that if one takes polluted water one will become sick and some will die. And if Hindus die then this Indian culture and faith will go. The two are related. Can we not just see this and use all the resources of faith, science, technology, and politics to protect this body of fresh water?"

VBM himself has contracted polio, hepatitis, smallpox and recently jaundice; a necessary price to pay, I presume. Yet he still bathes in the river every morning. His position seems very ambivalent, as if he can't figure out in the end how to reconcile the two. I wonder which side he would choose if push comes to shove.

I think the real hidden killer may not be sewage or garlands of

---

[33] Ganga can be "dirty" but not "polluted" in the eyes of the faithful. Dirt is man-made and can be removed. Polluted means defiled. Sanctity has been attacked and compromised. The problem of language makes it easy to mobilize educated, middle-class urban Indians, but a lot harder to fire up the less educated according to some of my NGO friends, such as Eco Friends in Kanpur.

[34] He's not the only Indian scientist who seems to have little problem living with both metaphysical and scientific explanations of natural phenomena — see Chapter 5.

flowers but toxic heavy metals, which bizarrely the Sankat Mochan Foundation laboratories at Tulsidas Ghat don't test for, whether deliberately or for lack of funds. That's what I'd really be afraid of.

~

I'd arranged with Indu to meet Satyindra Mishra, panda and president of the Dhasaswamedh Ghat. He wants to use his position to create public awareness. We bat ideas around — many of his are well-meaning. But I've yet to see any evidence that Indians really possess any civic sense. They are meticulous in keeping their own private space clean, but it stops at their front door. Private cleanliness, public squalor.

The panda says composting garlands is feasible but household sewage remains the main culprit. He agrees that Vinod Tare has it right — it's better to inculcate Brahmapurana and stop shitting into the river. It would be better to ban plastic bags and involve people; create a national trust of religious heads and get people involved this way. All worthy ideas, but unlikely to get us very far.

Satyindra Mishra makes the usual distinction between the river and its sacred function — the water is impure, the goddess pure. But something is still missing. I can't quite see what, not yet.

We go to meet Prema Tivari, wife of another panda, in her tiny apartment in a nearby alley. "Yes, I worry that if the river gets too dirty we will have to compromise our rituals."

Her husband Raj Kumar arrives. The conversation suddenly takes on a more interesting direction. "People will only really understand if and when Ganga dries up. Until then they're quite happy going on making this distinction between river and goddess."

Indu sees her opening: "We live as multi-faceted personalities and don't have a contradiction to try to resolve. For example, the idea of Ganga as goddess and river are two entirely different thoughts. How can a polluted river purify a human soul? Because the goddess is in our minds. That we can't see it doesn't make her any less real."[35]

Ganga therefore really can be both river and goddess — the two

---

[35] Diana Eck says Westerners also operate with multiple ways of thinking, "we just don't recognize it. And we certainly don't consciously and comfortably live with complexity and contradiction as so many Hindus do." She adds, "Westerners are often victims of a scientific fundamentalism as acute as any religious fundamentalism. It makes our thinking rigid. We start to be convinced there is only one way of thinking, when in fact most of us operate just like Indians." Interview with the author, September 12, 2005.

happily co-exist. There simply is no either/or for those who believe.

Raj Kumar Tivari adds, "Of course, if we keep poisoning the water then even the amrit [nectar] will turn bad."

Veer Badre Mishra is not the only person to make the connection between Ganga as goddess and Ganga in a liquid form. But he shied away from tackling how poisoned amrit could compromise the river as goddess. Instead, he argued that the physical decline of the river might weaken one of the pillars of Hindu culture. Hinduism would be the ultimate victim, not just the goddess as a myth or a river.

But even this will not convince a true believer, such as Chandra Bahl Misra, the blind judge in Allahabad, who anticipated VBM's argument two weeks ago in Allahabad.

"If you consider her as a river then she can be polluted and die. But if you consider her as goddess then she can never die. Faith will always win out in the end."

I see no way of refuting his statement. It explains why the physical river can be polluted, may dry up in places, even die. The river as goddess always lives on. This is very much an argument from within Hindu culture. If you really want Indians to save their river you may have to find a way to de-couple the river from the goddess.

*****

CHAPTER 5

The Mysterious Factor X

Why do so many priests, pilgrims, and aam aadmi — the common man — believe Ganga purifies their souls and cleanses them of sin? Does Ganga jal have some special cleansing properties that make it unique?

Many people who bathe in and drink Ganga jal indeed do get intestinal bugs. But there have been no recorded pandemics at any of the great bathing festivals — Kumbh Mela, Sangam, Kartik Purnima, Makar Sankranti — where you'd most expect them. No cholera, no typhoid, no dysentery. Why?

Indians who drink Ganga jal simply don't get sick. Again, why not? Surely it can't be faith alone. Devout Hindus of course believe bathing in the waters of the goddess Ganga will remove their past sins, that if you are cremated upon the banks of the Ganga and your ashes scattered in the river, particularly at Varanasi, this will ensure your liberation from further rebirths. Or that if you can't make it to Ganga or to Varanasi, then a drink of Ganga jal will at least ease the pains of dying. This is why it's very common for pilgrims and devotees to take pots of Ganga jal back to their homes, either as offerings to their household deities, or as a final elixir for a dying relative.[1]

~

Most of the early travelers' tales commented on Ganga jal. The great Arab writers Al-Biruni and Ibn Batuta noted that Muslim rulers always sought out Ganga jal.

The Mughal emperor Akbar's preference for "the water of immortality" from Ganga for drinking and cooking is described at length

---

[1] This is obviously an impulse common to most religions. Christians are baptized with water; Muslims perform ritual washing before prayer in the mosque.

in the *Ain-i-Akbari* by Abul Fazl. Akbar would serve only Ganga jal to guests at weddings because of its soft, sweet taste.[2] He made sure he had a ready supply on hand both at court and on his travels. The water would be collected from the river and sent to him in sealed jars at Agra or Fatehpur Sikri. The practice continued and expanded under Akbar's successors, even after the Mughal empire began its slow disintegration.

The great French traveller Jean-Baptiste Tavernier made five trips to India between 1640 and 1667. He casually mentions[3] that both Hindus and Muslims drink the water because it contains no "vermin," and is believed to have some medicinal properties. I think his "vermin" are the same "insects" mentioned by the family from Jhansi I met at the Sangam in Allahabad.

The British East India Company also swore by Ganga jal. When ships set out from Calcutta for the three-month journey back to England they only carried Ganga jal from the Hugli (one of the dirtiest reaches in all of Ganga) because they insisted it wouldn't putrefy en route. Water taken on board in England, on the other hand, could not survive the outward journey. By the time boats reached Mumbai it was putrid and foul to taste.[4]

When I told R.K. Sinha, a zoologist at Patna University, about the British taking supplies of Ganga jal on board at Kolkata, he simply refused to believe it. Sinha thought that all water probably stank so badly onboard ships that carrying Ganga jal may have reflected less on its merits than on the awfulness of the competition. Sinha doesn't believe in any special properties of Ganga jal. But he did admit he'd never really studied the question. It was just scientific commonsense — all water putrefies. Why should Ganga jal be any different?

Eric Newby in his book quotes from Swami Sivananda's *Mother Ganges*:

"A well-known French physician, Dr. D. Herelle ... observed some of the floating corpses of men dead of dysentery and cholera, and was surprised to find that only a few feet below, where one would expect to find millions of these dysentery and cholera germs, there were no germs at all. He then grew germs from patients having the disease, and

---

[2] Cf Jagmohan Mahajan, op. cit., pp 23-31.

[3] Tavernier's main focus was on Hindu customs — the bathing in and drinking of Ganga jal. His observations about the potential physical properties of the water are offered almost as an afterthought.

[4] C.E. Nelson, editorial in *Environmental Conservation* (1981), quoted in Bhargava: "Nature and the Ganga," pp. 307–317, Vol 14, No 4, Winter 1987.

to these cultures added water from the Ganges. When he incubated the mixture for a period, much to his surprise, the germs were completely destroyed."[5]

My friend Munni Sircar, a housewife in Kolkata, remembers many customs relating to Ganga jal and its supposed medicinal qualities when she was growing up in Kolkata. Her grandmother used to walk down to the Ganga ghat close to their house, bathe, and then walk back home and do her pooja every morning, every day, whether in winter or during the monsoon. Little Munni used to ask her why she had to go every day and bathe in the river. Grandmother explained that, "If you bathe in the Ganga every day, it will cleanse you of all sins. Not only sins but diseases also."

"So when you told me about this Mysterious Factor X, I suddenly realized that people of my grandmother's generation really believed that," Munni told me. "Even the pooja bogh, the food offered to the gods and goddesses, used to be cooked in Ganga water because it was thought to be clean, absolutely clean and pure."

A man would be hired to go and fetch water from the Ganga. "Every fifteen days this man used to come. It was his job to go to the Ganga and fetch water and store and fill up that copper drum. We kind of thought that whenever food had to be cooked for the gods or goddesses or some kind of pooja, it had to be cooked in Ganga water."

This is tantalizing stuff. Is there, could there perhaps be some truth to the old belief that there is indeed something special about Ganga jal — the water of the river? The obvious place to start is in the Himalayas.

~

B.D. Joshi, a professor of biology at Haridwar, has long been convinced Ganga jal indeed does have special properties. He maintains it must be due to the interaction of ice-cold water temperatures of the Bhagirathi, Alaknanda (and all the other mountain streams that go to eventually make up Ganga) with "medicinally important flora" special to the mountains.

But quite how chemicals and plants interact is something Joshi cannot explain. If truth be told, he's not really that interested, a characteristic of not a few Indian scientists. Quite why there is this lack of curiosity is still a mystery. I continue in my quest to discover what sets Ganga jal apart from other rivers. I next ask Diana Eck at Harvard.

---

[5] Newby, Eric: *Slowly Down the Ganges*, Hodder & Stoughton, London (1966, 1998) pp. 246.

"I remember bathing in Ganga in Haridwar and coming out of the river glittering with Ganga. The water is just full of mica from the Himalayas." The image is enticing and Diana is at pains to remind me she is not a scientist. But it doesn't add a lot. Vinod Tare of IIT Kanpur — very much a scientist — has just finished a study that suggests the reach of Ganga between Devaprayag and Rishikesh may have slightly higher than normal radioactivity. But only slightly higher than the normal, and he hasn't tested this out in the plains.

These ideas are interesting, but they'll soon be history anyway because the Tehri Dam will effectively destroy whatever the Bhagirathi may be bringing down. That leaves the Alaknanda, but no scientist seems very interested in investigating that river and its myriad streams. Again, the lack of interest is curious.

Besides, it's all a bit moot anyway. Since 1854, the Ganga Canal has siphoned off almost all the winter flow of the river at Haridwar. If there ever was or still is anything special in the waters of the river it would have long since been diverted at Haridwar for irrigation.

So end of story? Not quite. Enter one D.S. Bhargava to upset the entire applecart.

"Ganga has some special properties that I call the Mysterious Factor X."

Devendra Swaroop Bhargava is now a retired professor of Hydrology from Roorkee University. He somehow survives in the family home on Bhargava Lane in Haridwar, where he lives on a pittance of a pension in a single room. Bhargava did his doctorate at IIT-Kanpur under Professor G.D. Agrawal (important because he was also interested in the study of Ganga jal), then worked at the Central Pollution Control Board before returning to academia at Roorkee and retiring to pursue a new career as intellectual gadfly. He's well suited to the role, but it has perhaps unnecessarily made him enemies.

In the 1980s and 1990s, Bhargava published many papers in respectable international journals, arguing that Ganga has special chemical and biological properties that allow the river to absorb organic wastes at an astonishingly high rate due to a remarkable ability to re-oxygenate itself.[6] One that stuck in my mind was the claim that animal

---

[6] See the bibliography for a partial list of his papers. The most accessible to non-specialist readers are: "Scientific Explanations for Mysteries Associated with Holiness of Ganga," pp. 6–8, *Civil Engineering Today* (USA), Vol XXVI No 3, May-June 2003; "Sacred but Unclean," pp. 13–16, *Asia Water Environment,* July 1998; "Nature and the Ganga," pp. 307–328, *Environmental Conservation* (Switzerland) ,Vol. 14 No 4, Winter 1987. But there are many others, most highly technical and requiring a good understanding of advanced mathematics.

bones submerged in a tank at IIT-Kanpur had been dissolved within three days.[7]

Words and ideas tumble out of D.S. Bhargava's mouth as enthusiastically as Ganga herself out of the Himalayas. If your attention wanders as much as a half-sentence, he's disappeared around some corner, rushing into a new thought. You can try and slow him down but he'll just accelerate again as soon as your foot is off the brakes. Bhargava is exhausting, and fascinating, if you can keep up. Trouble is you may never catch up.

His arguments and conclusions set me off on a parallel yatra to find out if the broader claims that the waters of Ganga purify men's souls and prepare them for the next life, have some basis in scientific reality. I don't pretend to have discovered the Mysterious Factor X, a title Bhargava and I made up together as a convenient shorthand back in 2001, but I have uncovered enough to suggest there is urgent need for some major research project to resolve a host of unexplained loose ends that cannot be dismissed as old wives' tales or "just blind faith," with no scientific basis.

"Ganga water does not putrefy." This is just the first of Bhargava's astonishing assertions. Putrefaction occurs when there is an absence of oxygen, causing pathogens (harmful bacteria) to grow. This is what makes water stale and smell. Bhargava is adamant because, "studies show pathogens do not survive in Ganga jal."

In the 1980s, he carried out a simple experiment with two beakers of Ganga jal. The first he boiled, then added pathogens once the water had cooled. The pathogens survived and the water putrefied. The other beaker he did not boil and the pathogens died. But Bhargava was unable to isolate and so identify the substance present in either beaker. He therefore concluded that whatever had been removed by boiling must be volatile in nature.[8]

Bhargava didn't carry out his field experiments in the Himalayas, but in the plains, and not once but all the way down from Kanpur to Varanasi. So whatever was or is present in Ganga either can survive Haridwar and the Ganga Canal or else has a completely different origin. Nothing to do with the source of Ganga in the Western Himalayas — he doesn't rule out the foothills which recharge the river between Haridwar

---

[7] Cf "Nature and the Ganga," Ibid & Sampat, Payal. "The Ganges: Myth and Reality," *World Watch*. Vol. 9, No. 4. July/August 1996. Also, Bhargava interview with the author on October 16, 2004.

[8] Volatile means capable of evaporation or conversion into either vapor or gas.

and Kanpur — or the great tributaries: Gandak, Ghaghara, or Kosi that flow down from the Nepalese Himalayas. But since these huge rivers enter Ganga east of Varanasi, whatever Mysterious Factor X they could contain would have had no effect on Bhargava's experiments or his other conclusions.

"It has to be something it picks up along its course." Bhargava's going so fast one Sunday morning I have to struggle for oxygen myself. "In other words something in its own river bed?"

"Yes, something unique to Ganga."

Bhargava notes that if left alone most rivers have a surprising ability to purify themselves. They are able to replenish themselves with oxygen and so break down most of the organic waste dumped into them. But Ganga can also purify itself ten to twenty times faster than its neighbour the Yamuna.[9]

Bhargava says Ganga has these extraordinary self-purifying abilities, specifically "because of its high content of dissolved oxygen (DO), extraordinary high rate of re-aeration, long DO-retention abilities, and the very fast assimilation of the putrefiable organic matter that has been discharged into the Ganga river."[10]

Ganga can therefore absorb a lot of human and animal wastes. Bhargava in fact claims the river removes fully sixty percent of all organic matter in the first thirty to forty minutes, while other rivers take days. "There is something in Ganga that kills pathogens twenty-five times faster than any other river." [11]

In our first conversations in 2001, Bhargava had suggested temperature was an important factor, but when challenged in 2004 he agreed that doesn't really hold up because whatever he discovered happens in the plains. Here there's really no significant difference between Ganga and any other north Indian river. They're all shallow, essentially flat, so

---

[9] This is highly technical and involves two coefficients and something called a Phelps value. Details can be found in "Nature and the Ganga" and the various references there to his other papers. As far as I know no other scientist, Indian or foreign, has published papers on this re-oxygenation ability of Ganga.

[10] Bhargava D.S., "Nature and the Ganga," p. 308, *Environmental Conservation,* Vol 14 No 4, Winter 1987 (Switzerland). Bhargava has always claimed that whatever special properties exist in Ganga are not found in the Yamuna, which rises at Yamnotri, just a handful of kilometers from Gangotri in the Himalayas, and flows within a hundred kilometers of Ganga until the two finally merge at Allahabad.

[11] I've already witnessed this amazing ability at self-healing purification south of Kanpur in Chapter 4.

the current is sluggish at best; they are baked by the unrelenting sun and receive extraordinary increases in volume of water — and hence oxygen — once a year from the annual monsoon. Size is also not a determining factor because Ganga is by no means the largest river in south Asia.

A lot of what Bhargava has long been saying — often in the wilderness because his papers have been published almost exclusively in the West — makes sense.[12] Obviously, whatever is present in Ganga jal cannot come from Gaumukh because it is present as far south as Varanasi, and it is organic because it dies when boiled.

In many ways he's replicated and confirmed a seminal paper by M.E. Hankin, the chief medical officer for Agra, that was published in 1896 by the Institut Pasteur in Paris. Then, as now, the Institut Pasteur was *the* authority on bacteria. Although English was his native language, Hankin's study was indeed first published in French, and only subsequently translated back into English.

For several years I could not find a copy of Hankin's original. I was dependent on Bhargava's summaries, in print and in person.[13]

Hankin had observed that "what protects the Indian people from getting infected with some water-borne disease in spite of their drinking (for religious rites) even the sewage-contaminated Ganga water, has been a question that has been baffling the minds of environmental technologists, scientists, and physicians, for a long time." This, Bhargava argues, is because people develop immunity over time, although I think that answers only one part of the question and doesn't take into consideration either his or Hankin's observations.

This is Bhargava's abstract of Hankin's thesis:

"Dr. E. Hanbury Hankin's research of the nineteenth century relates to the disinfecting/antiviral power of the Ganga's water. Hankin (1896) reported that cholera microbes did not survive for long in the

---

[12] While one might wonder if Bhargava's claims for Ganga are intellectually "clean" (research on particular diets or the benefits of certain drugs often turn out to have been financed by multinationals), he seems to have paid his own way. Bhargava devised his own tests and even built his own simple equipment. It's all documented in his article "Nature and the Ganga," pp. 308-09, *Environmental Conservation* Vol 14, No 4 Winter 1987, which states when he did his field work (both summer and winter months), and how he did his research (equipment, field laboratories, etc).

[13] They were all I had to go on, which was unfortunate because Bhargava drew important (and I believe incorrect) conclusions because he read Hankin's paper only in the French, which he is manifestly uncomfortable with. Nowadays both English and French versions are available at *www.gangagen.com/sitemapframe.htm*.

Ganga's waters. He conducted his studies on the Ganga at Varanasi, where he collected samples below the cholera-infected dead bodies that had been thrown into the Ganga, and found that the cholera microbes died within a few hours of their contact with the Ganga water."

He then goes on to summarize Hankin's tests, which he himself would essentially replicate a hundred years later: "Hankin inoculated cholera microbes in two beakers — one containing Ganga water and the other containing sterile distilled water — and noticed that the microbes died soon (in less than three hours) in the beaker containing the Ganga water, whereas no great change took place in the living concentration of cholera microbes even after forty-eight hours in the beaker containing the distilled water."

"Hankin, however, noticed that the Ganga water lost this strong disinfecting property after it had been boiled in an open container. For some of his observations...it is noted that the Ganga water, even if not heated, will, in less than three hours, kill any cholera microbes that may have been added. However, the same water, if heated, lacks this power. Hankin therefore attributes the disinfecting property of the Ganga to the probable presence in it of some volatile material" (Hankin 1896).

Hankin's conclusions are the same as Bhargava's. The only difference is that Bhargava concludes that the Mysterious Factor X exists in the river bed itself. It makes sense. It accounts for why he can replicate his test right the way down the river to Varanasi. For the rest, one must travel further down the river, wait, and see.

~

Two weeks later at his ashram in Bilhaur, south of Kannauj, Swami Ramesh Chand Das seems to confirm Bhargava's theory.

"It is gandhak — sulphur — and that's why no germs can live in this water or pollute the water. Gandhak is found in the river bed."

"Why do you think no scientists have yet discovered it?" I'm a bit skeptical.

Ramesh Chand is not.

"Whatever is said in the Veda scriptures, we consider that the truth. I don't know why the scientific people are not getting their information from the Vedas and other places. It is written there, this sulphur is the only thing which is keeping this river's water unique."

Ramesh Chand's argument is dashed the following week by A.C. Shukla, a professor at Christ Church College in Kanpur.[14]

---

[14] Dr. Shukla taught Botany and was head of the Biopollution Study Center at Christ Church College, Kanpur before his retirement.

"Yes, there are sulphur springs in Ganga. But sulphur kills off everything, the good as well as the bad. And there is something in Ganga that is very beneficial called bacteriophage which would be killed off if sulphur was really present in such massive quantities. So I don't think the Mysterious Factor X can be sulphur."

"What is a bacteriophage?" I've never heard the term before. Dr. Shukla is economic with words. They're precious things, not to be wasted in useless verbiage. He takes a sip from his tea before addressing my question.

"Ganga is unique because of this bacteriophage. It comes from the Gangotri glacier and flows downwards. This bacteriophage has the capacity to totally kill off bacterial pathogens. This phage grows so vast and so rapidly that it can spread throughout the entire length of Ganga from Gangotri to Ganga Sagar in just twenty four hours"

"Twenty four hours? Twenty six hundred kilometers? That's phenomenal!"

"The growth of this killing virus is very rapid. It comes up in the water, it grows and multiplies and then vanishes automatically in twenty four hours time."

Presumably leaving no trace. Here today, gone tomorrow and Ganga has been swept clean of disease. Extraordinary.

So have scientists been able to identify this bacteriophage?

"Yes, it's called bacteriophage *Gangeticum.*" He says that a Canadian researcher (Shukla doesn't know his name, but I now know it has to be the French-Canadian Felix d'Herelle) identified this bacteriophage in the mid-twentieth century. But what existed then can no longer exist today because there will soon be no more continuous flow of Ganga out of the Himalayas. The Tehri dams will be the death of Ganga's extraordinary self-purifying capacity.

Dr. Shukla is adamant that water from the Nepalese Himalayas, which feeds into Ganga lower down through the great Gandak, Ghaghara and Kosi, cannot by definition carry this special bacteriophage. It can only come from Gaumukh and Bhagirathi. At the time it seems stupid to ask why.

He dismisses Bhargava's theory that the Mysterious Factor X could exist in the river bed throughout the plains. I explain that Bhargava has found Factor X from Kanpur to Varanasi and in the last twenty years.

"That's impossible, because the flow is no longer continuous. If you interrupt the flow of the river at Tehri or Haridwar then the phage can no longer travel down the river into the plains. There is a time-space connection. This may have happened fifty years ago, but conditions have totally changed today. Fifty years ago, you could put a few drops of Ganga jal into polluted water and it would kill all the bacterial growth. It has been recorded."[15]

So to summarize our search for this Mysterious Factor X to date: Bhargava says there is some special disinfectant agent in Ganga jal between Kanpur and Varanasi, but it's volatile and he hasn't been able to isolate and therefore identify whatever it is. He suspects it's somehow present in the bed of the river itself, because he's found this Mysterious Factor X throughout the plains, where very little of the original Himalayan water has trickled down ever since the Ganga Canal siphoned most of it off back in 1854. Once the Tehri Dam is complete, probably not even that small amount will get through.

Shukla doesn't even acknowledge Bhargava. But he says there is something called a bacteriophage that kills all bacteria in a great wave that sweeps down from the Himalayas to the Bay of Bengal in just twenty-four hours, and then disappears as mysteriously as it came, leaving no calling card. It had been discovered in the last century but its powers are much reduced because it comes from Gaumukh and is hence already curtailed by the Ganga Canal at Haridwar, and will soon disappear completely when Tehri channels the flow of the Bhagirathi into its turbines.

Finally, we have Swami Ramesh Chand Das who says the answer is springs with gandakh in them — and it's all described in the Vedas. Shukla says there are indeed sulphur springs which kill bacteria. The trouble is they also would kill everything else.

All very tantalizing but too many of them seem to cancel each other out. I had hit a brick wall. Some interesting snippets of ideas[16] but

---

[15] This conversation took place on a Sunday afternoon at the house of Dr. Shukla's colleague Dr. Vandana Asthani, who teaches political science in Kanpur. Dr. Asthani and Rakesh Jaiswal were convinced that the Indian government knew the Bhagirathi contained a secret miracle substance, that they had therefore suppressed a scientific report (which may or may not exist) on the effects of the dam on the water quality of Ganga jal above and below the dam once completed. As far as I know there is no substance to this conspiracy theory.

[16] Graham Chapman, a geography professor, who has walked and studied much of northern India, later told me Bhargava's river bed theory shouldn't be dismissed out of hand, "There was a sea linking the Mediterranean and the Bay of Bengal called the Tethys before the Eurasian and Indian plates collided. When the two landmasses bumped up against one another they formed a trough at least seven kilometers deep. The alluvial deposits in the Ganges basin are therefore the deepest of any river deposits on the planet. So yes, it's entirely possible there are strata that could contain sulphur or something else."

nothing to sink my teeth into, until I received an email from a colleague several months later.[17]

"I've just met an Indian scientist and he's got something very important to tell you about the Mysterious Factor X and Ganga," she wrote.

A rapid exchange of emails and a few days later I was talking on the phone to Dr. Jay Ramachandran, the founder of Gangagen, a biotechnology company named in honour of M.E. Hankin's discoveries, with research laboratories in Palo Alto and Bangalore.[18] Ram, as his friends call him, has done enormous work on bacteriophages. Dr. Shukla had introduced me to the word. But it was Ram who made it real and could answer all my impatient questions.

On the phone he explained: "Bacteriophages are literally bacteria eaters.[19] They can destroy a virus such as cholera before it's even got out of bed. If you study them under an electron microscope, they look like those moon lander spacecraft. They have long legs that attach to the bacteria host. They penetrate and destroy the chromosome and multiply exponentially. In thirty minutes, one hundred phages become ten thousand, and so on."

Instinctively, Indians may always have known about phages. Ram reminds me that many temples have a little tank outside where people wash themselves and some of them have developed a reputation as curative powers: "This could be due to phages."

Ram also sent me the original French and English texts of ME Hankin's papers from 1894-96. I could finally read for myself what Bhargava had been talking about. But there were still many unanswered questions. Most of my scientific colleagues in the United States were very skeptical. Why had they never heard about bacteriophages? Most of them assumed Ram must be claiming his discoveries would kill all diseases in Ganga, from skin rashes to low-grade intestinal infections.

---

[17] Dr. Kelly Alley is an anthropologist in Alabama who spends much of her time working on Ganga in Kanpur and Varanasi. She has written extensively and perceptively on Ganga, notably in *On the Banks of the Ganga — When Wastewater Meets a Sacred River*, University of Michigan Press, Ann Arbor, 2002. I am forever indebted to her for her chance meeting with this "Indian scientist."

[18] Gangagen is focused on the development of bacteriophage-based products for the prevention and treatment of bacterial infections, particularly infections that are resistant to antibiotics.

[19] The Greek word *phagos* means to eat.

In 1917, the French-Canadian scientist Felix d'Herelle, working at the Pasteur Institute in Paris, was asked to investigate the outbreak of dysentery which was afflicting soldiers fighting in the First World War in northeastern France. He quickly found that the dysentery was caused by the shigella bacteria. He cultured the bacteria to study their growth and noticed that sometimes clear areas could be seen on plates of bacteria. He recognized the significance of the clear areas (plaques). Something was killing the bacteria. D'Herelle wondered if he could use whatever it was as a treatment to cure the dysentery.

He took samples of a patient's stool, filtered out the bacteria, spread the mixture out on glass plates, and lo and behold one morning the plate was clear. The bacteria had vanished. There was no trace left. D'Herelle had a moment of epiphany: "What caused my clear spots was in fact an invisible microbe, a filterable virus, but a virus which is parasitic on bacteria."[20] This was the pre-antibiotic era. Unless one had natural immunity there was no way anyone could survive. So when d'Herelle published his paper on how he had cured dysentery in a whole village with bacteriophage treatment, it drew a lot of attention and literally dozens of companies were formed to sell phages.

For ten years, bacteriophages were all the rage. D'Herelle's success stimulated commercial production of phages for treating a broad variety of bacterial infections both in Europe and in the United States. D'Herelle came to India, and phage therapy was tried with impressive results in Punjab and Assam. The number of cholera deaths plummeted. But few doctors in India or elsewhere understood how bacteriophages actually worked, that bacteria could indeed also build up resistance, "capture" phages, and turn them back on themselves.

Then in 1934, the American Pharmaceutical Society published a less than ringing endorsement. It concluded that phage therapies were inconclusive. Simultaneously antibiotics became widespread. Antibiotics were inexpensive, easy to produce and could be used to fight any bacteria.[21]

The British in Assam next abandoned phage therapy for different but no less revealing reasons. The health authorities in India wanted to make proper sanitation their top priority. So any therapy that reduced the emphasis on the need for better water and sewer systems was seen as

---

[20] D'Herelle, Dr. Felix: "The Bacteriophage," *Science News,* 1r4:44–59 (1949).

[21] Summers, William P. *Felix d'Herelle and the Origins of Molecular Biology*, pp. 218, Yale University Press, New Haven, Connecticut 1999.

threatening. I think a lot of professional skepticism in the West today still reflects that view. Ironically, phage therapy continued to be used and developed successfully in the Soviet Union, right up to its collapse in 1989.[22]

"Today the boot is on the other foot. There's a 'perfect storm' brewing," Ram told me in his office in a Bangalore suburb.

"More and more people are developing resistance to antibiotics. I saw it myself at AstraZeneca.[23] It's becoming increasingly uneconomic to develop new drugs. So I think phages are the way of the future. They've been keeping bacteria in check for three and a half billion years."

In person Ram puts me to shame. At age seventy, he's tall, fit, and bears a striking facial resemblance to the Austrian classical music conductor Nicholas Harnoncourt. For many years his mandate at AstroZeneca was to develop therapeutics for tuberculosis and malaria, two of the most serious diseases in the developing world.

"So I was very much involved with infectious diseases. And what I saw convinced me that antibiotics are not the solution, that we have to look for alternative therapies." When he retired he simply kept on working because he was so worried at the growing ineffectiveness of many antibiotics.

Ram confirmed that what Hankin had discovered back in 1894 were indeed bacteriophages in (both) Yamuna and Ganga. Bhargava had never said much about Yamuna.

"First of all you have to remember that all this happened over a hundred years ago. He was working in very primitive conditions although he was pretty convinced that he was doing the right thing by the standards of the day. He was using the latest equipment — ceramic filters, that Louis Pasteur had developed to filter out the bacteria and debris. He then took a culture of cholera-causing bacteria, and when he added water from the Yamuna and Ganga he observed that within three hours, the bacteria were dead."

Ram explained that Hankin boiled the river water and then added the pathogens. They survived and multiplied. How come? Because the bacteriophages had been killed off by the heat. Although phages are

---

[22] Stalin established the first-ever world bacteriophage institute at Tbilisi in Georgia.

[23] For many years Ramachandran was head of the Asian branch of the Swedish pharmaceutical company AstraZeneca in Bangalore. When he retired he founded Gangagen.

remarkably heat resistant, above a certain temperature their structure simply breaks apart.[24] There was nothing left to kill off the bacterial pathogens.

Hankin instinctively realized that both rivers contained something that killed cholera bacteria, although it would only be identified as a bacteriophage twenty-odd years later.[25] Ram says bacteriophages are micro-viruses rather than bacterial anti-bodies and are present everywhere on the planet. In fact they are the most abundant entities on the planet. It is estimated that there are ten raised to the power of thirty-one — an astronomical number — bacteriophages on the planet. And in fact the bulk are in the oceans. If you go to any ocean and take a millilitre of sea water you will find between one to ten million bacteriophages.

There are phages for all bacteria. A cholera phage can only attach to a cholera bacteria, an E. coli phage only to that specific E. coli, and so on. They simply bide their time until they can sense that bacteria. But when they do, all hell breaks loose. The moment the phage gets into the bacterium it multiplies exponentially. In a few hours you can have billions of bacteriophages but almost no more bacteria. They've fled. Bacteria are always looking for something or someone to feed on, so those that survive will disengage, move away to comparative safety, until sooner or later the appropriate phage finds them out again, and the whole process starts all over again. This is why there's usually a state of low level truce with bacteria kept in ecological control.

"Why can't we see bacteriophages in the water?"

"They can hang around in shady waters for years, but you won't notice them because there is no host. They will only express themselves when there is a bacterial host." So the bacteriophage doesn't disappear after twenty-four hours, as Shukla had stated. It simply becomes dormant.

---

[24] Ram says his laboratory usually heats phages up to sixty to seventy degrees centigrade to isolate phages from hospital sewage or other sewage water. But if you heat the phage to a hundred degrees centigrade then it dies because its structure breaks apart.

[25] When Felix d'Herelle actually discovered the presence of bacteriophages, he couldn't of course see the phages because they are micro-viruses. That would have to wait the invention of the electron microscope in the 1930s. It was d'Herelle who showed that these ultra microbes are particles and gave them the name 'bacteriophage.' The discovery that phages are essentially strips of DNA that attach themselves to, then penetrate the cells of bacteria, would have to wait till the 1940s. The nature of phage as DNA and protein came from the work of Max Delbruck and several other scientists, in particular, Alfred Hershey and Martha Chase at the Cold Spring Harbor Laboratory in the 1940s and formed the basis of the evolution of the science of molecular biology.

One of the major problems in using phages as therapeutics has always been their extraordinary specificity. The phage that will kill cholera will not kill shigella dysentery even though they are both diarrhoeal diseases. And one that kills shigella will not kill typhoid, and so on. The challenge is to perform the diagnosis of the infection properly, and then match the right phage to that infection.

Unfortunately, this specificity simply wasn't understood back in the 1920s. The physician had to properly diagnose the infection. He had to know if it was cholera or shigella or some other type of diarrhoeal infection, Montezuma's revenge or whatever. And then find the appropriate phage to treat it. This was a very difficult proposition. Even today it is complicated, and in those days it was practically impossible because they didn't have the right tools, specifically the electron microscope, which had yet to be invented.[26] So the inappropriate phage was often applied to the wrong bacteria. Predictably, it failed to do the job.

The development of penicillin effectively ended the use of bacteriophage. Penicillin was and still is the miracle panacea because it's a broad spectrum antibiotic. The physician can therefore say "ahah-infection-fever-penicillin." So most physicians simply said forget about phages, we'll go with antibiotics. Doctors also didn't understand that phages can only kill bacteria. Back then, for example, doctors wanted to use phages to kill herpes. But herpes is a virus. So failure and discredit of the bacteriophage lasted for more than fifty years. Until today, when doctors are quickly encountering massive bacterial resistance to antibiotics that have cost a king's ransom to develop. Hence the re-emergence of the lowly bacteriophage.

All rivers contain phages. There's nothing special about Ganga. Hankin found phages in the Yamuna at Agra. Bhargava reported he had found this Mysterious Factor X at Varanasi and Allahabad. So the theory they are somehow unique to Himalayan waters or to below-normal temperatures is a red herring. Because bacteriophages exist throughout the entire river, damming or diverting the flow of the Himalayan Ganga at Tehri or Haridwar will probably have no impact on their presence, and therefore on the ability of Ganga to purify itself.

But any radical alteration in the state of the river, such as massive chemical pollution, or a complete breakdown of oxygen due to algae or other vegetal growth could have very negative consequences. The persistence of bacteriophages is undoubtedly affected by temperature

---

[26] It was invented in the early 1930s.

and direct sunlight. It's reasonable to assume that a significant increase in salinity or another chemical change could also be disruptive. The trouble is we just don't know how or what.

The bacteria which phages feed on can come from human sewage, or from human bodies when they bathe. The human body in water in fact acts as a catalyst. The higher the concentration of bathers the more food for the phages to feast on. So wherever there are major bathing festivals (the various Kumbh Melas) and high numbers of bathers (Varanasi, Allahabad) phages will flock.

"When you have a Kumbh Mela, I really believe that phages help. When sixty million people bathe in a small area, huge amounts of bacteria are rinsed off from their bodies. Suddenly the bacterial concentration is very high. Even though the phage concentration is initially very low, the chance of the proper bacterium meeting a phage is very likely. Having found out its prey, the phage will multiply and the whole area suddenly becomes rich in phages. So a few days after a Kumbh Mela you should find a lot of phages there."

Music to my ears. The 2003 Ardh Mela at Nasik (on the Godavari river) confirmed Ram's hypothesis. "Six million people bathed there. We took water samples and found about eight or nine different phages in that water." Just about what you'd expect when several million take a "holy dip" together.

As more people bathe in Ganga, the river seems to acquire greater powers of self-purification. Environmental purists would be horrified, just as the British in Assam health authorities were horrified at the idea of downplaying sanitation as their number one health priority.

To some it may also sound like an open invitation to encourage people to dump untreated sewage into Ganga. No one is advocating this. But maybe one doesn't need to get quite so hung up on expensive and complex sewage treatment plants that are heavily dependent on electricity. Settling ponds and bacteriophages seem a low-cost and effective alternative to high-tech methods — using nature to repair the damage man has done to the environment.

An environmental science colleague in the United States has worried that if the bacteria are wiped out then all the phages must also be killed. He bases this on what happens to wildlife. But Ram says the analogy is wrong. My colleague is confusing ecology and microbiology. Phages bring the bacteria back down to within acceptable levels. They don't eliminate them entirely. There's no need. The phages can take a breather until the next alert. When the bacteria are back within acceptable levels, the phages have done their work.

Which is why there are never any cases of mass epidemics at bathing festivals such as the various Kumbh Melas or Kartik Purnima or Makar Sankranti. Western common sense and hygiene insist there must be. But there never are because phages have killed most of the bacteria within twelve hours. "The devastation is exponential," as Ram says.[27]

At Varanasi, the Sankat Mochan Foundation laboratories report E.coli levels millions above permissible World Health Organization levels.[28] And yet there are no resultant pandemics. Skin diseases, stomach disorders, but no devastating epidemics. This might well be the reason why.

Today, Gangagen has built up a library of over 450 phages. Ironically, Gangagen gets many of them in the raw sewage collected from hospitals in Bangalore: "Human shit is a wonderful thing because it contains most of the phages we need to treat common epidemics like cholera, typhoid, gastro-enteritis. We shouldn't try to banish shit from our lives, if it contains the very microbacteria that prevent us getting sick."

I find it strange that so few Indian scientists seem intellectually interested in phages. Fragmentation of scientific knowledge? Ignorance? Jealousy? Ram thinks all of the above. Many Indian scientists simply separate out science from their religious beliefs. They accept and pass on to other subjects. Ram says: "I have known many particle physicists who will not move to a new place unless the stars are in the right position. They simply accept this is how it has to be. Once the astrologer has reassured them they can go back into the lab as if nothing has ever happened. Total divorce between the two."

---

[27] Specifically, Gangagen isolated very potent phages against Staph Aureus from Nasik after the Mela in 2004. Today, they are developing phages for the control of Staph infection in healthcare workers and patients entering surgery or dialysis. A Canadian subsidiary in Ottawa is developing phages for the control of E. coli 0157:H7 (this is the cause of the "hamburger disease") in cattle prior to slaughter to prevent contamination of meat.

[28] The figures are truly frightening. The World Health Organization limit is five hundred parts per million. R.K. Mishra, head of the Sankat Mochan Foundation laboratories in Varanasi, told me they regularly record readings many thousands of times above that permissible level. But Ram says ninety percent of all E.coli are actually beneficial. He therefore wonders what sorts of E.coli Sankat Mochan are actually measuring. Do they differentiate between the good and the bad E.coli? Do they also understand how bacteriophages work?

The bacteriophage is undoubtedly a part of the Mysterious Factor X. But it's not the entire explanation. Bacteriophage is indeed Bhargava's "disinfectant" that kills cholera and dysentery germs. They're not however unique to Ganga. The extraordinary high rates of re-oxygenation that Bhargava identified may be. But they are two completely distinct phenomena.[29] Bhargava's mistake was to confuse and collapse them into a single phenomenon because he had misread a badly-printed copy of a hundred year-old journal in French.

Hankin writes that his discoveries were made in the Yamuna, in Agra where he was chief medical officer. He could see bodies literally rotting on the banks of the river. So he carried out his series of simple experiments with samples from Yamuna and at local wells. Hankin also took comparative readings in Ganga, but at Allahabad. He saw with his own eyes that the cholera germ was present in epidemic proportions at Agra and at Allahabad. He nowhere writes that he observed cholera at either Haridwar or Varanasi. Bhargava simply misread the French. This is where much of the problem begins. Bhargava assumed Hankin has carried out his experiments only in Ganga and came up with his startling — and false — claims for Ganga jal.

The bacteriophage explains why there are no pandemics in Ganga. But the true Mysterious Factor X, the quality that Ganga possesses that no other river does, is perhaps its extraordinary rate of re-oxygenation. Bhargava found Ganga has a rate many times greater than Yamuna. The question is why? Nobody to my knowledge has even attempted or hinted at a plausible answer. Neither temperature nor velocity offer a remotely convincing answer. It's back to something in the actual river bed.

~

If Bhargava hadn't gone on to document the extraordinary re-oxygenation rates of the river and its ability to dissolve organic matter fully twenty-five times faster than any other river in India or elsewhere in the world, he'd probably be just a footnote in scientific papers. But he did discover these attributes. And they argue that there is something other than bacteriophages in the water. The river does have some extraordinary rejuvenating powers.

---

[29] My colleague David Black believes re-oxygenation and bacteriophages are somehow related. I reminded him that all rivers possess bacteriophages, but only Ganga has this extraordinary rate of re-oxygenation. He is still to be convinced.

Miah M. Hussainuzzaman, a young geomorphologist I met in Kanpur in December 2005, mentioned he was researching for arsenic in the area. "How did it get here?" I wondered.

"Probably brought down thousands of years ago, lying dormant ever since. Then other chemicals — maybe man-made, maybe totally innocuous like oxygen — interact with it. The original material suddenly stirs, changes its nature. It's called geochemistry," Hussainuzzaman casually explains, then goes on to more esoteric subjects.

But my interest has been piqued. Bhargava's eyes would have lit up. Something in the river bed — the germ of another theory has been sown.

* * * * *

Ganga in Bihar and Jharkhand

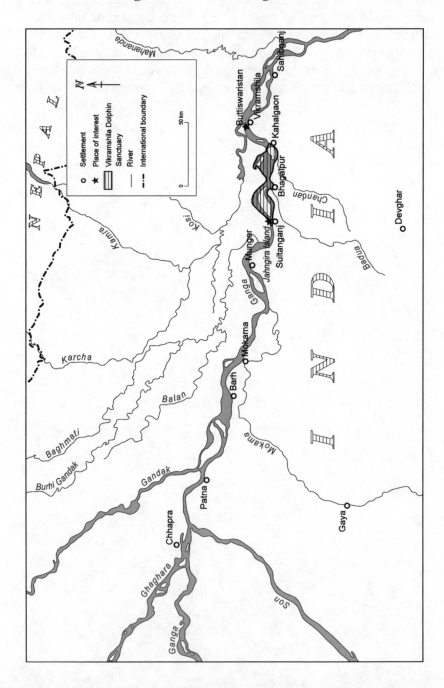

CHAPTER 6

Dacoits and Dolphins

New cast, new river. A butterfly starts life as a chrysalis, grows into a caterpillar that voraciously consumes anything around it, and finally emerges as a fully-fledged butterfly that will travel far and wide. It is much the same with Ganga. In its first stage from Gaumukh to Allahabad it crashes turbulently down the Himalayas, then slows into a languid, almost comatose lethargy until it reaches Allahabad. Here it metamorphoses thanks to the unexpected injection of fresh water and vigour from Yamuna. There will never again be any danger it will dry up and die of overuse. Between Varanasi and Patna it enters into a state of transition. Less than a hundred kilometers beyond Varanasi at the border with Bihar it changes shape once again to its final adult state — a physically imposing and dangerous river.[1]

From one end of Bihar to the other, no more than five hundred kilometers, Ganga triples in size. Four huge rivers flow into her: the Son running off the Deccan Plateau to the south, then the Ghaghara, Gandak, and Kosi from the Nepalese Himalayas. Not surprisingly, her nature in the human imagination also changes. Gone is the benign goddess. In her place Ganga becomes destroyer and creator.

Everyone — farmers, city dwellers, engineers has to learn to live with this elemental force, bringing life but also destroying land, animals, and human lives in her wake.

~

In Hindu iconography Ganga is usually depicted as a goddess who rides a strange-looking fish. It looks like a dolphin but it has a very

---

[1] We traveled this short section in the Scorpio and then raced to Kolkata to deposit valuables and unnecessary clothes and get back to Patna in time to make our departure date.

long snout and teeth. And it really does exist, as we first saw back where Ramganga entered Ganga at Kannauj above Kanpur. It's called *gangetica platanista*, susu in Hindi, the world's oldest freshwater dolphin. But Ganga's mythical mount is in danger of becoming myth; there are maybe only fifteen hundred left. The dolphin's main habitat is in Bihar, which is also India's most notorious state for dacoits or bandits.

We spent three weeks on our twenty-five-foot long country boat (appropriately christened *Dolphin*), with five local fishermen and five Indian scientists, rowing eight hundred kilometers from Patna to Kolkata. This was the longest unbroken period of time we spent anywhere on the river. It's difficult to be more intimate with a river than this. Our immediate goal was to survey the remaining dolphins. We saw very few. Luckily, very few people saw us either.

"You're mad! No Indians in their right mind would travel between Bahr and Bhagalpur. Julian, don't do it, please!" counseled one of my oldest Bihari friends, Mithu Gupta. The previous year, Mithu's own mother in Patna had asked her not to bring the grandchildren for a December visit because of dacoiti. "She said they'd get kidnapped." If you know anything about Indian families, you'll appreciate how unusual (and therefore serious) her request was. Mithu complied. "And you want to travel all the way down to Kolkata by boat?"

But plans have been set in motion. A twenty-seven-foot country boat has been built to our specifications on the Gandak, a major tributary of Ganga just opposite Patna. *Dolphin* is custom-built for this yatra. She's broad-beamed, with a ten-foot-long well in the middle. Benches line either side with bamboo backrests on one side that also stores spare oars, a sail, and long bamboo poles to steer the boat. Under the decking at either end are watertight compartments where two kerosene stoves, giant cooking pots, plates, plastic cups, and basic supplies — atta, various dals, rice, and potatoes — are kept. At the other end Khalid can store his scientific tools — sonar, batteries, notebooks. Naively, we'd imagined when we first saw *Dolphin* in the river at Patna that there would also be plenty of room for our supplies. But no sooner had we taken all our equipment down on rickshaws than we had to take it all back up again and store it in the Scorpio.

Our skipper is Ravindra Kumar Sinha, a professor, probably the professor of zoology at Patna University. Sinha has assembled a crew: four oarsmen — Subhash, Mahesh, Arjun and Raju — and a cook, Mohan. Sinha has serious qualifications for this particular job. His speciality is the gangetic dolphin. Every year he sails a section of the river as part of his field research. At least once he has sailed the entire navigable river from Haridwar to Kolkata. This particular stretch from Patna is his stomping ground. It's where most of the remaining dolphins hang out. Subhash and Mahesh have sailed with him many times. They used to be full-time fishermen. Then the bottom fell out of fishing. Now they work for Sinha several months a year to get by.

Together they make up the traditional image of Bengali boatmen — Mahesh performs bhatiali songs (a musical form popular in this region), Subhash skippers the boat. Mahesh is the singing half— he's the more outgoing and has a fine tenor voice. Before noon, he sings melodic songs about the river and the life of a boatman. His pièce de résistance always makes hearts melt, a film song from a very old movie, *Baiju Bwara,* which goes like this: *Tu ganga ke mauj mein jamuna ki dhara tumhara rahega milan yeh hamara hamara* (like Yamuna meeting Ganga—we will melt into each other and flow as one through the rest of life).[2]

After lunch, tummy filled, he extemporises bawdy lyrics to film hits, which have us all in stitches. Sample: "Ganga is changing course so much and is so unpredictable, she is more difficult than my wife!"

Subhash, on the other hand, is the quintessential taciturn boatman, standing tall at the tiller, face muffled in a woolen scarf, always looking for the most favorable current (or a dolphin). I've never heard Subhash so much as hum a tune, but occasionally a shadow of a smile softens his face, usually at the more outrageous of Mahesh's improvisations.

Mahesh and Subhash inspire confidence, so much so that after a few days Martine takes them with her to buy fish, meat, and other supplies in local markets. They, in turn, trust her. For Arjun and Raju this is their first time. They're much younger, physically fresher. The rest of the year they eke out a living as fishermen in Patna. All four are married with families in Patna.

Mohan is the baby of the team. His job is to turn out vast quantities of carbohydrates three times a day for the oarsmen and us — chawal, sabji, and rotis — all in the well of the boat on two kerosene stoves. It later turns out he doesn't know how to swim.

The "scientists" are more varied. Khalid Mahboob Khan is tall and rail-thin. A postdoctoral fellow from Dr. Sinha's zoology department in Patna, Khalid's job is to meticulously record sightings of dolphins, great and small, and to record our course every kilometer with a sonar and GPS. A man of few words, Khalid is unfailingly courteous.

---

[2] It continues in the same vein: "If you are the ocean I am the river, If your heart is the boat then I'm the sailor. You can't sail the boat alone. You can't find the shore without me."

The other three permanent fixtures are James Ashby, Dr. Tej Razdan, and the captain, R.K. Sinha. James is doing postgraduate research in geomorphology. His mother and Martine went to school together. James was working in Nepal and asked if he could tag along for the ride in exchange for an endless supply of biscuits and help with logistics. He bears a striking resemblance to the Australian fast bowler Jason Gillespie. Although culturally an American, James understands that cricket is what turns most Indians on, and plays to the constant gallery of small boys who pester him for his autograph.

Tej Razdan is a doctor from Rajasthan. It makes sense to have a doctor aboard, with a full array of pills and ointments. Tej is an adventurer. He seems to have been just about anywhere and everywhere in India. He and his long-suffering wife, Nancy, are originally from Kashmir — they run a private clinic in Udaipur, or rather Nancy does. Tej absconds (his word) on two-month trips. A very neat man, Tej is also a gizmo freak. He's brought along a mini camcorder, a mini cassette recorder and at least two cell phones. Our every step is somewhere recorded and in storage in Udaipur. Tej is dependable, a good man.

Ravindra Kumar Sinha — bearer of the Gold Fleece of the Netherlands, something his curriculum vitae is very proud of — is something else. R.K., as we familiarly call him (we never actually asked if he minded), is large for an Indian. Large does not mean fat. R.K. is certainly not that. He's just big. Six feet four, broad shouldered, he looks a natural sportsman. And he has a voice and an ego to go with his size. He knows his science, but he's also obsessed with money and shares one of the less attractive Bihari character traits — an instinctive taste and talent for corruption.

He figures he's got us over a barrel, so he tries to skim us, and the fishermen, for everything he can. Sometimes, it's legitimate (sort of); other times it's so outrageous we come to blows — both verbal and physical. We settle on a sum of money to pay the families of our boatmen during their absence on the river. Sinha signs for the money. We assume he's disbursed the four hundred rupees each per day to Mahesh, Subhash, Arjun, Raju, and Mohan.

But when we get to our penultimate camping spot at Barrakpur near Kolkata, the fishermen confide in Khalid, who in turn informs Martine, that they are actually being paid one hundred rupees a day. R.K. has told them this was all we're prepared to pay them, take it or leave it.

Martine is minister of finance on board *Dolphin*.[3] The net result is that she gets mad and confronts R.K. on the Esplanade in Kolkata. Unfortunately for him there's that receipt from Patna. He's not only signed it but also specified in writing how much and what for.

Martine takes the missing pay out of what we owe R.K. and personally gives it (along with new lungis) to each of our crew in front of Dr. Tej. They're so used to being cheated and short-changed I think they're still in a bit of shock. They promise her everlasting allegiance. R.K. jumps into a taxi and takes the first plane back to Patna, never to be heard from again.

And then there are the sometime *compagnons de route* — Gopal Sharma, Graham and Anne Gerd Chapman, and Saju Rai.

Dr. Gopal Sharma was Khalid's predecessor as research assistant, and now works for the Archaeological Survey of India in its Patna office, responsible for marine life along Ganga. It annoyed me then and annoys me still that we end up paying the freight for another of R.K.'s research assistants. I can't prove it but our suspicion is that the Archaeological Survey is also shelling out to R.K. for Gopal Sharma's expenses.

We have no real quarrel with Saju Rai. An old student colleague of R.K., Saju Rai is an up-and-coming BJP politician in Jharkhand. R.K. informs us he will be traveling with us from Sahibganj to Rajmahal. The pro quid quo is that he will arrange for a decent bed and meal at the circuit house in Sahibganj. Saju Rai has some interesting thoughts on Ganga, so we get along fine the days he's with us.

For a week the boat is really crowded to the gunwales— Graham Chapman, a geography professor whose speciality is the Gangetic basin, and his Danish wife Anne Gerd have always wanted to travel this area of Ganga. At the time, before the advent of Gopal Sharma, there was space. So we agreed. Graham has the unnerving habit of quietly putting R.K. in his scientific place. He's a Renaissance man — mountaineer, scientist, humanist, novelist — who happens to know much of Ganga well, and its geography and geomorphology even better. R.K. soon learns not to pontificate or pull the wool over our eyes while Graham is around. Anne

---

[3] Finance and Supplies. A week into the voyage, the boatmen start telling anyone who'll listen they urgently need protein because they're spending prodigious amounts of calories to row us every day. Chawal, sabji, and roti isn't going to do it much longer, so the next day Martine goes ashore with Subhash and Mahesh in the Scorpio to the nearest market and buys two huge squawking chickens and flats of eggs. The chickens are stowed on board and eaten later that day. From then on, trips by Martine, Subhash, and Mahesh to buy fish, chicken, fruit, and eggs become a regular feature of the voyage.

Gerd sends R.K. into paroxysms of apprehension. She's probably every Indian's fantasy of a Scandinavian woman — tall, blond, and slim. The first time I met Anne Gerd, I too had problems linking her to the very ruddy-faced Graham. They're both great travel companions and can rough it with the best of them.

Anne Gerd's job is to call out sonar and GPS readings every kilometer to Khalid. GPS locks on to four or five satellites to give an instant reading of your position accurate to within a few meters. When used with a topographical map (popularly known as a Topo map) you can pinpoint your position in the remotest corner of Ganga. But even the most up-to-date topo maps are only indications of where the river actually flows. There's an additional complication: the government of India does not allow anyone, Indian or foreign, to buy topo maps of any region less than one hundred kilometers from the country's borders, for security reasons, presumably a consequence of the Chinese invasion in 1962. Raja and I once went to the offices of the Archaeological Survey of India in Kolkata to see if they would make an exception. Nothing doing, not even for R.K. Sinha.

The Indian government was slow to wake up to the implications of Google Earth. During a temporary window anyone could download satellite images of the entire Ganga in the Himalayas and along the border with Bangladesh. Then someone in the Indian government caught on. Google Earth was blocked. So for the entire river from Bhagalpur to the Bay of Bengal we are dependent on out-of-date satellite images to pinpoint our position.

Ganga can shift course radically every year. Sinha, Mahesh, Subhash, and Khalid have traveled this stretch of Ganga as recently as two years ago. Khalid has brought along their readings. On more than one occasion the river had shifted so violently that our day's journey is either lengthened or shortened by as much as seven to ten kilometers, which translates into an hour more or less until nightfall or land. For tired boatmen that's a hell of a difference. On more than one occasion we row at night at a furious cadence, hoping our destination will eventually come into sight.

"Come into sight" is miraculously achieved using cell phones, GPS, and the topo maps. We have all three with us on the boat, as do Tivari and Raja. By the end of the yatra Tivari has revealed himself a gizmo nerd. Cell phones are of course second nature to Kolkata taxi drivers. But he masters the GPS far faster than I do. So every morning, he and Raja, and anyone else who wants time off the boat, have a lie-in, pack up the tents and equipment, load them into the Scorpio and head for the next rendezvous. It typically takes them no more than a couple of hours. Then they quietly check out a possible landing and camping spot, as secure and inconspicuous as possible. We prefer ashrams because they have electricity to charge recording equipment, cooking and washing facilities, tend to be on the river bank, have open space to pitch our tents, and are usually very secure.

It takes time to drum into Raja that he is not to head off to the nearest chai stall and start telling all and sundry about this boat that's travelling down Ganga on a yatra. Poor Raja — one of nature's innocents. He's been robbed or otherwise taken to the cleaners for all he possessed several times. Loose lips and all that wartime talk. But eventually, after the Indian members of the boat have reinforced our lectures with their own, he becomes a good boy, even if it means curbing his natural instincts.

We usually cast off somewhere between 8:00 and 8:30 every morning, leaving Raja and Tivari to break camp behind us. We row until five, then hopefully make land. Some days, when we know we have more than the average fifty kilometers to cover, we'll be out on the river by 6:30. Mohan starts us all off with chai, and then prepares breakfast by ten. The men take turns to row and eat. When they're really tired, James or I try our hand. Lunch is served around 2:00, and dinner at 9:00 once tents are safely up, bodies washed, and the landlubbers are ready to turn in.

Mornings I interview R.K. and Graham Chapman on everything connected with Ganga. R.K. bellows and Graham tries to reduce the decibel volume. Occasionally, they even agree. Afternoons people read or snooze, lulled to sleep by the constant rhythm of the oars. Ganga through Bihar is broad and beautiful, and often boring in a very pleasant way. The countryside is flat and generally unchanging. The only humans we see most days are the occasional ferry or an isolated farmer riding his tractor or lifting water from Ganga to irrigate his fields.

Parts of the riverbank seem little changed from when English artists and adventurers such as the Daniell brothers, William Hodges and Lieutenant Forrest first journeyed up Ganga in the 1790s. Their watercolors of Rajmahal, Kahalgaon, Jahngira Island (the Daniells knew it as the Fakeer's island at Sultanganj), or the fort at Munger are virtually unchanged.

Some of their descriptions are a bit fanciful (I would never compare Jahngira Island to the Chateau de Chillon in Switzerland, or Ganga to Lake Geneva) but when you see their paintings in either *Oriental*

Scenery[4] or Jagmohan Mahajan's indispensable books on Ganga, you automatically say: "I've been there. That's such and such. Remember?" They're that accurate.[5]

The rhythm of two men rowing, the sun beating down and a full belly are hypnotic. Reading is out of the question. It is best to surrender to a nap. Let Ganga cast her spell over you. What are we even doing here in the back of beyond? Why do we want to travel on Ganga through Bihar and Jharkhand? Good question. It's a huge logistical challenge. But what is the alternative? There are no hotels and precious little direct access to the river, even for the all-terrain Scorpio. This is also the one area that nobody has really traveled. Or if they did (the Newbys in 1964) they went fast. They were more interested in Varanasi or Kolkata than the badlands of remote Bihar. Besides, they traveled before Bihar acquired its reputation for total lawlessness.

I am only too aware of the physical and political obstacles. In 1975, the river had been blocked by a mile-long barrage at Farakka, just after it turns south towards the sea. When I was planning the yatra this seemed an insurmountable obstacle. We would have to haul the boat out of the water, physically transport it round the barrage and then put it back in the river. Easy enough to do with a kayak. But with a twenty-seven feet long boat and a ton of supplies? No one could suggest a viable alternative. Then one day I phoned R.K. Sinha in Patna with some question or other about the Gangetic dolphin. That's when he told me he'd traveled the entire navigable length of Ganga.

"But how do you get round Farakka?" I wondered.

"Simple, we go through the lock." he told me.

"What lock?" "Just before the barrage they've built a lock to allow cargo vessels to continue upstream between Patna and Kolkata. But only Indians are allowed to use it. You would have to get out and walk across to the other side, then climb back in. Or you could ask permission from the manager at Farakka."

R.K. Sinha had made my day. I found the contact numbers, asked Nidish to phone the manager. Two days later, Nidish emailed me in frustration. We were almost back to square one: Mr Gani, the manager

---

[4] Daniell, Thomas & William: *Oriental Scenery: One Hundred and Fifty Views of the Architecture, Antiquities and Landscape Scenery of Hondoostan,* Longman, Hurst, Rees, Orme and Brown, London 1812-1816.

[5] See Jagmohan Mahajan's *The Ganga Trail: Foreign Accounts and Sketches of the River Scene,* Indica Books, Varanasi, 1984 & 2004, especially Chapter 5, "Up the River," pp 78-95; or Mildred Archer's *Early Views of India - The Picturesque Journeys of Thomas and William Daniell 1786-1794,* Thames & Hudson, London, 1980.

at Farakka, passed the buck. We had to get a letter for him from the Ministry of Fisheries in Delhi. Nidish spent weeks on the phone and in person trying to convince the Permanent Secretary at the Ministry to issue us a letter that would allow us to travel through the lock at Farakka. Eventually, he gave up in despair. "This is what is wrong with my countrymen," he lamented. There was only one option left. The next day, I phoned the permanent secretary and, surprise, surprise, got through immediately. He was affability itself, and two days later, a shocked Nidish had the precious letter in his hand.

~

For days on end the river is empty, except the occasional ferry loaded down with people, bikes, and cattle. In the Vikramshila Dolphin Sanctuary we see one naval vessel. That's it. No commerce, no trade.

One would think that it's the empty quarter of Ganga when it in fact it bisects the most populous part of an already populous state — Bihar. This is India seen from its unattractive backyard. People get on with their lives, backs turned away from Ganga. The river is simply there to be used as a garbage dump or for free irrigation. Ganga is respected in the breach, not in the act.

This emptiness also means any group of men on or near the river is unusual and immediately suspect. "No money. No passports. No jewelery. No makeup," R.K. Sinha has ordered. Martine and I therefore leave jewelery, money, and passports in a safe deposit box in Kolkata. Not all though. We have to buy food, pay our crew, and keep something in reserve for the unexpected (ransom perhaps?) So Martine and Tivari devise places to hide all of the above inside the Scorpio. Even I never know where everything has been hidden. We can never forget the murder of that German couple ten years ago.

"This is Jhauabahiar — very notorious flat plain. A few years ago I was held up here." RK casually turns round in the boat and points to an innocent expanse of land on the northern bank. We are rowing at a steady seven knots on our second afternoon between Bahr and Mokama bridge, one of the few places where a road crosses Ganga. "I and my crew have been held up here at gunpoint three or four times."

"Just as well we didn't know this beforehand," I offer a bit lamely.

"I will show you the various places where they intercepted us and what they did with us. Almost all the instruments were taken." Sinha has reason to feel worried, and it doesn't just happen in Bihar. "First time was in December 1996 between Haridwar and Naoara," precisely the area Thoma Gokhale had advised us to avoid.

Then all Sinha's photographic equipment had been stolen. He appealed directly to the president of India in Delhi, who in turn ordered the police to track down Sinha's equipment (at the time surveys of dolphins came directly under the patronage of the president of India). "Eventually they found them in Chor Bazaar in Delhi." It turned out R.K. was an unwitting pawn in a quarrel between the government and a notorious dacoit they were already holding in jail. The latter had ordered his men to get a bargaining chip for his release. Their eyes fell on Sinha and his boatload of precious equipment. The government brought the dacoit boss to Delhi, threatened to shoot him unless he told them where to find the equipment.

On the other occasions the dacoits suspected the survey crew must really be police in disguise, or else in cahoots with other gangs or castes, so they were prepared to kill them. I knew enough about Bihar's reputation not to take this lightly. In 1998, R.K. and his research team were once ambushed near Mokama. They'd landed on a sandbar to answer the call of nature. "And we saw that one person on a horse was watching us. Then he rode off downstream very fast, as if he was going to warn somebody that a boat is coming." In the middle of the river was an island. There was a hut and some men nearby with a boat. R.K. assumed they were fishermen. The men hailed them in a not-so-friendly manner: "If you don't row over here we will fire on you." They all carried AK47 Kalashnikovs. R.K. and his crew were cooking. The noise of the stove drowned out the precise threats, but R.K. decided it was better to do as they asked. Gopal Sharma, then R.K.'s assistant, got so nervous he fell into the water. Luckily it was only waist deep.

"They aimed their guns straight at us and ordered us to form a queue. We will shoot you one by one. I decided I must lead by example, so I stood at the head of the queue. I ordered my students to follow me. I told the dacoits: 'I am a poor teacher and these are my students. Shoot me first!'"

He was careful not to disclose he was in fact a university professor.

R.K. also happened to be holding a guide to local birds in one hand, a pair of binoculars round his neck, and a GPS in the other hand. The dacoits began to waver. "What are you doing here? Who are you?" R.K. now realized they would probably not shoot. He became more concerned they would kidnap him and his students in exchange for ransom. He tried explaining he was doing research on dolphins. The dacoits still didn't believe him. They assumed he had been using the binoculars to spy on them.

R.K. tried another tack: "I need the binoculars to identify birds. If we get too close to them they get frightened and fly away." Fortunately that guidebook was in his right hand. He showed them Gopal Sharma's logs of bird sightings. The leader of the dacoits was coming round: "There is force in your logic."

Logic was an unusual word to hear from a bandit. R.K. reasoned the man was literate. He started to explain the team was also carrying out water analysis. They had a small portable laboratory on board.

The man's tone softened, became more respectful: "Master Sahib, we have made a mistake. We should not have held you up. We thought you were spying on us, carrying firearms in this boat. It happens all the time. We have a feud with the local fishermen. Do you know who we are?"

It so happened R.K. did. They were Gangota — a milkman caste, at war with the fishermen. Some of the dacoits had already helped themselves to the fish R.K.'s crew had been busy cooking. The boss told them to hand it back. "Now you are free to go."

But some of R.K.'s crew were scared, especially Subhash. They didn't want to go on; they were of the fishermen caste. So when they reached their next stop, they donated the boat to the local temple and abandoned the trip.

Two days later, we are approaching Bhagalpur, best remembered, by most Indians, as the scene where members of a lower caste were blinded by acid in the early 1990s. But for R.K., Bhagalpur was the scene of yet another brush with dacoits.

We tense. This area is known to be especially dangerous because dacoiti here is mixed up with smuggling. The flood plain in this section is wide. R.K. explains there are many mid-channel islands and sandbars where antisocial elements (the usual euphemism for criminals) can hide. The nearest paved road is many kilometers away, so Chinese silk yarn is smuggled down from Nepal and across to Bhagalpur where there are local silk factories. Silk yarn is expensive in the open market, hence the attractions of smuggling across from Nepal. Dacoits know this, so they are on the lookout to intercept the smugglers and their cargo, and hold both to ransom.

That was probably how it all started. Poor farmers annually lose their lands to the monsoon and the consequent shifts in the river. So they said to themselves, if they can make money by kidnapping and robbery, why not us? The flood plain is so inaccessible to the police and their vehicles that the poor farmers realized they could start start robbing anything in sight, including boats carrying out surveys of the dolphins.

R.K. appealed to the chief magistrate in Bhagalpur for some action. The chief magistrate threw up his arms in despair: "I can do nothing. Why don't you carry a large banner so everyone can see you are trying to save the dolphins? That way you may be spared."

It didn't do R.K. and his team much good. A year later, they were again in the area, but this time in a mechanized boat, so they could get away if pursued. Once again, they were engrossed in cooking and eating. They didn't hear the dacoits till they were almost upon them. Same routine as before: take the boat into the bank. Gopal Sharma was again held up, a rifle in his face. What was that big box he was guarding so preciously? Did it contain silk, yarn, or bullets?

Gopal, scared out of his wits, obligingly opened the box. Voilà — just glass vials and chemicals. Profuse apologies and once again they were allowed to leave, but with the warning — "Next time, please come when you're called. We might shoot first."

Dacoits thrive in the area round Bhagalpur for other reasons, not least this long and bitter feud between the Gangota (milkmen) and the fishermen. Local zamindars and mafiosi have played the communities off one against the other for many years. Not just the milkmen: the zamindars and mafiosi also force the fishermen to cough up their own version of water taxes. Much of this breakdown in law and order obviously has its roots in poverty and economic injustice. Sometimes, it takes extreme form: ten years previously, some farmers wanted free electricity. The local powers that be refused. The farmers then seized the deputy superintendent of police, poured kerosene over his jeep and burned him alive.

So why are we then going on this mad trip?

We do have a few near misses. At Munger Fort, where we are camping one night, a local TV news crew gets word of our presence and chases me and Sinha down to the boat for an interview. Sinha gives them a few sentences about a scientific expedition and we are off like bats out of hell. The implications of seeing equipment and white skins on local TV could be irresistible for men with guns wanting to make a quick buck from stealing expensive equipment or ransoming a white woman.

Later that same day, we are snoozing in post-luncheon induced bliss when all four boatmen suddenly seize the oars and start rowing at a strike rate worthy of an Olympic crew. Sinha and the fishermen have spotted nine or ten men with rifles sitting on bikes along the bank of an island. Luckily, they're looking north as we pass them in the southerly channel. R.K. orders Martine to collapse her camera tripod. He's taking no chances. She never uses it again. Our strike rate is positively olympian. Luckily, the dacoits do not turn round.[6]

We also know that further south, where the states of Bihar, Jharkhand, and West Bengal meet, is especially vulnerable—a real no-man's land. There are islands in the river that my friend Kalyan Rudra doesn't want us to go near. Dacoits use them as their base. They have been known to shoot out in their motorized craft, do their business and then scoot back again to safety. They commit their crimes in one state and nip across the river to another, where local police can't pursue them.

The same is true lower down where there is nothing between India and Bangladesh but the river and sand banks. Vast herds of cattle are reportedly raised in northern Bihar then smuggled across the river via West Bengal to Bangladesh where they are sold at market. We are lucky, very lucky to get out of Bihar and Jharkhand scot-free.

~

The empty quarter also used to be full of Gangetic dolphins or susu. The original susu are a common ancestor of both toothed and non-toothed dolphins. They are blind. They have a retina but cannot differentiate between light and dark because they have no crystalline lens. They swim on their sides using sonar, are about six feet long when fully grown, have the same body as ocean-dolphins, but with a very long thin snout armed with teeth. Gangetic dolphins, being mammals, come up out of the water to breathe every few minutes. They sleep only five minutes at a time. Subhash says they eat four to five kilos of fish every day, in the early mornings and late afternoons.

The dolphin bridges the divide between mythological tales of how Ganga came down to earth and contemporary ecological concerns about the need to respect the environment. My colleague Vinod Tare always reminds me mythology is a way of teaching illiterate Indians to respect the natural world; after all, they could end up as an insect in their next life.

---

[6] Normally two boatmen row at a time, while the others eat or rest or take turns at the rudder. So this was equivalent to a full-court press, to use a basketball expression. All hands to the oars!

Of course, all of this is now slowly being lost.[7] Who or what is to blame? Dr. Sinha is inclined to blame modern ideas of science. He believes science is a tool to learn the laws of nature, not a tool for controlling or exploiting nature for man's benefit. He adds, malevolently, "as in the West." India will not be able to have sustainable development if the country apes the West. It's a delicate balance. India has to learn from its past yet move forward, all the while trying not to chase the mirage of westernization.

RK calls the Gangetic dolphins "living fossils," the original ancestor of all cetaceans.[8] For him it's simple — they are the oldest known cetaceans with a secum or appendix situated between the large and small intestines. He tells me scientists have found fossils of Gangetic dolphins in Kashmir that date back fifty-five million years. Sinha claims they are the original common ancestor of both toothed and non-toothed cetaceans because no other whale or dolphin or porpoise in the world has this secum. This suggests they were originally herbivores (chewers of the cud like cows) who gradually evolved into carnivores. But they still retain that vestigial organ.

How come the common ancestor of all these mammals — whales, porpoises, or dolphins — is the freshwater Gangetic dolphin? It's linked to how India and Ganga were originally formed over seventy million years ago. I knew nothing about geomorphology when I began this yatra but the explanation I've gleaned from books and conversations with geomorphologists goes something like this:

---

[7] Vinod Tare argues that traditional Hindu culture "has always been able to translate complex scientific principles into simple myths and stories that anyone can understand, for example the worship of various plants and animals at festivals, of snakes at Nag Panchami during the month of Shravan. Similarly, we worship rats, cats, all sorts of animals. We give them dignity by explaining they are the mounts for all our gods and goddesses — the rat for Ganesha, for example. People can understand this.

"Likewise, we have particular days for different trees — ladies worship the banyan tree on a particular day in a particular month — and this is how we were taught to respect nature because when you worship something you are not going to harm it."

[8] Cetaceans include whales, dolphins, and porpoises. There are about eighty-five species of cetaceans in the world, of which roughly half are dolphins, and just four of these freshwater dolphins, including the Ganges and Indus dolphins. Cetaceans can be divided into two further groups — toothed and toothless — so Sinha reasons that because the Gangetic dolphin has both characteristics it must be the common ancestor of all other cetaceans.

When the Indian plate collided with Eurasia, it trapped pockets of water that formed an internal sea that geologists call the Tethys. As the two plates pushed up against one another this sea was squeezed. Its sediments (soft crustacean shells) were deposited on the northern side of the resulting Trans-Himalayas.[9]

I've read one account that calls the shrinking Tethys to the south of the Trans-Himalayas the Ganges or Himalayan sea, though Graham Chapman, for one, has his doubts.[10] However, it makes good sense to me, the non-scientist. How Ganga was formed is naturally a bit more complicated and may also have significant bearing on why the river has its own very unique magical properties.[11]

But if something like this did indeed happen then the herbivorous Gangetic dolphin would have found itself trapped in an inland sea that later shrank down into at least two major rivers — the Indus and Ganga. Hence the phenomenon of a freshwater dolphin being the oldest living fossil. I'm sticking to my explanation until someone proves I'm barking up the wrong tree. But I don't think I'm totally wrong. One thing this whole yatra increasingly suggests to me is how narrow even the most brilliant brains (not minds) can be.[12]

R.K. Sinha was born seventy-five kilometres south of Patna, and Ganga. His earliest memories of the Gangetic dolphin go way back to when he was eight years old.

"I remember as a child taking a holy dip. I saw all these black creatures jumping out of the water, then diving back under water. Adults screamed: 'Come out, the susu will drag you under the water.' I never forgot."

Later, when Sinha became a student at Patna University in 1970 -71, he found himself drawn to the banks of Ganga, watching the black

---

[9] The Trans-Himalayas form a barrier that blocks rain-bearing clouds from the south, which are turned back and drop their moisture on the southern slopes. Hence the phenomenon of the monsoon.

[10] Subba, Bhiman: *Himalayan Waters: Promise and Potential, Problems and Politics,* Panos South Asia, Kathmandu, Nepal, 2001.

[11] See Chapter 5.

[12] There are exceptions — Graham Chapman and Vinod Tare are striking examples — but many scientists (Indian or Western) have become so specialized they seem unable to see beyond their ever-narrowing fields of study. And forget about scientists who can admit the validity of non-scientific explanations of the world around us and how it has evolved. They are very few.

mammals diving and leaping. He was hooked. When he graduated, he decided to learn more. He got his first teaching post at Munger University.

"On Kastarni Ghat I used to sit for almost a year every evening and see hundreds of dolphins. Every morning and evening. So I decided I must find out more. I began to talk with the fishermen. They explained this is not a fish, sir, this is just like a human being. It suckles its young."[13]

Then Sinha realized the numbers of susu were declining in a big way. But nobody seemed to know or care. Sinha devoured the literature. The only report had been compiled back in 1879 by a John Anderson. That was it. So R.K. decided to take on the dolphin as his particular challenge. He started gathering data. An additional secretary in the Indian government read one of R.K.'s reports, flew to Patna, met him, and asked him what he needed.

A scientist from the Thames Water Authority in the UK was sent to make an assessment of Sinha's work: did he have what it takes? Did he need an institutional infrastructure? Mike Andrews came to Patna, spent two days with Sinha out on Ganga, and never revealed who'd sent him or why. A few months later, the Government of India funded Sinha's proposal — the Dolphin Conservation Project — to study the plight of the dolphin between Buxor and Farakka, and subsequently extended it from Allahabad to Kolkata.

The Gangetic dolphins were declared endangered in 1996 by the I.U.C.N.[14] (The Chinese dolphin may already be extinct. The Gangetic dolphin is most definitely under threat.) Just two thousand officially remain, no thanks to man. Of these maybe five hundred are in the Brahmaputra, the remainder in Ganga. There are two obvious culprits — changes in the dolphin's habitat caused by reduced flows of water and pollution, and illegal poaching because the meat is cheap. Susu meat also makes good bait to catch much more commercially valuable hilsa or ruhi, which fetch more than one hundred rupees a kilo ($1/lb). But their entire habitat is also threatened by poor management of the river, and by pollution.

Poor river management is a fancy way of saying man built first, then thought of the consequences afterwards. After India's independence dams and barrages were built on many of the tributaries flowing down from Nepal — Gandak, Ghaghara, Kosi — to generate electricity. The

---

[13] R.K. told me that in the early 1970s not even the zoology faculty at Patna knew this creature they could see from their laboratory was in fact a mammal.

[14] International Union for the Conservation of Nature. Its headquarters are in Geneva, Switzerland and its web site is *www.iucn.org*.

consequence? The dolphin was suddenly prevented from swimming up these rivers. Populations became cut off. The critical mass for breeding was threatened. Small communities of dolphins did the only thing left — they inbred. The only group large enough to flourish was left in Ganga.

And it wasn't long before they too were under stress. Increased human population means more pollution, but also more and more water taken out for irrigation. At Sultanganj the river used to be fifty feet deep ten years back. When Khalid and Anne Gerd measure it with the sonar this time it is just thirty-five feet deep. The only truly deep water is in mid-channel at Kahalgaon, probably a hundred feet deep. At most places Ganga is now no more than fifteen feet deep. Gangetic dolphins, however, need deep water for their habitat, and hydrological complexity, another way of saying a contoured underwater landscape of hills and valley.

Dolphins are also slowly being made sick by all sorts of toxic compounds, principally organo-chlorines and carcinogens. At the confluence of the Champa nullah and Ganga, just before we reach Bhagalpur, they are being poisoned by effluents from the local dye industry. Sinha has found many forbidden substances here, all with nasty sounding prefixes — poly, biphenyl, buta, dibuta, tributa — derived from local plastic and paint factories. Most of these organo-chlorines from the local factories are lipofilic, which means they are soluble inside oil. So once they get deposited in the dolphin's body they gradually spread throughout the entire body. Many of these compounds are also known carcinogens.

No one knows exactly how they will affect the animals' reproductive systems because dolphins are classified a Category One species, which means they can't be caught, even to be tagged. So in his laboratory Sinha can only examine and dissect dead dolphins.

The dolphin, like the equally endangered tiger, is basically an indicator, or flagship species. This means both stand at the apex of their respective food chains. If you have a good number of tigers that means there's also a good number of their prey available, which in turn means there's good vegetation, in other words the forest system is balanced and in good health. Similarly, if you have a good number of dolphins that means they are getting good food in the form of small fish and other invertebrates, which in turn means the river has sufficient bio-diversity. So if the dolphin is in trouble, fish lower down the food chain are probably under even greater stress.

Sure enough, the last thirty years have seen an almost total collapse in the catch of hilsa in this stretch of the river. Hilsa is a migratory species,[15] so during the monsoon huge quantities of hilsa used to migrate up Ganga as far as Kanpur to breed. During past monsoons fishermen caught a very great quantity of hilsa. R.K. tells me that Subhash used to earn so much he would boast he could afford to take the whole of the following month off from work.

Even the construction of the Farakka barrage in 1975 should not have been a problem. They would build a fish ladder. Unfortunately nobody could agree on the technical specifications, with the result it has never actually worked. So the local fishermen in Bihar have been agitating against anyone and everyone in a people's movement called Ganga Mukhtia Andolan. If local fishermen can't catch hilsa they go after smaller fish, and so the whole system unravels and collapses.

I've brought along a fancy underwater microphone to record the dolphin. This hydrophone can record to a depth of thirty feet. I asked the manufacturer in Boston, why only thirty feet? Seems a bit arbitrary. "The US Navy doesn't allow anyone, I repeat anyone, to record at depths below thirty feet because it could interfere with their nuclear submarines." And the same goes for Ganga. The microphone works well enough but the dolphin is a bit disappointing. Maybe I was expecting too much.

Dolphins are usually sighted (and therefore recordable) wherever two or more rivers meet. The two currents churn up the mud, flush out the fish dolphins feed on. Simple. Even I can't miss them leaping at the confluence of the Barhaya river with Ganga at Mokama. I lower the hydrophone. Something must be wrong. I hear an electronic whistle with occasional fluctuations in tone, punctuated by morse code, the sound of firewood crackling, dog barks, pig squeals. When I play the tapes back my engineers assume there's local static. No, I explain: those are dolphins talking in electronic Hindi or Sanskrit.[16]

One night off Kahalgaon I keep Subhash, Mahesh, and the others out way past their bedtimes while I wait for dolphins. They never come. Great to have done once, but if you've got something better to do, do it. Listening to Ganga from within, on the other hand, is more rewarding. No matter the depth the river sounds opaque, like liquid metallic glass. Water magnifies everything: a diesel engine can be heard even a kilometer away. Similarly, oars and people talking on land or in a boat.

---

[15] Hilsa is capable of anadromesis, which means it can move happily between salt and fresh water and back again. This is why hilsa can swim up Ganga to breed, and then return to the sea.

[16] Khalid and Gopal Sharma assured me these are sounds all dolphins make.

And water rushes. It's never static. It's always in movement. Once I imagined I was Ganga ma listening to my devotees bathing at Varanasi. This is fascinating, especially when bathers let fall drops of water between their fingers or immerse themselves according to the prescribed ritual.

In 1991, the government of India established the Vikramshila Dolphin Sanctuary on the fifty kilometer stretch between Sultanganj and Kahalgaon, precisely because this stretch of Ganga had enough depth, good meanderings and many sandbars, all of which go to make up that necessary complex habitat for dolphins. RK says in past trips they've usually sighted 130 dolphins in the sanctuary. But this time we spot no more than a dozen.[17] Apart from all the other threats, part of the problem is that there is as yet no management plan and no regulation of illegal fishing. The wildlife department of the Ministry of Environment and Forests is officially responsible for the sanctuary.

But that's precisely where the problem lies according to RK, because "unfortunately in Bihar and most of the states in India, even at the country level, wildlife has not been separated from forest so the forest officials are still dealing with the river, and forest officers are more interested in forests than conserving dolphins, or gharials."[18]

That means there's really no one to police poachers. After a series of newspaper articles, the Patna High Court asked the central government to put some teeth into management of the sanctuary. Some large naval patrol boats were purchased — we actually see one cruising in the river — but they don't seem to have stopped poaching.

Sinha estimates ten to twenty dolphins are still killed in the sanctuary every year, either for their meat or for oil that fishermen use as bait. Up until the mid-1990s nobody ate dolphin meat. Then the price of chicken and mutton started to escalate. Susu at twenty-five rupees a kilo suddenly becomes very attractive to the poor.

---

[17] This wide disparity in official versus observed numbers of dolphins reminds me of the scandal uncovered in the Sariska Tiger Reserve in 2004. For years, officials at the reserve had published accounts that demonstrated a healthy tiger population. Then environmentalists started examining the evidence for these numbers and discovered they were circumstantial or totally spurious; no tigers had in fact been actually sighted in Sariska for several years, pug marks cited as evidence for the presence of tigers turned out to be old museum casts. The story is covered in *Sanctuary Asia*, 2004/2005. Old numbers can be accessed at *www.sanctuaryasia.com*.

[18] The gharial is a fish-eating crocodile found only in south Asia. It does not attack humans and is distinguished from a normal crocodile by an extremely long snout.

Sultanganj is home to a famous temple on Jahngira Island, much loved by painters and photographers for over two hundred years (the so-called Fakeer's island). It's also a tirtha from where it gets its name and its legend. It's a nice if familiar story. A yogi called Jannu is meditating on the rock. He'd have certainly been undisturbed until Ganga and King Bhagirath came along, on their way to restore the sixty thousand sons of Sagar to life at Ganga Sagar. The saint was annoyed because they'd entered his territory. Bhagirath, just like his great-grandfather Sagar, always seems to have problems with rishis. Ganga also became very annoyed and turbulent. Bhagirath realized it was up to him to play the peacemaker and prayed to rishi Jannu, who in turn cut his own thigh — allowing Ganga to continue on her way. And this is why Ganga is also called Jahanavi.

So every winter, thousands of devotees come here to collect Ganga jal, which they then carry the 105 kilometers to a Shiva temple at Devghar in the interior of southern Bihar, many not stopping even for the call of nature. The most enthusiastic, and fit, run the whole way, carrying the Ganga jal on their shoulders. I have been told it takes a minimum of sixteen hours. If you opt for the slower method — walking and stopping to rest and relieve yourself — it takes maybe two or three days.

For years I have been seduced by a famous photo by the late Raghubir Singh of devotees gathered with saffron turbans and trishuls waiting for the ferry to carry them across a few hundred meters of Ganga to the island. That photo was taken in the 1970s. Imagine my horror and surprise as we row up from Munger. Where's the island? There's a fairly steep river bank. And there, maybe a hundred meters inland, surrounded by fields, is Jahngira, the fakeer's rock, firmly landlocked. Washed up like an old tramp steamer by the tide. The island is simply no more. Extraordinary!

The Ajgaibinata Temple still stands on top of Jannu's rock. Around its base are carved fascinating depictions of this and other stories from the past. On the rooftop I have a strange conversation with the mahant — Prem Shankar Bharti. He's taken a vow of silence and all his answers are written by him in chalk on a slate which Tej Razdan does his best to decipher and interpret back to me.

The obvious question: why has he taken this vow of silence? In 1992 Ganga changed course and suddenly left the island high and dry. So the mahant took a vow of silence that he would only break if Ganga changes course and swings back to return the landlocked rock to an island. As simple as that. But it takes half an hour of scribbling, rubbing out, more scribbling because Tej is extremely conscientious at getting it exactly right. While all this strange conversation is unfolding I gaze down at what was once river. Now it's a dusty cricket pitch where young boys are playing an enthusiastic game of cricket. As long as they hit to leg, the tennis ball is safe. Woe betide an extravagant square cut or lofted cover drive. That will surely end up in Ganga.

"Why do you think Ganga flowed away from this island?" Five minutes of coughs, scribbles, explanations, elucidations to give birth to the answer I should have guessed from the beginning. Two reasons: Farakka and the pollution of the river by untreated sewage. "We are degrading the river," the mahant writes. The only way to reverse this destruction is by a return to ancient, traditional values.

That certainly can't do any harm. But unfortunately, man's departure from traditional values is probably not the only reason why Ganga has shifted its course so violently. The whole topic has more than its share of red herrings and jargon.

The red herring is the common belief, especially amongst environmentalists, that deforestation is the major culprit that has caused Ganga to shift course so radically so often.

Deforestation and de-vegetation (the clearing of land for agriculture) certainly increase the silt load that gets washed into the river. But they're by no means the major causes of silt loads. Most silt in the mountains in fact comes from the normal scouring of loose rock by monsoon downpours. Deforestation probably accounts for less than twenty percent. In the Himalayas, monsoon rains scour softer rocks, not just loose topsoil. Ironically, some of this debris is probably material that had once been lifted up millions of years earlier when the Himalayas were formed, and deposited on the shores of the Tethys sea to later become the Outer Himalayas or Shivaliks.

In the plains there are the same ratios, but most silt again comes from the river scouring the fields on its banks and carrying that soil down before depositing it no more than a few kilometers further down. Contrary to conventional wisdom, silt from the Himalayas is not carried very far. It certainly isn't the cause of the massive erosion and meandering in the plains. Graham has estimated most coarse silt travels on average only ten kilometers a year.[19]

---

[19] Graham Chapman, who came on the boat with us, edited a volume in 1995 that has specific chapters on this very subject. The more recent Panos Asia volume *Himalayan Waters* confirms what most geographers, but not enough environmentalists, know.

A river such as Ganga carries basically two sorts of loads. The first are fine suspended particles that can be carried all the way down to the Bay of Bengal in a single season. So it's perfectly possible for the finest of silts from the Himalayas to travel the entire length of Ganga in a few months. These fine particles are essentially the clays that will form topsoil. Clay is in fact a very fine mixture of sand and silt full of organic material and other vegetation that get entangled with the fine sand to form humus. This mixture also retains water, so the building blocks for fertile top soil are all present.

But the river also carries soil and rock too heavy to be carried very far. These coarsest sediments, called "bed load," move only a few kilometers. In a river such as Ganga huge boulders are the first to be dropped. They form an underwater obstruction to the river's current. So what does the river do? The heaviest solids pile up against the obstacle, form underwater sand dunes. Over decades, centuries, millennia, what began as a straight channel acquires curves and bends. The gradient obviously helps. A steep gradient and the river will be very fast and carry all before it. But from Patna to Farakka the gradient is just six centimeters every kilometer. It's essentially flat. So it flows very slowly and therefore drops all but those finest sediments, which will make it to the Sundarbans delta.

The next bit I understand instinctively but not intellectually. Graham has tried many times with diagrams and terms such as kinetic energy, and there comes a point beyond which I simply cannot follow any longer. So, rather than commit a crime against science, let's leave it like this. The river has two banks and two different speeds. It goes faster on one bank than on the other. Please don't ask me to explain why. On the slower lane it will drop more of its suspended load. The stuff piles up, juts out, the river swings to avoid it, and this is the part I don't understand instinctively, the current switches from one side to the other. So you get a constant zigzag which can become more and more exaggerated until you have a river that loops like a never-ending string of the letter *S*.

R.K. argues that extreme meandering is a phenomenon of what he calls tropical rivers. Graham says that's nonsense: all rivers meander. Just as all rivers to some extent perform the same basic four functions — weathering, erosion, transportation (carrying silt), and finally deposition (dropping the silt or bed load) on the slower-flowing bank. It's nothing unique to rivers in south Asia. Even rivers in tranquil England meander.

But R.K. is correct that there is a distinction between a tropical and a temperate river, at least two major differences that can drastically accelerate the phenomenon of meandering. The differences are the

Himalayas and the monsoon. The two are inextricably linked. Without the Himalayas there could be no real monsoon. And without the combination of the two there would be no annual washing down of rock and soil into the plains. And in the plains the engorged river erodes the river bank, especially the looser alluvial soils.

And now another counter-intuitive idea: I have always assumed (prior to this yatra) that the topsoil is the first to be eroded. We all probably remember images of fierce winds whipping up dust bowls or sandstorms. But the exact opposite occurs with a river such as Ganga. Right at the beginning of the voyage RK points to the river bank.

"You see how it is stratified. The lower layer is the coarse sediment. That's the first to get deposited. Above you can make out the successive layers, always finer. The topsoil is the finest of all — clay. But when the river erodes the bank it attacks the base which is also the loosest. It saps it, cuts into it, until a section of the bank above just breaks off and topples into the river, to get carried further down, and then in its turn deposited."

So it's the foundation that caves in first, not the fine silt on top, the cause of that extraordinary fertility that makes Bihar still in theory one of the richest agricultural soils in all of India. If only they didn't have all those other manmade problems.

Sometimes there is so much coarse sediment the current simply can't move it on. In the late 1980s a massive earthquake in Assam caused landslides into the Brahmaputra. Next monsoon there was a huge increase in the amount of sediment from the landslide. It choked the river. There are many who believe the late 1980s floods in Bangladesh were to some extent caused not just by rainfall but also by this great mass of coarse material choking the rivers in Bangladesh.

Rivers such as Ganga or the Kosi beyond Kahalgaon Island always find the weakest link in the river bank and carve out new channels. On at least two occasions we find our day's row is shorter or longer than when Sinha and his crew last sailed this reach. The first time, going from Barh to Munger, someone tells us this river has made a short cut at the bottom of a huge loop. We save an hour. The next time we are less lucky. It's deposited so much silt that it's made a far more exaggerated loop that takes us an extra two hours to row around. That's the day we arrive at Sahibganj in Jharkhand by flashlight.

Normally a river such as Ganga oscillates back and forth within a fixed distance in seventy year cycles. Ganga should therefore swing back eventually, but I don't think the mahant at Jahngira will live to see his wish fulfilled. Ganga only swung away in 1991. And this idea of a cycle can be disturbed, perhaps fatally, by human actions (or inactions). Ganga would call it "meddling in her affairs."

A few days later we are rowing through the most desolate reach in all of Ganga. Not a sign of life for hours, not even a dolphin. Suddenly to our right an apparition: green hills and at the foot of the hill, a large white temple complex. No town, no other houses, just this solitary temple gleaming against the green of the hill in the early afternoon sun.

Why here? There is no mention of it in our guidebooks. But R.K. Sinha knows. It's the temple at Buttiswaristan, famous all over Bihar because it marks one of the very few places (Varanasi is another) where the river flows due north. Up close the temple appears in need of a good coat of whitewash, happy occasion or otherwise.

A few kilometers beyond the excitement of Buttiswaristan is one of the strangest monuments you will see anywhere up and down Ganga: five huge brick arches advancing from the flat plain on the north bank a few hundred feet into Ganga. Preliminary pilings for a stillborn bridge, presumably from colonial times, judging by the age of the brick work (today they'd use poured concrete). Coming from nowhere? Heading nowhere? Why here of all places? No major town in sight. And to the north the most notorious of all Bihar flood plains — the Kosi Fan.

The Kosi rises in Nepal as several rivers that come together into a single wild river, and is reputed to carry more silt than any other river (except the Hwang Ho in China) in the world. Kosi has a bad reputation. In Hindu folklore if Ganga is the all-forgiving mother, Kosi is said to be a woman who dreads marriage. Rural women drop a packet of vermillion in the water when she floods in northern Bihar to warn the river to mend her ways, or else she will be married off. The British were so much aware of this legend they called the Kosi "a libertine woman who changes her bed every night."[20]

In two hundred years her outlet into Ganga has shifted two hundred kilometers from west to east. She now comes straight down out of Nepal and takes a right angle parallel to Ganga before surreptitiously easing her way sideways into the latter. If ever there was a case of a river meandering, it's Kosi. The destruction of land, life and property must be an annual nightmare.

But misguided human intervention has only made things worse. Voters want relief. So governments have tried to tame Kosi. They've built long and massive embankments to control her in an orderly fashion when she enters Ganga, just opposite Buttiswaristan. Guess what happens!

---

[20] Quoted in Bhim Subba, op. cit., p. 56.

Kosi pours over and then through a broken embankment, so every few years there is more massive expenditure, to rebuild and strengthen the broken stretches of the embankment (maybe those pharaonic pilings were to bring heavy earth moving equipment across the river?). Or if the Kosi doesn't break its embankment, it backs up and floods the land to either side. The water can't drain away, so the land becomes waterlogged. Nobody wins. Why even try?

The so-called Kosi Fan is one of Graham's specialities. He says that in the 1950s there were just 125 kilometers of embankment in all of Bihar, and twenty-five thousand hectares were affected by floods. Forty years later, there were 3500 kilometers of embankment and seventy thousand hectares of flood-affected land.

So instead of solving the problem the embankments compounded it. Peasants cut the famous embankment to let the water drain out into what remains of the flood plain, and into Ganga. An entire natural system of drainage has been destroyed by arrogance. (One of the many paradoxes of the Indian mind is an all-too human belief that man can indeed control nature.) Worse, many people have contracted kala-azar — a disease of the eyes from living in such waterlogged areas. Is it any surprise that the Kosi fan is also the poorest area in an already-poor state, and therefore gives rise to the greatest incidence of crime in Bihar?

~

At the far end of the Vikramshila Dolphin Sanctuary are three rocky islands that lie opposite the town of Kahalgaon. Only one is inhabited. It houses the temple of Shanti Dham. This would be a great camping spot but Kedarnath (the priest) says no one can stay here. We have to pitch our tents just opposite on the mainland, in the grounds of a school. But Kedarnath does agree to be interviewed later that evening.

The islands are very, very old. Rishis have always lived here and will continue to do penance as long as Ganga flows. The original name of the place is Kaholgram, which of course is the starting point for what even Kedarnath warns is a long story. Here goes. This one is fun.

Kahol rishi is praying here with his wife. She is pregnant. There are just the two of them. Suddenly, Kahol hears a third voice. Where could it be coming from? There's no one else on the island. He leans closer to his wife. It's coming from inside her womb. It's the baby, and he's telling Kahol he's made a mistake in his prayer. Kahol takes this rather badly. "If my child is already telling me off before he's even born what's he going to be like when he's actually flesh and blood and fully grown? He'll humiliate me the whole time."

So he does what all rishis do. He curses the unborn baby so that all his limbs will be twisted and deformed. And then it gets too complicated (somewhere I have the full Hindi text). At some point King Janak, the father of Sita, gets involved. But at the end of the day everyone lives happily ever after, or sort of, except Kahol, who has to pay for his original curse, and so ends up here on this island.

Actually, this is not the real reason Tej and I have rowed over to talk with Kedarnath. He's famous because a few years ago he made all the local fishermen take an oath never to kill the Gangetic dolphin because "The dolphins are living beings who live inside of Ganga. I asked them to take an oath because if the dolphin survives then Ganga will be clean. There will be no pollution. Water will be clean and diseases will be less. So Ganga will survive."

But if poaching continues and the dolphin die, then Ganga will also dry up. He's traveled and seen for himself. At places the river is very, very shallow. The water has been taken out by farmers up and down its length.[21] Kedarnath says Ganga jal at Kahalgaon now putrefies. He blames this on pollution and the decline in dolphin numbers. For him the two are linked. The fishermen, however, have obeyed the oath. Not just here but everywhere in Bihar, because they are afraid of what they see happening to the river.

"There is fear everywhere that if we kill the dolphin we will also die."

Kedarnath confesses something unheard-of for a Hindu priest: he no longer drinks Ganga jal. "I get ill if I drink it. So I drink tube-well water and filtered water from the town. This is very sad."

Next morning, before setting sail, Subhash and I walk down to the shore to confirm what Kedarnath has told us the previous evening. Fishermen are sitting next to their boats mending nets. Yes, they took the oath and they've stuck to it. It hasn't always been easy because mafiosi have stepped in and ruined their livelihoods. These so-called fishermen use dynamite to kill entire shoals of fish. The locals have another immediate problem — a power plant runs by the National Thermal Power Corporation (NTPC).

---

[21] I've seen figures that state that fully 90 percent of all water in India is used for irrigation. The global average is 69 percent. See Bhim Subba, op. cit., p. 93. The author also says fully two thirds of all irrigation water is wasted. That's scary.

And if that isn't bad enough, there's Farakka. Kisan Sahani is adamant. "It's killed our livelihoods. We used to catch hilsa, panas and ruhi. But now the fish don't come up any more." The culprits, they insist, are those poachers and that non-functioning fish ladder.

"We're part of Ganga Mukhtia Andolan, a movement against the threat to our livelihoods. Some of our number have been jailed. My father Dasrath is still in jail. His case comes up next month."

Kisan's getting very worked up: "It's so difficult to make a living. I'd like to destroy Farakka, blow it up. It's a disaster for us, a curse!"

Farakka. It's time to see for ourselves.

*****

Map of Farakka

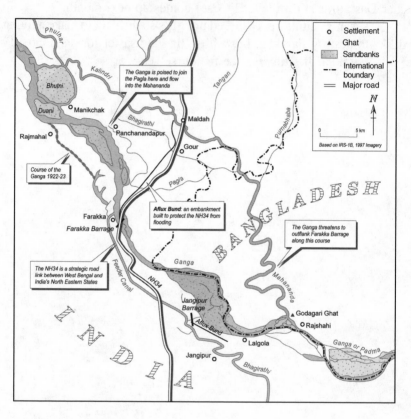

The Ganga is poised to join the Pagla here and flow into the Mahananda

Aflux Bund: an embankment built to protect the NH34 from flooding

The Ganga threatens to outflank Farakka Barrage along this course

The NH34 is a strategic road link between West Bengal and India's North Eastern States

Course of the Ganga 1922-23

Settlement
Ghat
Sandbanks
International boundary
Major road

N

0   5 km

Based on IRS-1B, 1997 Imagery

Phulhar
Kalindri
Bhutni
Duani
Manikchak
Rajmahal
Bhagirathi
Panchanandapur
Maldah
Gour
Tangan
Purnabhaba
BANGLADESH
Pagla
Farakka
Farakka Barrage
Feeder Canal
NH34
Ganga
INDIA
Jangipur Barrage
Aflux Bund
Mahananda
Godagari Ghat
Rajshahi
Lalgola
Jangipur
Bhagirathi
Ganga or Padma

CHAPTER 7

Farakka

Ganga flows due east for a further one hundred kilometers after Kahalgaon until it takes a right turn and begins its final descent to the Bay of Bengal. As it senses the sea, it loses all shape and form. It divides, subdivides, then seeps out through a myriad of smaller rivers and vast mangrove forests called the Sundarbans, which straddle India and Bangladesh. The estuary of Ganga in the Bay of Bengal is so broad[1] atlases call it "the mouths of the Ganga."

Ganga doesn't change much in eastern Bihar until its final descent at Farakka. It's sluggish (the current is no more than four kilometers per hour), broad, and flat as far as the eye can see. In the early afternoons, our eyes become drowsy from a combination of Mohan's cooking, the hypnotic rhythm of two men rowing, and haze from the heat of the sun. The clean line of demarcation between water and sky blurs. Blue, grey, earth brown, so vivid and clean at eight in the morning, merge into a general wash of color which defy precise identification. The river is empty of traffic, even of villages. Just the occasional town, Sahibganj or Rajmahal, until the barrage at Farakka.

If Kanpur (and to a lesser extent Varanasi) represents institutional failures, Farakka is surely an example of man's arrogance in assuming he can manipulate nature without paying the consequences. For many, Farakka is indeed the ultimate swear word. In India itself the government is acutely sensitive whenever the word is mentioned. It therefore asked me to exclude specific mention of it in my documentation when seeking permissions from the various ministries to undertake this yatra on Ganga.

In the early 1970s, the Indian government built a huge barrage at Farakka on the border between West Bengal and Bangladesh to regulate

---

[1] Approximately three hundred kilometers.

and manipulate Ganga's flow. But they failed to anticipate the consequences to the river's hydrology. Ganga during the monsoon floods has always eroded land, especially in Bihar, largely because of the sheer volume of water pouring down into it from Nepal; it's inevitable, natural. But the Farakka barrage has exacerbated the annual ritual of destruction. Ganga has been driven to extremes, her natural rhythms and cycles disrupted. Entire villages have been destroyed because the barrage has altered the hydrological dynamics of the river well beyond Kahalgaon.

Ganga is seen as a munificent goddess from Gaumukh all the way down to Varanasi. Then she swells threefold from the huge inflow from Ghaghara, Gandak, and Kosi and becomes the Nepalese Ganga — a destroyer of land, animal, and human life. Not surprisingly, not many people seem to worship her here as a benign, generous goddess, giver of life.

~

Dr. Kalyan Rudra, a geography professor in Kolkata, has asked us to stop and meet him at a village called Panchanandapur in Maldah District in West Bengal. He wants to show us Farakka and its consequences firsthand.

We set sail from Rajmahal on the southern bank of Ganga.[2] In the middle of the river lie huge islands where dacoits are rumoured to hang out, all the better to catch unsuspecting prey like us, then scoot back to the safety of their islands. On the far bank lies West Bengal, the same country but in many ways a different world.

Rajmahal is at the northeastern-most tip of the vast Deccan Plateau. It's granite and basalt, so the river can't cut into it. Not coincidentally, between Sahibganj and Rajmahal the southern bank is full of quarries and stone crushers, building materials destined for West Bengal. The river therefore has to run along in a straight line eastwards until it finds an opening and plunges south towards the Bay of Bengal.

As we row across Ganga from Rajmahal to West Bengal, both Graham and I simultaneously have the same thought: we're heading into delta country. The vegetation is no longer the same. On the West Bengal side are thick forests of palm trees, muezzins sound the call to prayer, tractors race up and down, small fishing boats dart in and out of the shore,

---

[2] The town used to be in Bihar until the creation of the new state of Jharkhand, carved out of eastern Bihar. Jharkhand is largely populated by tribals and is a beautiful state, full of rolling hills and lakes. It is rich in mineral deposits, but dirt poor.

everywhere there are large electricity pylons. The countryside literally hums with activity. Graham and I instinctively feel at home here. This is a place we're familiar with from past journeys.

Tivari and Martine have crossed ahead by ferry in the Scorpio to find our contact in Panchanandapur, a young activist called Torikul Islam. Torikul heads an organization — Ganga Bhangan Protirodh Action Nagarik Committee — that helps rehabilitate villagers in Maldah District displaced by the annual floods.

Finally, Panchanandapur comes into view. At the top of the very steep river bank a huge crowd awaits us on a wide stone embankment. We clamber up. On the other side lies another river, effectively separated from Ganga by this embankment of earth and huge boulders. After the traditional garlands and speeches, the village welcoming committee asks us the usual questions, why we are travelling down Ganga, etc. Kalyan Rudra takes us inside a thatched bamboo hut while the others go to set up the tents in the garden of Jalaluddin Ahmed, the village patriarch.

Kalyan Rudra is not the sort of man who'd stand out in a crowd. He's the complete opposite of RK Sinha; small in size, voice, and ego. RK Sinha didn't even realize he was a fellow professor when he first met him and treats him as someone of no particular consequence. However, Kalyan Rudra has a highly original mind and is accepted by these villagers, even though everything about him says city man. For some reason he's here in a relatively nondescript college in northern Kolkata, but the quality of the man and his work are extraordinary.[3]

Kalyan rolls out a map, explaining Ganga's drastic shifts these past thirty years. The river has traditionally oscillated back and forth within clearly-defined boundaries. But now there's evidence Farakka has accentuated this shift. The crowd press against every crack of the bamboo walls, trying to peer in and get a glimpse. Kalyan then explains the role of Torikul's organization. More than eight hundred thousand people have lost their homes in Maldah District to Ganga in the past ten years. Some have moved across to new sandbanks or chars on the south side of Ganga, back towards Jharkhand.[4]

His colleague Monatosh Shah takes me on a short tour of the village to explain Ganga's effects on its land. Monatosh was born here

---

[3] Graham Chapman immediately realized Kalyan's worth back in 2000 and has co-authored research articles and at least one book with him.

[4] There are three moribund distributaries of Ganga nearby — Chotti Bagirathi and Kalandri and Pagla — the river separated from Ganga at Panchanandapur by the stone embankment. Their significance is still unclear to me.

but now lives in Kolkata and has accompanied Kalyan on the overnight train to Maldah[5] expressly to meet us. Monatosh says this embankment is brand new. It was rebuilt last year after Ganga destroyed the old one. I'm shown some slides taken the previous year by Mehedi Hasan,[6] a geography teacher in Maldah City, twenty kilometers away. I don't recognize any of the places — the embankment the slide shows is now a hundred meters out into the river.

Mehedi puts up another slide: a two-story brick building surrounded by forest. He says the building was called Ganga Bhavan. It housed the offices of the West Bengal Irrigation Department. It also used to be right here on the river bank in Panchanandapur.

"I didn't see it today," I tell Mehedi.

"You won't for a few more years," he tells me. "Maybe in a few years it'll reappear." The school and police station have also disappeared in the last year. I am filled with shock and disbelief. "You mean this river moves two hundred meters a year?"

"Sometimes more, sometimes less. Everything has become distorted because of Farakka. Thirty years ago Panchanandapur was eight kilometers inland. By next year it may have entirely vanished into the river. My father's house will be no more."

Before we turn in — it's been a long hot row — Ruhul Islam, a local musician, sings us some vaviyas, traditional Bengali folk songs. The bittersweet lyrics are all about how Ganga takes away people's land and houses. Some vaviyas deal specifically with the devastation in Panchanandapur. Floods, erosion, and loss are central to these people's lives. In one song, Ruhul Islam lists everything he's personally lost to the floods, beginning with his boat. Out of eight hundred thousand people who have lost their land in Maldah District to erosion and floods, two hundred thousand of them have emigrated from the district entirely, presumably permanently to points south.

West Bengal is an area where Islam and Vaishnavite Hinduism coexist fairly peacefully. A few days later this impression of communal harmony is graphically reinforced in unusual surroundings. Raja has arranged for me to take a detour and go with him to record two traditional singers — Ghulam Mohammad Mustafa and Jalaluddin Sheikh — in

---

[5] This whole area had once been a prosperous kingdom. Gour was the fifteenth century London of Bengal. Now it's deserted and in ruin: the river moved away overnight, leaving Gour high and dry, much like Jahngira island at Sultanganj in Bihar. But if the river moved away it can also return.

[6] Mehedi is the son of Jalaluddin Ahmed, our host in Panchanandapur.

traditional bhatiali (boatmen songs) and baul songs by the great Muslim poet Nazrul Islam. The setting is unusual — a boat on a beel[7] near Baharampur south of Farakka — but it's quiet, no one can interrupt us. It's astonishing and gratifying that Islam and Vaishnaivite Hinduism can still be brought together through Sufi mystical songs, perfect examples of the fusion of religions and cultures. The songs again are a never-ending litany of loss and destruction caused by Ganga.

After dinner in Panchanandapur, I sit with Jalaluddin Ahmed, the bedridden patriarch of the house whose garden has become our temporary camping ground.

"I remember how forty years ago this village was a prosperous port," he tells me. "We traded a lot with Rajmahal. There used to be an indigo factory. The British built it. We had extensive mango and bamboo groves. Then the erosion began in 1969. Within a few years it was all gone. I lost everything. Nothing I could do about it. Everything just disappeared in front of my eyes." The indigo factory from British times has long since been washed away. Jalaluddin personally has already lost seventeen acres of land.

The next morning at the chai stall I sit and talk to as many villagers as have stories to tell, most Muslims. Jalaluddin Ahmed appears fortunate: he still lives in the same house he grew up in.

Chittaranjan Sarkar says, "I've lost my house six times. Some of us are now actually seeing old fields reappear on the other side where the river has shifted. I saw my own farmland reappear over there," he points to the chars on the far bank of Ganga. "But West Bengal refuses to grant me — or anyone else here — legal title. Why?" He promptly answers his own question: "I'll tell you why. It's because the CPM [the Communist party that has ruled West Bengal since the 1970s] doesn't want to give our sitting MP a few hundred thousand new voters. He represents Congress and he's a Muslim. So they prefer to keep us stateless."[8]

---

[7] A small inland lake. This particular beel is called Bandar Dhaha beel.

[8] Panchanandapur and all its land were always on the left (northern) bank of Ganga, part of West Bengal. For the last thirty years Ganga has eroded this northern bank and shifted its course towards West Bengal, away from Jharkhand. So farmland originally in West Bengal has collapsed and been swallowed up by the river. Thirty, twenty, even as little as ten years later, the river having shifted yet further north into West Bengal, the farmland and even buildings that had disappeared into Ganga, start re-emerging, only this time on the southern side of the river. The villagers of Panchanandapur set out across Ganga to reclaim their farmland and start farming it again. But is the new "old" land in West Bengal in Jharkhand or in a legal no-man's land? The owners want to vote in West Bengal state elections. The government in Kolkata refuses.

Khider Bux was born in old Panchanandapur village in 1973. Old Panchanandapur was back then eight kilometers further west, towards Jharkhand. It's only now slowly re-emerging from Ganga. He's especially bitter that the West Bengal government has never offered him compensation while it spends crores of rupees dumping heavy rocks along the embankment. But heavy rocks don't protect them. The weight of the boulders is more than the coarse sediment at the base of the river bank can hold. It merely accelerates erosion.[9]

Ganga once flowed into three small rivers on its northern bank — the Pagla, Chotti Bhagirathi, and Kalandri — which used to be old distributaries of Ganga in past centuries. Now they are each cut off from Ganga by huge stone and earth embankments, like streets in West Berlin that would suddenly be brought to an abrupt dead-end by the Berlin Wall, healthy limbs amputated for no apparent reason.[10] What were the authorities afraid of? PK Parua, the former Chief Engineer at Farakka, later told me in Kolkata that it was the villagers who had insisted the West Bengal apply these vast tourniquets. If they did they soon realized the error of their ways. The natural flood plain of Ganga had been disrupted. So Ganga did what all rivers do: it tried to break through the embankments and follow its old course.[11] The results have invariably proved worse than the original condition.

Saidul Islam still lives here, but he has a similar identity crisis. Every morning, he takes the ferry to the newly-emerged char land on the other side of Ganga. He now farms fifty acres there that he claims were his before they were swallowed up by the river.

Monatosh Shah chips in. "The real tragedy is that people here in Panchanandapur are paying the price of keeping Kolkata port open. But why should this be at our expense?" Monatosh was born here in 1949

---

[9] Amit Nath, a researcher at the River Research Institute, West Bengal, says placing heavy boulders actually accelerates erosion, taking the *toe* out of the embankment. At best it's a very short-term fix.

[10] The river at Panchanandapur (separated from Ganga by the stone embankment) is the Pagla.

[11] In 1994, the Mississippi and Missouri rivers in the central US plains also flooded. The US Army Corps of Engineers had built concrete embankments along much of the rivers to protect farmland and wealthy homes. The inevitable happened because the natural flood plain had been disrupted. The Mississippi swept over the embankments and destroyed homes and farms. Many people suddenly woke up to the fact you can't alter flood plains without people paying the consequences.

and lost his family house and mango orchards to Ganga only three months ago. He's not just angry with the West Bengal government in Kolkata; he's mad at New Delhi as well.

"They never thought of the consequences of building Farakka. All they could think about was hurting Pakistan. The barrage doesn't work anyway. Half its gates are closed because of silting."

Monatosh tells me, "The West Bengal government has spent two hundred seventy-five crores this year shoring up this thirty-kilometer stretch of the river. For what? Money thrown into the river. They should have given it to the villagers. You cannot control the river. You have to learn to live with the river."

He lugubriously adds, "Otherwise Panchanandapur may be gone if you come back next year."

One day Kalyan takes me across the river to a village called Kashmiuldalla or Little Calcutta, ten kilometers as the crow flies; three hours by boat in and out of the braided channels that are Ganga here as it regularly throws up fresh chars. Five thousand former residents of Panchanandapur have established themselves here on the new char lands that have reappeared on the southern side of the river. Most of the chars are just fields, their banks hidden by tall Ganga grass, like new fuzz on an adolescent's chin. Then, round a bend, something more substantial comes into view — large farmhouses, radio antennas, sheep and cows grazing at the water's edge. We have arrived at Kashmiuldalla.

Jaffar Ahmed, the village elder, greets us with a predictable complaint: "We want to be West Bengalis but West Bengal won't acknowledge us. We have Jharkhand voter registration cards and they have given us three health centers and ration cards. But we have to rely on solar power for our electricity. Neither state wants to give us the connection." Jharkhand is simply too far away; the nearest stores are back in Panchanandapur and Maldah in West Bengal. I still don't really understand why West Bengal doesn't want to have anything to do with them. The villagers huddle together to confer.

Finally Jaffar Ahmed decides to tell me what the villagers believe is the real reason. It's not just that they're Muslim and a potential vote bank for the Congress MP Ghani Khan Choudhary. It's a tale of corruption. Relief moneys are given out from Kolkata. The ruling CPI(M)[12] reasons if they refuse to acknowledge these people even exist

---

[12] Communist Party of India (Marxist), one of several brands of Communists in India, and the ruling party in West Bengal.

they can skim off money with relative impunity. Obviously, I can't prove this. But it's what the villagers in Kashmiuldalla believe. Who knows where the truth lies?

Although Mohammed Faqir Ali lost his farmlands back in 1990, he claims there are definite advantages to living here. The land is very fertile. Since West Bengal has done virtually[13] nothing for them — no roads, no electricity, no medical facility, no school, no ration or voting cards — they've built their own mobile tower and solar panels to power their new homes. "And, of course, we don't pay any taxes."

And yet, every year, the West Bengal government spends crores of rupees trying to prevent nature taking its course.[14] It's the Indian version of the Anglo-Saxon story where King Canute tries to prove his dominion over the ocean, seating himself on his throne on the beach and ordering the tide to stop and retreat. The tide ignores him and his courtiers rescue him from this gross act of insubordination.

Sourav Sarangi, a young Bengali film-maker friend of Kalyan Rudra, made a film called *Bhangon* (erosion) in Panchanandapur in 2005. It shows, graphically, the folly of attempts to make the river behave according to a bureaucratic dictate. In it we see (and hear) huge sections of the river bank — often complete with palm trees — cracking, splitting, and then falling into Ganga like huge chunks from an iceberg in the Antarctic. The villagers can only watch helplessly. It's sobering to see Ganga eroding land you've just walked on.

The unspoken fear this day in December 2004 is that Ganga will burst through its embankments and link back up with Pagla, Chotti Bhagirathi, and Kalandri. The three rivers are just waiting to be brought back to life. These new distributaries[15] of Ganga would then flow naturally into a bigger river — the Mahananda — which goes far north of Farakka near Gour before rejoining Ganga just inside Bangladesh. Farakka would effectively be bypassed.

---

[13] I've heard Kolkata politicians in Maldah promise on tape several thousand rupees compensation per person. The sums are derisory. Kalyan Rudra is surely correct that if moneys spent on trying to prevent Ganga flooding its northern bank had been spent on compensation and rehabilitation, the lives of thousands might have been made a bit easier.

[14] It's hard to find exact figures. I've heard a grand total of nearly six hundred crore of rupees over ten years ($130 million) from Kalyan Rudra, then twenty-three crore ($500,000) for a three kilometre stretch of river bank in Panchanandapur alone in 2004. Whatever the figures, it appears to be a substantial sum of money.

[15] A distributary flows out of a main river, often taking some water down to the sea.

Many other old distributaries of Ganga flow down to the sea beyond Farakka, where Ganga becomes Padma, and the river is the effective border between India and Bangladesh. One of these distributaries called Bhagirathi is now separated from Ganga/Padma by less than eight hundred meters at Fazilpur. The river here has wreaked its anger on the southern bank, meandering at will. The West Bengal government have once again spent crores of rupees constructing vast embankments to prevent Ganga/Padma breaking through the remaining land and flowing back down into the Bhagirathi. In 2001 I stood on that embankment: I could see both rivers separated by this narrow strip of rock and earth. I was told then by an engineer at Farakka that the embankment would halt the erosion. But the same man also said the same thing about the embankment at Panchanandapur.[16] In both cases he was adamant that it was impossible anyway for Ganga to flow into any of these old river beds because the latter are far too small to take the sheer volume of water from Ganga.[17]

After a few days of excellent food and company in the village we set out to row the remaining twenty kilometers to Farakka. The river has now become awfully broad and flat. The river divides and subdivides in a maze of broad, flat sandbanks. For the first and only time we actually lose our way. Which is the main channel? There are no discernible landmarks and the water itself has changed. It's become suddenly clear and still, and here's a hazy stillness, the feeling of rowing across a vast pond. But to where and what? Subhash standing at the helm peers into the haze. He utters just three syllables: "Farakka."

~

Seen from upstream the barrage appears a low faint line in the morning haze, all hints, suggestions and smudges of color, reminiscent of a Turner masterpiece.[18] Farakka the township is rather lugubrious.

---

[16] P.K. Parua was Chief Engineer at Farakka until 2002, when he retired.

[17] Parua says the bed of Pagla is far too small to accommodate Ganga because the monsoon flow of Ganga is 25,000 cusecs and the capacity of Pagla only 6,000 cusecs. I thought then there was something curiously static about this argument: events were sadly to prove me prescient.

[18] Of course the renowned Impressionist painter William Mallard Turner never came to India, though he did paint remarkable seascapes off Belgium and Holland, and masterpieces of the canals of Venice and the Thames in London. Many, many times I have seen scenes in the Himalaya or in the plains which make me immediately think of what Turner would have painted if he could have seen what I have seen. The Daniells and their colleagues are very good, but they are a bit literal — Turner is the painter who would have done justice to the spirit of Ganga.

On the southern bank of Ganga, its sole raison d'être nowadays is to regulate the flow of water through the barrage. Previously, it had housed all the construction workers and engineers.

It's a company town built for the sole purpose of creating the barrage. All neatly laid out, anonymous cream concrete buildings, living quarters subdivided by letter and number, barbed wire fences, half a day from Kolkata by train or road. What do wives do to while away the seasons, I wonder, while their husbands are shuffling papers in these musty offices? There's surely a novel to be written here, of petit bourgeois ambition, intrigue, boredom, and illicit sex.

The sight of Farakka prompts Graham Chapman to make one last attempt to set me straight. He's still horrified that I freely confuse dam and barrage. "Look, Julian, a dam stores water. A barrage is a weir with gates all along for letting water through. This is the basic difference."

Graham explains that dams and barrages look the same. But I beg to disagree. In my imagination, a dam is massive, concrete, solid, a vast still reservoir stretching far behind the dam at the expense of people, villages, animals, and perfectly good farmland. The massive Tehri dam in Garhwal is a good example. Lives wrecked, productive farmland flooded to make a lake thirty-five kilometers long — all to light the lifestyles of the burgeoning middle-class in Lucknow and Delhi.

But a barrage looks very different. It's low-slung, functional, flat. It screams engineering: a huge Meccano set, all metal and rivets and right angles. I could never fall in love with a barrage. The river behind the barrage looks like a normal flowing river, maybe tending to middle-aged spread as silt piles up, in engineering jargon pondage. A barrage has gates that can lift and descend to let the river through. Graham's correct in his geographer's precision.

I suddenly have a flashback to the village on the Thames where my parents lived. There was a small weir there too. Every year there would be a tragedy: some kids would get swept over in their boats and drown in the roiling white water below.

A barrage is usually designed to handle a river in flood. In the case of a monsoon river such as Ganga, where the flow can be a hundred times greater than in the lean season, it puts an immense strain on the barrage. This means an awful lot of gates and design. When the river is in full flood the whole structure presumably shudders and vibrates. It must feel exhilarating, or frightening. In Varanasi I had just bought Joseph Conrad's *The Typhoon*. (I actually read it the previous night in Panchanandapur.) I can easily imagine standing on that barrage, feeling the metal structure sway to breaking point — much like that obstinate skipper of the merchant hulk who misreads the clouds and his instruments, yet somehow makes it through the fury of the South China sea.

Graham got stranded just south of Farakka in the famous September 2000 Millennium flood. Engineers then worried that the sheer volume of water was such that the barrage could be damaged, so they opened the gates to the feeder canal and diverted part of Ganga's furies down south into Murshidabad District. But the many embankments constructed north to south to carry railways and roads trapped the flood water so it couldn't flow away sideways. It just kept on rising and devastated anything caught in its path. Farakka therefore didn't cause the floods, but it didn't help either.

Farakka Barrage is a defence installation, which means there are armed guards every twenty meters, and absolutely no photography allowed. Of course we all try to sneak a few in. But Farakka is so broad it's hard to capture its essence in even a few surreptitiously-snatched photos. Maybe only Turner could have done it justice. It's more than two and a half kilometers long and has one hundred and eight gates. Yesterday Monatosh Shah told me half of them are closed. In daylight it appears even more. It's built deliberately across the narrowest point of the river after it's made its big turn round the tip of the Rajmahal hills: important fact number one.

Farakka is also three hundred and fifty kilometers, as the crow flies, due north of Kolkata: important fact number two. As far back as 1852, the East India Company was concerned about the long-term viability of the port of Kolkata. It was silting up, I presume, for normal hydrological reasons. Sir Arthur Cotton, a leading company engineer, suggested diverting Ganga down into the Hugli,[19] to flush the silt out to sea. The idea was studied, then rejected. The Bengal Chamber of Commerce took it up in the 1930s, and again rejected it. I would love to know the reasons. Cost? Feasibility? Hydrological consequences? Whatever the reasons the Indian government decided to go ahead in the 1960s. Was it to punish Pakistan? They'd done this before: in 1948 as tit-for-tat for Kashmir, India shut off the water flowing from the Firozpor head works into

---

[19] Hugli is another name for Bhagirathi. Bhagirathi is an old distributary of Ganga that dried up a few hundred years ago. Since 1975 it has been re-activated by the feeder canal from Farakka, and it changes its name to Hugli at Krishnanagar because this marks the northernmost limit of tidal waters up the river and through Kolkata. So fresh water Bhagirathi, salt water Hugli.

Pakistan's Dipalpur Canal.[20] What we now call Bangladesh was then East Pakistan. So it sounds plausible.

Kolkata was of prime strategic and economic importance to India. The Hugli was obviously silting up and boats were getting larger and their drafts deeper. So they dusted off the plans and took the decision to build a barrage across the Ganges to divert low season flow through a feeder canal down the Bhagirathi-Hugli and "flush" the river at Kolkata.

But why a barrage at Farakka? Why not at say, Rajmahal?

P.K. Parua, the former Chief Engineer at Farakka, says they never would have chosen Rajmahal. The river at Rajmahal is five to six kilometers wide, and the feeder canal would have had to be a hundred and twenty kilometers long just to reach Bhagirathi. (The feeder canal from Farakka in comparison is thirty-nine kilometers long.)

Graham reminds me of another reason they probably opted for Farakka over Rajmahal. Before 1947, the old rail and road links from Bengal to Assam were via the Hardinge Bridge, now thirty kilometers inside Bangladesh (but at that time the arch enemy — East Pakistan). It would have cost a lot to divert both the railway line and National Highway 34 from Murshidabad District over to Birbhaum and up to Rajmahal; it did not make geographic, strategic, or economic sense. And on the other side? It was far more convenient to divert the pre-1947 rail and road links a few kilometers west and resume their path up into Assam. Farakka was the obvious place.

What is interesting are the basic questions they did not address.

Was the amount of water coming down into the Hugli already in decline? Could there be other reasons why Kolkata was silting up? Would an increase in water from Ganga into Hugli really "flush" the port of Kolkata and keep the Hugli open? Were there cheaper options, such as moving the port downstream? And what about the impact on Bangladesh?

The Indian government studied the project for a full twenty years, from 1951 to 1971. Pakistan protested but could do nothing. Then New Delhi finally made up its mind. They would build Asia's longest barrage on alluvial soil. They would divert Ganga down a feeder canal just before the barrage, increase the flow of water into Bhagirathi-Hugli, flush the silt out of Kolkata and keep the port open to shipping. Put like this it sounds eminently reasonable.

---

[20] Chapman, Graham: *The Geopolitics of South Asia*, pp. 178, Ashgate Publishers (UK), 2000.

They went ahead, built, and commissioned the barrage (1971–75) in the absence of any international agreement. Unfortunately, western Bangladesh is vitally dependent on Ganga in the winter months. So in the flush of Bangladeshi independence from Pakistan, a short-term agreement between India and Bangladesh was signed in 1977. But it was very short-term, and it wasn't until 1996 that a permanent treaty was signed, that has worked more or less well.[21]

The Ganges Water Treaty is far from perfect but it makes sense. The two countries get to share Ganga according to a sliding scale that favors one or the other country according to the time of year.[22] In 1977, the winter flow hit an all-time low. There wasn't too much water to share. Eventually, each country got half of the reduced flow, but neither was happy.

Bangladesh always wants to increase its share of the flow. So it periodically suggests regional cooperation with India and Nepal. However, trilateral talks with India and Nepal have always failed because India has resisted. The others want India to put up much of the finance. India balks. Instead, India proposes boosting the flow of Ganga at Farakka by diverting part of the Brahmaputra from Assam. After all, it's part of India. But this would mean building a canal half a mile wide and more than one hundred kilometres long across Bangladeshi territory with both significant control points on Indian soil and in Indian hands. It would therefore be unacceptable to Bangladesh.[23] Graham maintains it's a non-starter anyway because the canal would have to be brought over the Teesta river, which is about as stable as the Kosi.

---

[21] Cf: Graham Chapman's "The Nature and Human Environment of the Ganges-Brahmaputra and Meghna Basin (GBM)," unpublished paper given in March, 2005 at Lancaster University.

[22] If Ganga's flow at Farakka is seventy thousand cusecs or less both countries receive fifty percent. When the flow is between seventy and seventy-five thousand cusecs, Bangladesh receives thirty-five thousand cusecs and India receives the rest. When the flow is more than seventy, five thousand cusecs — presumably in the monsoon and post-monsoon periods — India receives forty thousand cusecs and Bangladesh receives the rest.

[23] The best references for this entire sorry episode, complete with charts, maps, and texts of the treaties are Chapter 7 of Bhiman Subba's *Himalayan Waters: Promise and Potential, Problems and Politics*, Panos South Asia, Kathmandu, Nepal, 2001, or Ben Crow's *Sharing the Ganges. The Politics and Technology of River Development*, Sage Publications: New Delhi, Thousand Oaks, London, 1995.

Bangladesh blames Farakka for everything. The main complaint is that the lack of adequate flow has caused salt water to creep up a hundred kilometers into the Sundarbans from the Bay of Bengal. This increase in salinity is then blamed for the alleged death of the mangrove forests. It sounds plausible until you remember that mangroves thrive on brackish water. What if the problems of the Sundarbans have other manmade causes such as the pressure on land and water from substantial population increase? Misguided encouragement of water intensive crops? Or expansion of irrigation via shallow tube wells that lowers the water table?[24]

~

All this time I have kept the precious original of the letter from the Permanent Secretary in Delhi in a plastic wallet. It's our permission to travel through the lock and down into the feeder canal, bypassing the barrage. Clutching this precious letter, I ask for the house of the assistant engineer Samir Kumar Pal. He looks at it carefully, pronounces it in order and says: "Be there with your boat at the entry to the lock gates at eight thirty sharp tomorrow morning."

So next morning, we row the half mile back up Ganga and find the entry to the lock. Mr. Pal beams down at us from the side of the lock, which is massive. It was intended to allow large cargo boats to pass through, keeping intact trade between Kolkata and its hinterland as far away as Patna. In practice very little of this has worked out. We did pass one steamer on its way up to Rajmahal, but the shallowness of Ganga (it can't be more than ten feet deep at Farakka) means it's very difficult to get big boats up into the river north of Farakka. R.K. Sinha proudly touts a recent Inland Waterways plan to resuscitate Ganga for commerce. But unless the lake behind the barrage[25] is deepened no large boat is going to use the lock.

Kalyan Rudra has calculated that to dredge this shallow lake to allow ships to use the river would require a convoy of trucks stretching thirty-four times around the equator and a fourteen-lane highway down to the Bay of Bengal, so that the trucks could dump it all into the sea. In return for this helpful calculation Kalyan Rudra was removed from the government's Advisory Board of Water Policy.

---

[24] Lowering the water table exposes a harmless form of arsenic to oxygen. Oxidisation then transforms the arsenic into a highly toxic form.

[25] This is what Ganga has become above the barrage. Its critics also call it a pond.

It beggars belief that the planners never thought about sedimentation. But the construction of Farakka has always seemed to ignore fundamental hydrological realities. If you effectively build a wall across a monsoon river, this will obviously upset the hydrological dynamics of the river upstream. For a start, where would all Ganga's sediment go? It can't all flow through the barrage — there's too much of it — so it builds up behind in an erratic pattern.

Kalyan Rudra says that since Farakka was commissioned in 1975, the river has dumped so much sand behind the barrage that the riverbed has risen over seven meters or twenty-three feet. This shallow lake above Farakka is therefore now no longer muddy, but clear and transparent. Ironically, Westerners would see this as a sign of good health. But the opposite is the case. Turbidity in India means a healthy river; clear water means no flow. All because most of the silt has been deposited in front of the barrage at Farakka.

Ganga historically oscillated within a thirty kilometer belt every seventy years. Kalyan argues the silt build-up behind Farakka has "made the river unstable." This thought never seems to have occurred to the engineers who designed Farakka. When I last met P.K. Parua in January 2005 and asked him whether Farakka has caused any deposits of silt he looked at me in astonishment: "How can it? The gates are all open during the monsoon. Therefore the sand will be deposited downstream, south of Farakka." Then he loses me in a bizarre twist of logic. "If there is any silt behind the barrage it must be caused by deforestation upstream. Farakka is totally innocent. Nothing to do with the barrage."

Some silt would indeed come from local deforestation, but most comes from the annual scouring of the bed and banks of the river by Ganga herself. Anyway, that's beside the point. Farakka is the culprit and cause of massive sedimentation that in turn alters the hydraulic dynamics of the river above Farakka.

P.K. Parua, bless him, seems to have no clue how a river like Ganga actually erodes its banks. There also seems to be total disconnect between his belief that Farakka can have no negative impact on the river's hydraulics and a paper he wrote in 2002 arguing precisely the opposite.[26]

---

[26] Parua, P.K.: *Fluvial Geomorphology of The River Ganga around Farakka*, Journal of Institution of Engineers, Vol- 82, February, 2002, pp 193-196.

When I first met him in 2001, Parua was still a civil servant. So his refusal to acknowledge massive sedimentation upstream of Farakka was understandable. But in early 2005 he'd been retired for two years, and in much demand at water conferences. He simply does not believe me when I say that half the gates are silted up, that the level of the Ganga above Farakka has decreased to less than ten feet, that the river bed has risen a full twenty-three feet, or that the presence of new chars in the Padma downstream is not evidence of Farakka passing through all Ganga's silt at all, but of erosion south of the barrage.

Parua feels it's unfair of Kalyan Rudra to characterize Farakka as a white elephant. He defends Farakka against the other charges made against it in India. He maintains that the drying up of the Jalangi, Churni, and Garai rivers (all distributaries that take Ganga down to the Bay of Bengal) occurred before Farakka. Nor does he share Kalyan's fear that Ganga will decide to flow through Pagla into the Mahananda and circumvent Farakka to the north. This seems to be based solely on his belief that Pagla is way too small to handle Ganga.

Sadly, events have since proved him wrong.[27] He agrees grudgingly that Farakka has been a disaster for the fishing community, but says the Bhagirathi has benefited from regular increased flow from the feeder canal. When he was a child, he used to cross the Bhagirathi on foot. Now it's a broad expansive river. Listening to Parua I feel I am in fantasy land. Although some of his points are true, he appears to ignore any proof of the colossal damage the barrage has created.[28]

~

But enough digression. In front of the gates is fifty meters of thick carpet of water hyacinth: the gates can't even open. Most of us have to land and walk up to the lock, while Mr. Pal and his lock workers

---

[27] See pp 202-204 in this chapter.

[28] The other surprise to me is his insistence that the 1996 Treaty with Bangladesh has been a disaster for both countries. He actually prefers the 1977 treaty because it allowed for a potential increase of flow into Ganga from the canal link with the Brahmaputra (a non-starter) and dams in Nepal. (It would take a chapter to analyze the arguments for and against). He maintains that if the canal from the Brahmaputra was built and could come out into Ganga above Farakka then Bangladesh would get its extra water, so everyone would be happy. He's also an enthusiastic advocate of river-linking. Given the economic and political problems associated with any canal in India all this seems total pie-in-the-sky.

throw down a line to drag our little country boat even up to the gates. Tej furiously cuts away the water hyacinth from the boat. RK Sinha, standing in the boat like an admiral, shouts for my benefit that water hyacinth absorbs heavy metals. It somehow seems inappropriate to the struggle at hand. Little Gopal Sharma sits in the boat as if waiting for the servants "to do the needful."

Finally, after half an hour of the combined efforts of Mr. Pal's staff and *Dolphin's* crew hauling on the rope, our little boat reaches the gates, which manage to open just wide enough to let her ease into the lock. Then it becomes merely a question of waiting for the lock to do its thing: once the tiny country boat is safely inside the massive concrete lock, water is pumped out so that the level inside the lock descends till it's the same as the level in the (lower) feeder canal. When they are equal, the lock gates open and *Dolphin* can proceed down into the canal.

Mr. Pal says they never envisaged little country boats (like *Dolphin*) using the lock. Big boats can cut through the water hyacinth. I ask him, "How many big boats actually use the lock?" "Maybe three a week." Scarcely the level of traffic envisaged. Yes, he admits they should clear the approaches. But what to do? Staff have been cut: there are only five men to maintain the lock. Budget cutbacks. But we do eventually get through and out into the feeder canal, thirty-eight kilometers of concrete-lined canal straight as an arrow all the way down to Jangipur, where the canal has revived the virtually-moribund Bhagirathi, and then on to the Hugli, Kolkata, and Sagar Island.

The Bhagirathi bears no family resemblance to Ganga. It appears a charming pastoral river, civilized, landscaped, the occasional temple to remind me this is India, not Surrey or Hampshire. As if on cue, the extraordinary palace at Murshidibad comes into view, a Bengali Hampton Court on the Thames. All that's lacking are the swans.

Of course, there's another way of looking at Bhagirathi and Sinha can't hide his disgust. "This is a totally artificial river. It has no hydrological complexity at all. Engineers cannot create a river in an alluvial area. You cannot iron out its irregularities. Nature does not make mistakes — trying to control it will always come back to bite you."

I would have put it more crudely: this is a river that's been castrated, or because Ganga is feminine, that's been desexed. All the awesome power we experienced in Bihar, even at Panchanandapur, has been taken away. Tej Razdan laments: "This river could never inspire faith. It has no majesty." Tej is depressed: "I can't feel the goddess." He's hit the nail on the head.

It never ceases to amaze me how few of those living outside of West Bengal seem to know that Ganga actually continues flowing across the border into Bangladesh, where it becomes known as Padma. If government officials had understood a bit about the basic geography of the Bengali delta they might also have had second thoughts about the wisdom and purpose of building Farakka. In a nutshell, for or against Farakka hinges on whether you believe Bhagirathi-Hugli or Padma-Garai is the natural and historical channel for Ganga to reach the sea.

"I do not believe that Bhagirathi is the way Ganga flowed into the Bay of Bengal for three reasons," Kalyan Rudra says. In medieval Bengali literature Ganga was always referred to as *Satamukhi* (having one hundred mouths). This being delta country, Ganga frequently changes course anyway, throwing up new and massive chars or sandbars. It's futile to expect to find a map — any map — that shows the main channel of Ganga, because few people ever agree on what or where that channel flows.

Massive earthquakes in the last two centuries, combined with shifts in the Indian and Asian tectonic plates, have today decisively tilted the river from west to east. Its natural inclination today is therefore to flow ever-east into Padma. Together with two huge Bangladeshi rivers — Meghna and the Brahmaputra — Padma forms a vast estuary that empties into the Bay of Bengal, but inside Bangladesh. The question is: has it always been so? Or is this a fairly recent (in Indian terms several hundred years) phenomenon?

This is where mythology and geology merge. One school — the Bhagirathi-Hugli camp — believes that Bhagirathi-Hugli is the natural and eternal path down which Ganga flows into the Bay of Bengal. If you are a hydrologist, this is important because construction of Farakka and a linking canal into the Bhagirathi are merely restoring the river basin to its natural path and flow, which has been interrupted by earthquakes and recent tectonic shifts. In this view Kolkata is historically a natural deep water port that should be restored to its proper function.

In Hinduism, traditional sanctity has been assigned to the waters of the Bhagirathi, presumably because King Bhagirath led the Ganga down along this distributary, now bearing his name. The defenders of the "Bhagirathi as Ganga" thesis believe the decay of Bhagirathi and the easterly flow of Ganga eastwards into Padma are in fact recent phenomena. They argue that the hydraulic change in the delta took place sometime between the twelfth and sixteenth centuries AD. As proof, they cite references to Bhagirathi and bathing at Sagar Island in the great Indian epics *Ramayana* and *Mahabharata*, or classical texts such as the *Vayu Purana*.[29]

When Kalyan was younger, he subscribed to the Bhagirathi-Hugli thesis. Then a couple of geography professors — one Indian, one English — put forward the radical notion that most distributaries such as Bhagirathi were in fact irrigation canals excavated and reused by Hindu rulers.[30] They argued that Padma had always been the main outlet of Ganga.

Today, Kalyan also believes Bhagirathi was never anything more than just a spill channel of Ganga. Bhagirathi indeed has a separate identity with its own tributaries — Mayurakshi, Ajoy, Damodar, Rupnarayan, and Haldi — that flow into it from the Deccan plateau to the west. Kalyan suggests these and not Ganga are the historical and actual partners of Bhagirathi-Hugli. These are the rivers that Bhagirathi has always taken down to the sea, not Ganga at all. The canal at Farakka is therefore an attempt to transform a myth into a reality.

The partisans of the "Bhagirathi as Ganga" thesis are unrepentant. They argue that this great easterly migration of Ganga took place as recently as the twelfth century. As proof they note that many other former distributaries to the east — Jalangi, Mathabhanga-Churni, Ichhamati, or Garai-Madhumati — have also been left high and dry.[31]

I know a little bit about Garai-Madhuma, having visited it several times since 2001. It flows out of Padma about fifty kilometers inside Bangladesh, near Tagore's country estates at Silaidaha, then flows south towards Khulna. The first time I went up there in 2001, Jan Prins, a Dutch dredging engineer, took me out on the river. It was late December and the river was maybe ten to fifteen feet deep. Imagine my surprise

---

[29] Many of the great travelers — Megasthenes (300 BC), Ptolemy (150 AD), Fa Hien (300 AD), or Yuan Chuan (639 AD) — describe Bhagirathi and Tamralipta as great trading ports on par with the rest of south-east Asia and the Mediterranean, which would tend to support the Ganga as Bhagirathi-Hugli theory.

[30] Willcocks (1930) and Chaudhury (1964) were the dissenters. The former identified all rivers of central Bengal including Bhagirathi as irrigation canals excavated by old Hindu rulers. The latter made a model study of deltaic rivers in his lab at Cambridge (UK), concluding that the Padma had always been the main outlet of Ganga water.

[31] But this doesn't necessarily invalidate Willcocks' and Chaudhury's revisionist theories.

when less than a month later I received an email from him saying he had just walked across the river bed at the same spot. In one month the river had completely dried up. How come?

One evening at his house in north Kolkata, Kalyan explained: "The Garai is like the Bhagirathi. It has what we call a hanging lip for nine months of the year. It's like a lintel in front of your front door. The street can be flooded, but if it doesn't rise above the lintel your house will stay dry. But if the Padma is below the lip than no water can flow into Garai." I'm curious how this lip was formed. "In the monsoon the river cuts a deeper valley on its southern, right bank. That leaves a hanging lip up to five metres higher than Padma."

So if you were sitting in a boat on Padma you'd have to look up, to find the entrance to Garai. Extraordinary! But when you've been there it makes sense. These rivers, like the Garai, really only come to life during and immediately after the monsoon. If the canal linking Ganga at Farakka to Bhagirathi had not been built it too would be just a monsoon distributary of Ganga; the rest of the year the Garai, Bhagirathi, and all the other southward-flowing rivers would be basically dry, in technical jargon "moribund."

Raja Chatterjee once took me up to the dry riverbed that marks the start of Bhagirathi. It's at least ten kilometers from the present course of Ganga, totally dried-up but with evidence of stone jetties and moorings. It is consistent with Kalyan's image of hanging lips. This is another reason why Kalyan firmly believes that Bhagirathi has always headed plain south, while Ganga has always flowed east. His final piece of evidence is the presence of millennia of sediment deposits to the east. If you take into account the subsurface geology and tectonics of the Bengal basin then he is positive Bhagirathi can't possibly be the original way Ganga made her way down to the sea.

He also thinks the reason the British did not go ahead with something like Farakka in the nineteenth and early twentieth centuries is because they understood the plate tectonics were against them. That's the real reason, according to him, why Farakka will always fail; the river wants to flow east, not south.

At first glance the idea that Ganga has always flowed into Padma and entered the sea (and hence the underworld) in what is now Muslim Bangladesh might appear to be damaging to Hindu mythology, particularly in an age of Hindutva. But on second thoughts, I don't think so. After all, Bangladesh did not exist until forty years ago. Islam was revealed to the Prophet Mohammed less than fifteen hundred years ago. It's perfectly plausible that a distributary of Ganga washed over the ashes of King

Sagar's sixty thousand sons at Sagar Island. This could have been merely one of several ways Ganga reached the Bay of Bengal and is unlikely to have much impact on faith. Was Bhagirathi-Hugli once the main course of Ganga? Who knows? Is it important in the greater scheme of things? Probably not.

What is much more relevant is that Farakka is basically not working as envisaged. Forty thousand cusecs of Ganga are diverted down the concrete feeder canal into Bhagirathi-Hugli, so the port of Kolkata can tick over. But no big ships come up. Dredging has increased threefold just to maintain the status quo. The first time I met Parua in his office at Farakka in 2001 (he was then Chief Engineer) he proudly told me:

"We are getting boats up in the port as large as in 1958."

I hated to spoil his day. "And how large is that?"

"Oh, eight to ten thousand tons."

My shipping friends tell me nobody carries anything today — oil, manufactured goods — in a cargo vessel of less than fifty thousand tons. Tankers and supertankers, of course, are at least twice as big. On that score whether the volume of water is the same or has increased is largely irrelevant. Modern ships simply cannot get up to Kolkata from the Bay of Bengal. They load and unload at Haldia. Kalyan says they're now thinking of building a port at the tip of Sagar Island itself.

I'm not sure that's such a good idea: the sea at Sagar Island is very shallow for a long, long way out. At Kolkata, just like every so-called port in the Sundarbans, channels are nowhere deep enough. There are simply no suitable sites for modern deepwater ports along the coast of the Bay of Bengal. They're at best inland ports like Dhaka and Mongla Port in Bangladesh, suited for the coastal trade.

A whole economic ecosystem has been destroyed by Farakka. Before Farakka ships regularly brought tea or jute from the north down the river to be processed in Kolkata's factories and exported. In return, finished goods came back up not just to Assam or Patna, but as far west as Allahabad. All carried up and down Ganga. All this world vanished for the mirage of keeping Kolkata port open.

One afternoon, before we had crossed Farakka, we passed something exceedingly rare — a freight steamer bound for Rajmahal. It was taking raw materials down to the sea and bringing goods back up again. But it was shallow draft. It had to be because of the shallow depth of the lake Ganga has been reduced to behind the barrage. What used to be thirty feet deep is now barely ten.

The Inland Waterways Authority has announced a wonderful plan to revive trade on Ganga. But it's a non-starter until they get serious about Farakka and this pondage upstream. Unfortunately, a "serious" solution would have to be rather drastic to be effective. I can't see Indian politicians dismantling Farakka. So Ganga will have to take the matter into her own hands.

In Kolkata I once rowed out to some barges moored midstream to talk to the crews. They were mostly Muslims who'd been working the river since before Farakka. Mohammad Shafiq and Sheikh Abdul Kalam were taking the *Jyoti* to Naranganj on the Sittla river, off the giant Meghna in Bangladesh. The entire journey would take them ten days.

"Yes, it's fairly slow. A lorry can do the trip in just ten hours. But then it can only carry ten tons. We can carry a hundred tons." In the sixties, both men had gone up to Patna and back, bringing down jute and taking back finished goods. They even remembered barges coming all the way down from Allahabad. "But since Farakka, that's become impossible. Business has declined dramatically, it's down to just a fifth of what it used to be. Mostly we now take occasional cargoes of fly ash for building sites in Bangladesh. Otherwise, we wait here in the Hugli and play cards."

I asked them as Indians and Muslims if the Ganga was sacred for them too.

"We swim in it because it is pak [pure]." Only in theory surely. Ganga at Kolkata appears about as dirty as at Jajmao in Kanpur. Shafiq sticks to the official line: "All rivers are sacred to Muslims, so we bathe in Ganga. It purifies us before we make our prayers to God. We don't worship images and idols. But this river is made by Allah, so it is pure and sacred to us."

I asked to be rowed to another barge in mid-channel. This one had just arrived.

"What are you bringing up?" I shout across.

"We're coming from Kidderpore dock, empty." Mohammad Sadiq, one of the boatmen, says they're going back down to Sagar Island tomorrow to bring back firewood. Going down empty one way is not very profitable.

"There used to be ten thousand barges here. Now there are just eighty. It's all because of the decline in the jute trade, and Farakka." I'm sceptical of the figure of ten thousand barges but not of the decline in the jute trade. The question is: which is cause and which is effect? Did Farakka accelerate the death of the jute trade or was it in decline already? In any event, the economic relationships between upstream and Kolkata are virtually dead today, like so many of the delta's rivers.

The failure of the fish ladder at Farakka has far more serious human consequences. All the fisheries as far back as Buxor west of Patna have been decimated. The fishermen at Kahalgaon are right to feel

Farakka is the cause of their misery. Coming down Bhagirathi-Hugli, our skipper Subhash blames Farakka for the plight of the traditional fisherman. But it's not only Farakka. He says many fishermen in Bihar have been driven to leave fishing altogether and have become labourers, rickshaw-wallahs, even vegetable sellers.

His colleague Mahesh says paradoxically, "There are more fishermen than ever." How come, if Farakka has cut catches? "A kilo of fish now sells for a hundred rupees. That's one reason why." It used to sell for twenty to twenty-five rupees a kilo. "Now any Tom, Dick, or Harry can earn a living because fish prices have increased." There are no cooperatives, no loans, no capital for investment. So there are now at least two distinct fishing communities — the traditional and the johnny-come-latelies.

The latter also use fine-mesh mosquito nets. "I think this is why the number of fishermen has increased," says Mahesh. "With these ready-made nets anyone can buy them off-the-shelf and catch their two kilograms a day. We had to learn to make our own nets. Today's youth don't even know how to tie simple knots." Subhash won't encourage his own children to become fishermen. "They need to get education to get better jobs. Anyway, the mafia's gotten involved in fishing. But if our Mother Ganga dies we will also die. We get everything from her."

Is there any solution? Saju Rai, up-and-coming BJP politician in Jharkhand (who hitched a ride with us for a day), thinks the answer is a river bypass. It sounds plausible. Even the arch-apologist for Farakka — Parua — says it has merit. He claims the West Bengal government considered such a proposal in 1998 and did not act on it.

But if you want to build a bypass before the existing canal at Farakka what becomes of the existing canal? If you build a bigger and better canal upstream with a lock, the problem of pondage doesn't go away. You can't dredge it for the reasons Kalyan Rudra suggests. Cargo boats can't use it, nor fish and dolphins. At best, you'd be back essentially to where we are today — barrage and feeder canal, while Ganga subverts man's best-laid plans and seeks out her old river-beds. At its worst, diverting the river would have unimaginable consequences on land and lives.

What are your options? Build a huge embankment across Ganga and divert the entire river southwards into the Bhagirathi, at vast expense and with who knows what hydrological consequences downstream and upstream? You can't divert Ganga a second time above Farakka unless you build another barrage specially for this. And what would this achieve, one wonders.

Our host Jalaluddin Ahmed in Panchanandapur thinks the only real solution is to break down Farakka, let the river behave normally again. But the Indian government will never countenance that; it has too much prestige riding on Farakka. To destroy Farakka would be to admit they'd been wrong all along. If Ganga can't flow through Farakka, will it simply find a way to flow round it — and will Farakka become the ultimate symbol of India's, and man's, hubris?

~

Nine months later, in September 2005, I get an urgent call from Kalyan Rudra to come back up to Panchanandapur as soon as possible. Something terrible has happened. Panchanandapur has fallen into Ganga. I meet Kalyan and Monatosh Shah at Sealdah Station in Kolkata to take the night train to Maldah.

Torikul Islam meets us next morning, drives us the twenty kilometers from Maldah towards Panchanandapur. The road is lined with makeshift tents — villagers forced out of the village inland. In this flood two thousand houses have been destroyed.

We're not coming in by the usual road. I soon discover why. On September 3, 2005, Ganga swept the embankment away and flowed into Pagla. Most of the village of Panchanandapur collapsed: it now lies deep beneath Ganga. The embankment has been almost totally destroyed. To go to Jalaluddin's house is now impossible by car. It's cut off by Ganga which is now flowing directly into Pagla. The only access to what remains of the village is by a swaying bamboo footbridge. We cross to Jalaluddin's house because he's invited us to spend the night. Hardly anything remains of the streets and houses I walked through less than a year previously. The chai stall, the whole area where we sat, is now buried deep under a vast new bay of Ganga.

After putting our bags down, we walk back across the rope bridge to what remains. We sit in the sole remaining dhaba. Monatosh says: "You can see for yourself. Pagla and Ganga have connected."

The previous winter the West Bengal Irrigation department had built three kilometers of bed spurs, a form of underwater barrage. The villagers had assumed they were safe, at least for 2005. I assume this destruction must have been caused by Ganga flooding but the river wasn't in flood — it simply ate away at the foundations of the bank until they finally collapsed.

Because not a single life was lost, I also assumed the erosion had taken place during daylight hours. Wrong again. When Tajmal Huq walked out of his house at two o'clock in the morning on August 24 it had already slipped into the river when he looked back.

The erosion occurred in two phases, on August 24 and then on September 3. On the earlier date 370 shops in four neighbourhoods collapsed into the river. But the decisive event took place on September 3. Ganga was already one meter higher than the Pagla. When the breach occurred, Ganga simply poured into Pagla for several hours until the levels had equalized. Kedarnath Mundal, a villager I'd met previously, told me what he remembered.

"We were sceptical about the erosion work the previous winter. We even wrote to the President of India. But we never believed this would happen," Kedarnath said. "I've already lost my home four times. My existing one is just three hundred meters from the river, so it looks like I'll be homeless again this time next year."

Kedarnath thinks the West Bengal Irrigation Department should open up the three small rivers — Pagla, Chotti Bhagirathi, and Kalandri — to allow Ganga to flood naturally. "If only we had been given land so we could move before the erosion," he laments. "No one died, but we've lost all our animals." Both schools have collapsed so his kids are no longer in school.

Over lunch at the dhaba Kalyan explains why and how it happened: "Imagine a river flowing straight into a massive brick wall. What happens? It rebounds and sets off a current back upstream. The effects of the barrage can be felt a hundred and ninety-five kilometers back upstream, and you know who has done these calculations? P.K. Parua,[32] the very man who declared in 2004 that Farakka could by definition have no consequences upstream."

But there's a wrinkle. In the lab, the current hits the wall at ninety degrees while in real life Ganga hits Farakka at an angle. The course of the river is no longer a straight line from Rajmahal to Farakka.[33] Farakka has exaggerated the natural meanders upstream, pushed the river to one side, so it approaches the barrage at a slant. As Kalyan puts it: "The whole hydraulic gradient of the river has been changed." And what's the consequence? "This causes a back rush, and the river seeks an alternative outlet sideways."

---

[32] Parua, P.K.: Fluvial Geomorphology of The River Ganga around Farakka, Journal of Institution of Engineers, Vol-82, February, 2002, pp 193-196.

[33] The map at the beginning of this chapter shows how the river has deviated between 1920 and today.

Precisely at its weakest point, at Panchanandapur. The cause of the collapse of the village therefore wasn't a storm or massive flooding. The new hydrological dynamics produced by Farakka had undermined all the careful efforts of the West Bengal government. The entire embankment — above ground and below water — had eroded. It was the weight of the boulders that actually triggered the collapse. But it was Farakka that was really responsible. It had forced Ganga sideways, so Ganga then undermined the bank from below. There's now nothing to prevent Ganga flowing more and more into Pagla and then into Mahananda. Now that it has united with Pagla the government is worried it could cut the railway and highway to North Bengal.

"P.K. Parua was wrong, wasn't he," says Kalyan, "when he said September 3 could never happen. I think he's wrong too about Farakka. It will become a totally redundant national asset, a white elephant."

Of course, the rich have already moved, the poor are condemned to stay.

~

The following day we take a motorized country boat out into Ganga to pay another visit to Kashmiuldalla village on the char lands on the other side. On the way back we stop the boat next to some heads of trees sticking out above the waves. Kalyan says this marks the spot we moored in 2004. We have a minute of silent thought about happier times. Then everyone on board starts talking all at once:

"We are like fish without water." (Idrish Ahmed)

"Unblock Pagla and allow Ganga to behave normally. You cannot control this river." (Monatosh Shah)

"I've lived here all my life. In a few years will Panchanandapur be just a memory?" (Tajmal Huq)

Will anything be left when I return?[34]

---

[34] Kalyan tells me that in June 2006 the West Bengal government once again built an embankment to separate Pagla from Ganga. Too late, the damage has been done: Panchanandapur is just a shadow of its former self. It won't be coming back. And Ganga? I'll bet it will again destroy that embankment this summer or the next.

Sagar Island & South 24 Parganas

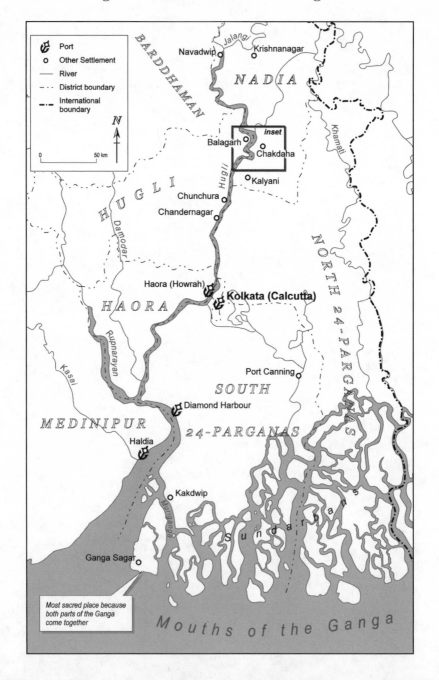

Legend:
- Port
- Other Settlement
- River
- District boundary
- International boundary

N

0   50 km

BARDDHAMAN

Navadwip   Krishnanagar

Jalangi

NADIA

Khamati

inset

Balagarh   Chakdaha

Hugli

Kalyani

Chunchura

Chandernagar

HUGLI

Damodar

NORTH 24-PARGANAS

Haora (Howrah)   **Kolkata (Calcutta)**

HAORA

Rupnarayan

Kasai

Port Canning

SOUTH

Diamond Harbour

MEDINIPUR

24-PARGANAS

Haldia

Kakdwip

Muriganga

Sundarbans

Ganga Sagar

Most sacred place because
both parts of the Ganga
come together

Mouths of the Ganga

CHAPTER 8

Makar Sankranti at Sagar Island

$\mathbf{B}$athing at Sagar Island on Makar Sankranti is the icing on the cake for Bijoy Tivari. For the past four months he's been able to live a dream come true — to bathe all down Ganga at its most sacred tirthas. January 14 will be the climax. And what a climax!

Makar Sankranti marks the date in the Indian winter solstice when the sun enters Capricorn, heads north — always auspicious—and the days begin to get longer. It's also the last day of the Bengali month of Poush. But why always on January 14? Why is this one always fixed? All other Indian festivals change dates every year. This puzzled me a lot and I never found anyone who could explain the reason, until I read that Makar Sankranti is the only Indian festival that is celebrated according to the solar, as opposed to the lunar calendar.

Remember why Ganga originally came down to earth? The sixty thousand sons of King Sagar had inadvertently angered the hermit Kapil Muni while he was meditating by the sea at the tip of Sagar Island. So he shrivelled them into ashes. It was Sagar's grandson Bhagirath who asked the gods to send down the goddess Ganga to restore them to life.[1] Ganga, of course, came to earth in the locks of Shiva's hair at Gangotri and then Bhagirath led Ganga down out of the mountains, across the plains to the sea, looking for that huge pile of ashes. They found them here. Ganga washed over them and the souls of the sixty thousand sons were liberated — they had found mukti to go to heaven.

So every January, on this festival day of Makar Sankranti, thousands come from all over India to bathe at this spot where Ganga flows into the sea, carrying with her the souls of all the dead whose

---

[1] According to some retellings of the story the gods leaned on Shiva to break Ganga's fall.

ashes have been consigned to her along her way. Makar Sankranti at Sagar Island is a Hindu equivalent of the Christian Easter Sunday, when souls arise from the dead. Bijoy swears that Allahabad is the Raj Tirtha, but most of the people here today are quite convinced this beats them all. Bathing here on Makar Sankranti for them truly is liberation, freedom.

There's another way of understanding Makar Sankranti as a rather different story of life and death. The Gangetic plain is the most thickly populated and the oldest settled plain in the world, and agriculture sustains that population. The whole story of the ashes therefore becomes a metaphor for the cycle of famine and drought. Every year, Ganga brings the land back to life.

The life-giving qualities of Ganga are ultimately what is conveyed through Makar Sankranti, just as the story of Ganga's descent and the imagery of Shiva's hair corresponds to the myriad mountain streams and rivers that flow down into Ganga. Imagery and mythology dovetail beautifully with one another.

~

If you've never been to a really big mela, it's a bit like an open-air rock concert at the edge of the sea, but with two important differences — no entrance fee and no age restrictions. Nobody advertises the mela. It just is. Everybody knows. You just get there anyway you can — by train, by bus, by foot. And once you're there you can sleep anywhere you can find, wash, eat, chat, meet people, sing bhajans, visit stalls selling just about everything — conch shells, beads, books, cassettes, even DVDs. At the mela at Ganga Sagar the only thing that is fixed and immutable is that on the great day you take your "holy dip." Precisely when is a bit more problematic.

In Kolkata a bamboo village has sprung up near Eden Gardens for all the villagers who are coming to Kolkata by train. But there are more workmen than residents. Has the tsunami scared them away? Bijoy goes down to see if relatives from Sultanpur[2] have come. They haven't arrived yet.

I know some Kolkata socialites who've traveled to Sagar for past Makar Sankrantis from Kolkata by motor launch. But they were VIPs and guests of the government. Ordinary people have to take the ferry across from Kakdwip.[3] We're not quite ordinary, but neither are

---

[2] His village in UP.

[3] Kakdwip is the embarkation point for ferries to Sagar Island (see map).

we special. However, we do need to take the Scorpio across and find somewhere to stay where our recording equipment will be safe and we can recharge our batteries. The hotel has been completely booked by VIPs for many months. We go to Alipore to see Mr. Choudhary, the additional district magistrate of 24 South Parganas. Letters are typed and signed; a pass for us and the Scorpio. "Go to the mela office as soon as you arrive. They will look after your accommodation."

We (Raja, Bijoy, James Ashby, and myself — Martine has returned to the US to deal with a fiscal deadline) leave early to get there before the crowds. Fat chance. The prime minister is in town, so most of the main roads in Alipore have become one-way overnight. Round and round in circles until we finally get out of the city. But it's a lovely winter's day with very little traffic. We're aiming to reach the loading bay at Kakdwip by 2:00 P.M., so we can get to the mela grounds while it is still light.

But when we get to Bay No. 8 at Kakdwip we find half of India already there (where did they come from?), and no ferry. Why the delay? Tides. We've missed high tide by thirty minutes. Now the water in the straits is so low the ferries can't load. They're stranded on the beach like exhausted, snub-nosed whales covered in mud and oil. We will have to wait another six hours. So we read, walk, and eat — samosas, pakoras, fresh coconut juice. When in doubt follow the driver; Tivari has always known where to eat.

Finally we reach the other side, along with thousands of other Indians. We drive off in our Scorpio. They are herded on to buses. But the destination is the same — Ganga Sagar, the spot where Ganga and the sea finally merge. Good roads, little traffic. Suddenly we cross a bridge and enter an immense fairground. Or is it a film set? Floodlights as far as the eye can see. And who is waiting for us but Mr. Choudhary from Alipore, transformed into mela officer, holding court in a small house on the outskirts of Sagar City. Another chit is signed: "Go to the Information Tower and give this to DICO." An attractive young woman called Malvika Goswami — the district information and cultural officer — is waiting to show us to our quarters as members of the media. It appears we are the only firangs.

We cross a broad avenue of loose sand and dart between two stalls, left down an alleyway, to our new home — individual bamboo and Ganga grass thatched huts with verandah, bedroom, open-air shower, and latrine. One lock, one chair, one bucket, one blanket, one electric light, one solid wooden bed — all enclosed by a wall of Ganga grass to keep curious eyes out.

There's a particularly noisy generator at the end of our block, doubtless powering the floodlights and the bulbs in all the stalls that front the avenue leading to the water. Throughout the night, a continuous stream of pilgrims shuffles down past our huts to the sea, to take a dip, chat, and then come back, stopping to buy conch shells and other souvenirs at these stalls. Some fall asleep on the sand in this broad avenue. Others head off to other areas in mela city — it's all signposted by block. At the head of the avenue is the only solid permanent structure — Rishi Kapil Muni's temple.

It's not the original by any means. The spot where the sage meditated is now way out to sea under the advancing tide. Inside the temple are three stone images: Kapil Muni himself, eyes wide open, looking out to sea with thousands of devotees waiting on his every word, with Ganga and King Sagar flanking him. The horse of the sacrificial yagna, which caused all the problems in the first place, stands off to one side. Next to the temple are rows of tiny stalls. Inside sit naked nagas, bodies smeared in ash, vaunting the size of their penises in proportion to the charms of female pilgrims (especially any foreign tourists) who have to pass their gauntlet to get to the temple and the sea. I ask Raja if the ash has some religious significance. After all Catholics smear their foreheads with ash at the start of Lent to signify that man comes from dust and will return to dust.

"No man, it's to keep warm. Smearing ash locks body heat in."

"Oh!"

So apparently does mud, which may explain another image that has haunted me for several years. In 2001, I watched as a man above Asi Ghat in Varanasi sat in what passed for the Asi stream and slathered himself with black mud. At the time this seemed the height of madness: that ooze was probably toxic, certainly full of pathogens. But maybe that wasn't the point?

Gazing at this vast scene, trite thoughts come to mind: this is truly a mela. Not for the tourists or the Indian middle classes. Definitely not a media event. Of the people, for the people, by the people.

~

The next morning Jeeta Babu is seated on a mat, holding court in the middle of the avenue just behind our compound. His fifteen-foot long tresses, like hawsers on a ship, are stretched out in front of him.

"I don't want to talk with you. I know all about you." Not for the first time microphones are mistaken for cameras.

"You will get a lot of money for my photo, won't you? I won't give anything."

Raja asks, "How much money do you want?"

Jeeta Babu is adamant. I can't blame him. "No, I won't give it."

Raja tries flattery. I'm staying well out of this fawning. It won't work, I know it.

"You know everything — you have such huge hair. You are a great man with great thoughts."

"Yes, I also think so."

Raja doesn't know when to stop: "This is a place for saints and peace."

"Yes I am for all people — but not for you."

No point in flogging a dead horse. Time to move on. I sympathize with Jeeta Babu. Of course, he's been spoilt by media attention up in Kolkata. His photo was in *The Telegraph* earlier this week. Now he will only talk with a substantial down payment.

Just behind Jeeta Babu are a group of some fifty peasants wrapped in winter woolens, sitting on the sand under the Information Tower, bundles around them, waiting for one of their group to turn up so they can leave the island. Most of them work carving temples in Udaipur. Their leader is Dhan Singh Kumaut.

"This is our pilgrimage. We will complete it and then we will go home. We came yesterday. We've already taken our bath. We leave tomorrow evening."

In fact they left Udaipur by bus back on December 27. They're taking six weeks off from work to go on a yatra around the entire country. They've already been to Haridwar and Rishikesh. After this they'll head south to Tirupati, Kanyakumari, and Rameshwaram ending up in Dwarka.

I ask my usual bathing question: "When you bathe in Ganga you wash away your sins — correct?"

"Yes."

"Now if that is true why do you bathe so often in Ganga, at Kartik Purnima, at other auspicious days? Do you have so many sins that you can't wash them away all at once?"

Silly question, really. Another silly question: taking a dip washes away one's sins and good Hindus bathe every day. Does that mean observant Hindus sin more than Indians who never pray, fast, or bathe?

Roars of laughter. That's a good one.

"No, seriously. It's not because of sin. We don't have a bath for washing sins away. We don't come for that. It's because our religion tells us to, that's why."

Other voices are now cascading in: "Your religion is yours and ours is ours. We wash to get clean for our journey to the next life. Nothing much to do with sins at all."

They've hit the proverbial nail on the head. Of course, there's a religious explanation, but the custom is nowadays more important. Not too many Indians really think about forgiveness when they bathe. It's just something you do. Period.

I'm still curious. It's a long way from Udaipur. "Why do you make a yatra like this? Purely for religious reasons?"

"We come to see the gods and goddesses and worship them." But there's also another very important reason. "In this way we'll meet people on this journey. So yes, it's also about meeting people. And it gives peace to the soul." What's important to them is just being here, seeing where Ganga has washed over the ashes of Sagar's sixty thousand sons, and discovering their country and countrymen. A wonderful reason to make the journey.

But one of the group is missing; the group needs to catch the ferry and get to Kolkata tonight so they can take the train back to Rajasthan. "We have informed the Information Center." That's why they're sitting here, waiting until the missing villager shows up. In the Watch Tower behind us the P/A is appealing to the missing person — Ganesh Pal — to come quickly. But another villager says there's no need to worry: "He will come here after wandering around."

VU3 JFA — Juliet Foxtrot Alpha — wears a T-shirt proclaiming he is a member of the Kolkata Ham Radio Network. His true name is Ambarish Nag Biswas, and his job is to find Ganesh Pal, and many others. The network debuted successfully in the tsunami relief two weeks ago. They liaise with the ferries at Kakdwip and on the island. Ambarish says the problems start back in Kakdwip before villagers get on the ferries to take them across the Buriganga[4] to the island:

"Some come to this side and some stay on the other side. It happens all the time. They come in more than one bus; some of them get lost back there and go back to the bus stand; some of them go to Namkhana [the thana on the mainland opposite the island]; some even go back to Kolkata. There are few phones here on the island, so the DM [District Magistrate] hired us to handle the missing persons, and we will get them back together again."

This is the first year they've done this, but is seems to be working. There are twenty-three of them: a couple at the club back in Kolkata, a

---

[4] See map on p. 206.

handful at Kakdwip and at Kachaburia — the ferry terminal on the island — and the rest here. They're at it twenty-four hours a day. It's been less than three weeks since the tsunami, but they've installed a high frequency set so they can be in contact with monitoring stations around the world, in case a new tsunami occurs. Ganga Sagar is so flat I wonder where they could evacuate all these hundreds of thousands of pilgrims to. There is no higher ground. A wave would just sweep through the mela grounds until it ran out of steam.

But their bread and butter is missing persons. Ambarish just got a message that a party of pilgrims got stuck back on the mainland over on that side. Some of the party boarded a launch and came across, the remainder are still waiting in Bay 8 at Kakdwip. When the first group arrived at Kachuberia on Sagar Island, the Ham Radio people sent out a message over the loudspeakers telling them to wait for the rest of their party to arrive. Otherwise, they'd all lose one another.

Of course, there are other times when the Ham Radio network is called into action. Ambarish tells me, "Sometimes it happens that someone got sick and can't get over. Then that person is made to stay behind at Kakdwip. When the person is well, he or she is sent over. If a couple is aged — and that's always possible because it is a mela for older people, then our people — the ham radio operators — they get a car from the DM and make arrangements to take them to the other side — that's how we work."

As if on cue a colleague springs into action:

"Delta alpha November India. This is Rajat from Sagar bus stand tower. Red Cross near bus stand tower. There is someone sick here. Repeat Delta alpha bravo..."

So someone has fallen ill at the bus stand. Another person from Varanasi has lost his wife. He is being escorted here. By the time he arrives maybe his wife will have been found.

But what if somebody is just plain missing? Like Ganesh Pal from Udaipur? Wandering aimlessly in the mela grounds with no idea where his friends are? He wouldn't know what the Information Tower is, where it is, how to get there. If he's anything like some Indians I've known he may try and hide because he is afraid of the police. So what happens then?

Every year in the mela some pilgrims do indeed decide to stay behind. When the mela camp is over, the Bajrang Parishad gather all the missing persons together. The rest of the villagers have already reached home and contacted their local thanas to tell them so-and-so is missing, probably at the Sagar Mela. When the mela is finally over, these people are taken back to Kolkata to the Bajrang office. They stay there. If they are physically fit but they need money, the Bajrang gives them their fare. If they are aged then someone goes with them physically. It can be anywhere — UP, Jammu, even Kerala — they are all eventually sent back to their villages, wherever.

Certain families also dispose of unwelcome senior citizens (and children) here. They just abandon them. They can be young or old. Usually one mouth too many to feed. Solution: lose him or her at Sagar Island. They want to be rid of them in any case. I'm not shocked. Many of the street kids I know in Mumbai were once abandoned in this manner by their parents. The kids were bewildered. I used to wonder what was going through the minds of the parents. I imagine here on Sagar Island, a few forget to tell the Bajrang Parishad the name of their thana, so the family member can't be returned. A mean little thought crosses my mind: that man from Varanasi who has lost his wife, what if he wants to lose her? Or she him?[5]

Officially one hundred and sixty-seven people have been lost. The actual number may be twice that many because so many villagers never report a person missing in the first place. All but fifteen, however, have been found.

~

There are a multitude of other little dramas being played out near the Information Tower. A woman from Bhagalpur in Bihar is frantically trying to find rupee notes she forgot in her green cotton sari while bathing. I can relate to that. It's easy to forget. It's the sort of thing I do. I often leave ten, even twenty rupee notes in the pockets of my kurta. Martine has a rule: "If I find money in the clothes to be washed it goes into the glass jar for the house. It's no longer yours to do with as you want."

But there's no Martine today and no glass jar here on the beach. This woman had seventy-five rupees wrapped up in the edge of her sari — twenty-five to get back to the ferry on the island, then fifty to cross to Kakdwip.

She laughs with bitterness. Money is obviously very much on her mind. Who can blame her? The whole trip from Bhagalpur (Bihar) has cost her five to six hundred rupees.

"And that's not counting food. We didn't get to eat either. Incidentally they're charging far too much for the bus and the ferry from

---

[5] I asked Ambarish, but he's far too diplomatic to go down that road. He did admit it's a possibility: "Who knows?"

Kolkata. It's normally thirty-five. But they told us: "Makar Sankranti on Sagar Island only happens once in a lifetime. So you have to pay extra."

Shri Budaram Das from Ayodhya is not quite certain why Makar Sankranti is important. "It just is. All pilgrimages are important. But there is only one Ganga Sagar, and we come for Kapil Muni."

Krishna Das from Chandigarh has no such problems. "I have come because it is important in our culture." And proceeds to tell me once again, but well, the entire story of King Sagar and the ashwamedha yagna horse sacrifice, with a few details I'd forgotten.[6]

Here on the beach everyone wants to tell me his or her life history. Kailash Baba, for instance, lives on the banks of the Sipra river near Ujjain. He's done the entire parikrama of the Narmada twice. ("Two circles, 2680 kilometers of the Narmada is the pilgrimage. I've done it twice.") He walked here from Nasik. After Ganga Sagar he's off to the Kamakshi temple near Guwahati in Assam — a long yatra. You name it, he's been everywhere: Gaumukh, Gangotri, Haridwar, Allahabad, three

---

[6] The details are interesting. For a start I hadn't realized that Indra was the instigator of the whole thing. To recap: in the ashvamedh yagna the horse is let loose to roam. That defines the territorial limits of the kingdom. For some reason I don't understand, if the horse was not caught, Indra could lose his throne to King Sagar. So it was Indra who stole the horse and hid it at Kapil Muni's ashram. And everyone knows the rest of the story: the sixty thousand sons blundered along, disturbed Kapil Muni's meditation, and were shrivelled up into ashes by his gaze. And that's how Ganga got involved; only she could restore the ashes to life.

But I didn't know all the ins and outs of the negotiations among the gods, or that Ganga also pouted. Sagar's grandson Bhagirath prayed for help to the gods. Brahma recommended he go and see Shiva. No dice. Shiva sent him on to Vishnu. Vishnu was a bit more helpful: "Yes, I can send Ganga down, but there's nothing to soften her fall and she'll flood the whole world. Go see if Brahma's got any suggestions."

Bhagirath returns to Brahma who in turn tells him to go see Shiva again. He does and spends the next thousand years meditating on one leg at Gangotri, until Shiva agrees to use the locks of his hair to lower Ganga to earth so her impact will not crush everyone and everything. The fly in the ointment now is Ganga.

In Krishna Das's words: "Ganga says I won't go, I'm upset, no one thought to ask me." To cut a long story short Nandi the Bull agrees to drink Ganga and that's the origin of how and why Ganga flows out of Gaumukh, the cow's mouth. Krishna Das's explanation of the role of the famous locks of Shiva's hair is novel to say the least: "At Gangotri Shiva shook his locks for twelve years and when he stopped Ganga was now flowing as five different rivers — Alaknanda, Mandakini, Bhagirathi, Satluj, and Indus." The last two rise in Tibet near lake Mansarovar, the other side of the watershed and flow out to the west of the Himalayas and into Pakistan. But it's amazing how geography gets all jumbled up. My geologist and geography friends would have a field day sorting all this out. Let it pass. It's what Krishna Das believes; that's what's important.

Haridwar, Allahabad, three times alone to Shiva's cave at Amarnath in the Himalayas. And with just a bundle on a stick slung over his shoulder.

"These are all your worldly possessions, I take it, you have on you?" I ask.

"This is bedding to lie down on; this is my blanket. That's all I have. If I get some food, that's okay. And there's always water from Ganga."

Tulsi Ram is burly, with close-cropped hair. He's dressed in a white kurta with an orange scarf. He comes from Mathura-Vrindavan. "Varsana, to be precise. Radha also comes from Varsana. [Note the present tense.] We call it Brij — the leela area — the playground of Krishna and Radha. My ancestors were friends of Krishna. [Another wonderful example of how time collapses — it's the event that is the defining factor. When is unimportant.] We're related to a friend of Krishna's — Sudama."

Tulsi Ram also says that tonight something wonderful will happen: "There will be a rain of amrit. That's why it's auspicious to bathe here. People will come from India and all corners of the world. The gods will drop a rain of nectar here on this area tomorrow, for the welfare of all the believers. Our souls will be released. This is why this day is so important." So when will Tulsi Ram take his bath? "Six o'clock, as soon as the sun god comes up." (I store that away for future reference.)

Meanwhile, the tide is starting to come in.

As if on cue, a group of villagers seated on the sand starts chanting "Radhe, Radhe." One of them wanders off, starts playing small cymbals, singing a bhajan to Krishna. Meanwhile, a brass band advances across the beach, preceding a village deity carried on a palanquin, conch shells blowing and women ululating. A hundred yards offshore, a large hovercraft is crisscrossing the bathing area. A Kashmiri terrorist group is reported to have threatened to attack bathers on Makar Sankranti, so the army is taking no chances.

A tall woman observes all this to one side, visibly not taking part.

"Have you just bathed?"

"No, I haven't taken bath and I will not take bath!" She makes me think of Raja refusing to bathe all those months ago in the sangam at Allahabad.

"Why not?"

"I don't believe in all this. I'm just waiting for my friend. I bathe at home in Ganga at Murshidabad. There are lots of other people here who also don't believe."

I ask her name: "Lutfa Begum." I mention the Muslim bargemen in Kidderpore in Kolkata who say they bathe in Ganga because the river is so pak (pure). But she's not buying.

"No. That's not the reason. I don't think this water is clean, that's all."

~

Lutfa Begum's dismissal of Ganga's still ringing in my ears, I see two women — Babli Jha and Pramila Mishra from Patna, doing something odd, scooping sand into a plastic bag. Not for sandcastles, I think.

"We will mix it in the foundations of our houses so our new houses will be blessed," they tell me. The thought had not occurred to me.

Equally odd: why are so many calves on the beach?

Raja is astonished I don't know the significance

"Gou daan — this is for gou daan [donation of the cow to the puja]. You should touch its tail. Then you will go to the next world."

"How?" I ask.

Raja mutters, "This is Baitarini."

Baitarini is an actual river in Orissa that is mentioned in several myths in the Ramayana. The devotees here at Ganga Sagar tell Raja that the waters of the Baitarini are red and its source looks like a cow's face. In Hindu mythology Baitarini is the river of life which you cross to get to the next world. So a cow with its tail painted red is the symbol of this river. If you catch its tail and take a few steps into the surf you're saved. Yet another way to be saved. Raja's disappointed I don't want to perform the ritual. The man leading the calf is not amused either.

The band is returning down the beach. It's probably time to leave and go back up past Kapil Muni's temple, brave the nagas, and find somewhere to eat. The tide washes over the pooja offerings — flowers, sticks of incense, pieces of coconut. Just above the high tide mark are a row of small pandals depicting scenes connected with Ganga. My favorite is the one depicting Behula and Lakhindar. Behula is yet another in that long line of Indian women whose chaste devotion to their husbands is finally rewarded — in this case Lakhindar is restored to life.

It's a Bengali folk tale, probably at least two thousand years old, written down in the fifteenth century. It's part of a much longer poem — the Manasa-Vijya. Manasa the snake goddess strikes me as a rather ambivalent goddess. One moment she's all benevolence herself — the great goddess all the other gods accommodate. The next, she's petty, mean-spirited, bent only on revenge. Anyway, the plot: Chand Sadagar, a banya, refuses to pay sufficient homage to Manasa, so she determines to make his life such a misery he will eventually have no alternative but to acknowledge her sovereignty. She murders his six sons with poison (a particularly delicate touch — poison in their rice), wrecks his ships, but still he holds out.

Then a seventh son Lakhindar is born to Chand and his wife Sanaka (who secretly worships Manasa). But there is of course a prophecy that is in reality a curse: the sage Bidhata tells the parents that Lakhindar will die on his wedding night, bitten by a snake. Worse, his bride Behula will take his body in her lap and float with it for six months on the river. But at the end of those six months Manasa will relent and yield to the power of prayer of Chand and restore Lakhindar to life.

Now Behula's really something to behold.

"Her face is like the stainless moon, her words are a cup of nectar, the mass of her hair is fuller and darker than the thundercloud. She is a girl most chaste and devoted. Her hair hangs long, tumbling down her back...oh, I have nothing to compare her with. She is a lovely girl. Her walk is more graceful than that of the most graceful swaying elephant. She is more beautiful than Tilottama. Behula Nacana is her name. And she is religious. [Oh how she's religious!] In every twelve-month period she makes twelve vratas, once on every full-moon day."[7]

Right from the start Behula realizes she has to fight Manasa and win her over if she is to have any hope of seeing her husband live beyond their wedding night. Chand builds a wedding chamber entirely of steel (apparently without ventilation) but Manasa has a tiny hole bored in one corner, through which a snake can pass. On the fateful night Behula strangles the first three would-be assassins with golden tongs. But the fourth snake gets through just after the wedding couple have eaten and finally dozed off to sleep. This snake — Kalanagini — doesn't want to go through with the mission; Lakhindar is so handsome. But the young man turns over in his sleep and his heel is accidentally pricked by one of Kalaganini's fangs. He dies.

What's a young girl to do?

In Behula's case she does what's written in her destiny.[8]

---

[7] Dimock, Edward C, edited and translated by, *The Thief of Love — Bengali Tales from Court and Village*, University of Chicago, 1963. I was introduced to the late Edward Dimock at a rather incongruous spot in Varanasi in 1986, a bar where he has drinking whisky. I then went out and bought this book and it has given me great pleasure ever since. Interestingly, he used as a basic source a Bengali version published in 1953 by Sukumar Sen, a renowned Bengali academic.

[8] Ibid, p. 259.

"I shall take my husband's body on my lap and float upon the river for six months. I shall, by the power of my former worship, make Manasa restore my lord to life. I shall fulfill my dharma: this I wish to do. Let no one stop me. Build me then a raft of banana-wood, and make it ready for the trip. Lash the logs together, and hammer in bamboo pegs. Prepare the raft and float it on the water."

So off they set, apparently down the Damodar, into the Hugli below Kolkata, and then into Ganga at Sagar Island.

The dead body stinks and rots — maggots eat away the flesh, a fish takes a bite out of what remains and removes the kneecap, and all the while Behula rejects any number of advances — from men old and young, infirm and lusty, till she somehow makes it to the triveni. This puzzles me a little because the only triveni I know in West Bengal is at Nawadwip which is where the Hugli and Jalangi meet. The other candidate is north of Sagar Island where the Hugli, Buriganga, and Rupnarayan (or Haldi) rivers all come together.

In any case, not even Ganga jal can restore the bag of bleached bones to life. The snake's venom is too powerful. It remains in Lakhindar's body. So Behula does what any self-respecting young woman would do — she dances in front of the gods to charm them into bringing her husband back to life. It works. Manasa is shamed by the other gods. She lifts the curse, restores Lakhindar to life, even finds the fish with the missing kneecap (without which the young man would be a cripple). The end has always felt anticlimactic: Chand finally swallows his pride and agrees to worship Manasa.

There are several oddities about the story: the parents of Lakhindar and of Behula are merchants, not Brahmins. Manasa, being both a goddess and the villain of the story is alternatively petty and magnanimous. Chand is weak yet proud and stubborn, while all the women in the story lead double lives — devoted to their husbands but also secret worshippers of Manasa.

In the pandals on the beach here at Ganga Sagar, Behula is cradling a visibly dead Lakhindar.[9] The importance for those here for Makar Sankranti is twofold: they floated down Ganga, possibly to Sagar; and a man is restored to life thanks to the chaste devotion of a wife. The people, here at Ganga Sagar, of course probably believe he's been restored to

---

[9] Until I recently reread it I swore that a crocodile tore off one of Lakhindar's limbs which was trailing in the water (crocodiles are big in my mental art gallery). Turns out as usual to be a figment of my imagination. I had also forgotten many of the other details.

life thanks to curative waters of Ganga ma even though the author specifically rules that out. But it's what people believe happened that counts, of course.

Throughout the day there's been a sub-text running: when is the correct time to bathe on Makar Sankranti? A good half of the people I've talked to say "at dawn when the sun rises." But the other half says at eleven in the morning. I can't figure out why. Even the official chief guest, the Shankacharya of Puri, says eleven o'clock. I press him during a rather bad-tempered conversation and he refuses to give a reason. Maybe he has the same low opinion of me as Jeeta Babu.

I had read that the Shankaracharya was willing to bridge the intellectual chasm that appears to separate secular environmentalism (Ganga as a river) from Hindu beliefs that Ganga is above all else a goddess. I guessed wrong. The Shankaracharya says:

"In January month the Prayag [at Allahabad] becomes a river of blood because the Muslims in Kanpur slaughter cows for their leather. This is a conspiracy against Hindus ... a conspiracy to pollute all the things that are important to Hindus ... not just the Ganga is polluted ... everything we Hindus believe in is being polluted, such as the mutths, the mandirs, marriages ... law, education, and security ... All of it is being polluted — this is an international conspiracy."

I remark that it's not foreigners but Indians, Hindus as well as Muslims, who actually pollute Ganga. He's not listening.

~

That night I never see a rain of amrit, not even a mist. I don't get too much sleep anyway. No one else can have slept either. The PA system from the Information Tower blares throughout the night. If there is an official start to the great day, I miss it. The guidebooks say the priest (Which one? From the mandir?) announces the auspicious moment has arrived and the crowds surge forward chanting "Kapil Muni ki jai" and plunge into the sea. This may have happened. But that's not what I witness.

I peer out at three in the morning. The tide is so far out and the beach so shallow you have to walk half a mile out before it ever reaches over your head. Crowds are indeed bathing to chants of Gangaji. There are also a lot of calves in evidence (mooing in protest or in prayer?), brass cymbals beating rhythmically on the beach, and everywhere lots of people talking, having a good time. A night out at the seaside. The conch shell stores are doing brisk business. I pad back to my bed.

Up again at six o'clock, in expectation of something momentous. Malvika Goswami, the Cultural Liaison Officer, told me yesterday, "The auspicious time is ten minutes before sunrise till ten minutes after. A window between six sixteen and six thirtysix."

But nothing seems to have changed much since my earlier sortie. The tide is still way out. To get to the sea one has to walk a long way. Same PA blaring, same cows, same clappers, same crowds — well, they do seem greater. Groups of women are seated on the dry sand near the Behula and Lakhindar pandals singing bhajans. So many people. Someone tells me huge crowds have arrived during the night. They surge down the avenue towards the sea. Village pandits are chanting "sab teerth baar baar, Ganga Sargar ek bar."

One group of villagers, swaddled in thick woollens, shuffle in lockstep, held together with a thick rope tied round their perimeter so no one will get lost on land or at sea. It's possibly the one and only time they have seen the sea, except on the ferry across. Certainly their first time actually in the sea: and all this less than three weeks after the tsunami. No wonder they look bewildered and apprehensive, while all around them there's a raucous cacophony of spontaneous joy.

Conversations with bathers are necessarily brief. Why get in their way? One fully-dressed man mummified in layers of woollens is watching the bathers to see how they do it. He says he lives on the island. Strange to think you could live here and not know all the rituals — the mantras and the turning seven times in the water. But there has to be a first time for anything and everything.

A man from Chhapra in Bihar has just come out and looks very cold. "Yes, I'm shivering a little bit. After you have a bath when you come out you always shiver. It's the air that's cold. But the water is warm. [This is true; when you bathe in the morning, water always feels warm because of the contrast with the outside temperature.] It's my first time, and I wouldn't miss this for the world. This bath is very important."

A husband and wife are scavenging discarded coconut shells at the water's edge, obviously offerings to Ganga left only an hour ago. Is there any fruit left inside? If yes, they'll take them back home to resell. They're quite unashamed about it. In the city or in the West that would be a big scandal. Dirty, a sign of poverty. Here at the mela it's so normal no one even thinks twice.

A boy has a pile of green coconuts on a handcart: "Fifty paisa. Need to make an offering? Coconuts. Fifty paisa." A villager asks: "Do you have any daab — green ones?" They're cheaper.

Three women from Nagpur are raking the wet sand.

"I'm picking up the coins that were offered to the sea," one tells me. I ask her how much she'll make.

"Oh about twenty-thirty rupees. Something like that."

No trumpets this morning, just big bass dhols banging rhythmically away, up and down the beach. A quick sample of bathers suggests the net has been cast pretty wide — Agra, Delhi, Nepal. All of them say the same thing: "This is the most important day of the year. If I take holy dip here, it will purify me and bring me closer to God."

A family from Mienpuri in Uttar Pradesh spontaneously burst into a round, each one singing a different line:

"This is about Kapil Muni maharaj. He had done a meditation over here. And all the sons of Raja Sagar, they had been burnt to ashes over here." (soprano)

"He had given a curse." (mezzo)

"And the Ganga is also here, and she..." (alto)

"Raja Bhagirath, he had done the meditation here standing on one leg." (tenor)

"And it is known as Ganga bath." (baritone)

"Sagar's sons they get back their life ... the Bhagirath brought the Ganga here." (bass)

And on and on it goes.

Two elderly swamis are holding court on the sand. They have come from Jharkhand, complete with trishul and bell. They're playing on a dumroo — a small drum that's played in one hand, with a string tied to the middle and beads at either end. When you shake it the beads hit the drum part and make the sound.

They bathed at four in the morning, spent an hour praying, and now they're ready to talk world peace to all and sundry. One rings a bell, then the dumroo, which is attached halfway down the trishul. His colleague then blows on the conch and they begin chanting "Ganga, Ganga."

Raja, trying to be helpful, asks them about Makar Sankranti. One of them starts telling the story rather well. His colleague interrupts and goes off on a tangent about a river called Ulta Ganga (which exists in West Bengal): "Normally the Ganga flows from west to east. But here on this day it is flowing the other way. It is Ulta Ganga. It flows the other way and at night." (The most extraordinary stories get told here.) They start arguing — verbally, then physically.

"I'm telling him about Makar Sankranti. I won't move. I've planted my flag here..."

"I'll cut off your..."

"What do mean? You'll cut off my..."

A policeman appears from nowhere, tells them to leave. "Come on you two, break it up. Or off to the thana."

Raja doesn't bathe or go into mandirs. He's been depressed much of this trip. But he's visibly energized today: "I just can't believe such a big bath. Amazing. People are crazy or we are crazy."

~

Seeing the Ganga at Ganga Sagar has filled me with hope. I have often felt fearful of Ganga's future during this yatra. Can she survive Tehri, toxic chemical dumping and Farakka, the demands of a rapidly developing India? At Ganga Sagar, with its air of jubilation, the river feels immortal and invincible. But is she really immortal?

Can Ganga die? The simple answer is yes, the river can dry up in certain places in the reaches between Haridwar and Allahabad for a few very simple reasons. Too much water is being taken out for irrigation or impounded behind dams huge and small to generate electricity for an economy thirsty for electricity (the problem can only get much, much worse as India urbanizes; a city dweller uses ten times as much water as a villager) and though the groundwater does get substantially recharged from runoff from the Shivalik hills there simply is not enough water coming in to Ganga to meet all the demands made on her. The Ramganga near Kannauj is the only substantial river in this whole eight hundred kilometer stretch. And it's not enough. This is a simple case of supply and demand, and supply is inadequate.

Indeed, the more I think about the pressures on Ganga the more I'm convinced we may also be doing everyone a grave disservice (and everyone means Indians and non-Indians) by only talking about the river in terms of either mythology or environmentalism. There's a word missing — economics.

If you think of the river as an economic resource, as a raw material then it should become possible to come up with solutions that can save this resource for future generations. People need water and they need things that are derived (such as electricity) from water. But there's nothing to say electricity can't be generated from other sources. It would be nice to save Ganga's environmental ecology. But all the time we should have been thinking of the role Ganga plays in economic life. After all, that's really why her environment is under such threat. Indians are starting to ask too much of this river. She needs time to recover before it's too late.

I'd also re-frame the pollution question. I'm not convinced Ganga will die from pollution. Yes, pollution from the tanneries in Kanpur is bad, very bad. But pollution can be mitigated by human agency. Supply can't. More water would substantially lessen the pollution problem by diluting the concentration of pollutants and flushing them away to quieter areas where they deteriorate in tranquil neglect. (But not toxic heavy metals. Only total prohibition can prevent them.) I'm not being complacent, just trying to be realistic. I have many friends and colleagues who'll be up in arms and probably never talk to me again because I appear to be minimizing the dangers of pollution. I'm simply saying Indians can do something about controlling what goes into the river, but they can't control how much water is in there to start with.

Yes, I know there's always river-linking. But does anyone seriously think that this will ever come to pass? There are basic hydrological and geographical reasons why you can't link river basins. Another idea, building giant dams in the Nepalese Himalayas isn't the answer either. What do you do about the silt washed down by fierce monsoon rains? Reservoirs have to be at rock bottom before the monsoon, which means they don't have enough water to generate electricity or irrigate fields at precisely the period of year when both are in short supply. Other ideas such as storing water in vast underground aquifers such as the Bhabar in the Shivaliks are too futuristic to be taken seriously. No, if Ganga is not to dry up in stretches less water has to be taken out, and what water there is needs to be stored better in small check dams, then used in micro-hydro electric schemes. Or farmers have to find more profitable and less thirsty crops. Small is still beautiful, no matter how many times you have to repeat it.

Will this change the status of the goddess? Can Goddess Ganga survive if the river dries up? Will rituals wither away?

The last is probably the easiest to answer. No. Rituals evolve, they're always evolving. Millions no longer bathe every morning in Ganga, not just because it may be polluted but because they no longer have the leisure to do so. Whether you agree or not, the pace of life even in India is accelerating. I know many city-dwellers who bathe at home, not in Ganga: they simply add a few drops of Ganga jal to their tap water. That's not going to change. For birth and death ceremonies much the same thing: add a few drops of Ganga jal. Those who believe in the water's medicinal powers will continue to drink it.

But can Goddess Ganga retain her place in people's hearts and cosmos if the river shrivels up in places? I see no reason why not. After all, the river is simply the goddess in liquid form. The important thing is she is still a generous goddess. If people no longer bathe every morning she may become less immediate in people's daily lives, but she won't die as a goddess. It's romantic to link the possible disappearance of the susu — Ganga's mount, to the disappearance of the river. But how many people north of Varanasi have even seen a susu? It's in their imagination: actually seeing it won't diminish the role and place of Ganga in their hearts.

Indians I respect argue that Ganga has to be protected because, "it gives life so I must protect it. I cannot protect something unless I respect it, therefore it is sacred." Not because it's a goddess, but in order to protect Indian society and civilization.

My friend Sharada Nayak in Delhi goes further: "Sacred means giving importance to the natural life-giving substance, to the function. For instance I gaze on a tree that is held to be sacred: that doesn't mean that I am worshipping the tree. I am emphasizing the importance of the tree. Sacred therefore means to me respect for nature.

"I am not that religious. But I go all the time to worship Ganga as the goddess. To me Ganga is sacred, in the sense that life comes from the land. And anything that happens to nature affects my living and therefore is sacred. It is my relationship with a life-giving force. I think all the temples along Ganga reaffirm the sacredness of our natural heritage. What would happen if all the snows of the Himalayas melt because of global warming and the rivers cease to flow? The Tehri Dam therefore hurts me personally."

I agree with Sharada that taking care of Ganga should be reframed as an anguished plea in favour of sustained development, for trying to live in harmony with the environment. If Indians allow Ganga the river to be raped and pillaged, it means they are destroying their own habitat, their own birthright. Ganga is therefore a symbol of that birthright, a metaphor for India's future.

"If ecology and mythology were linked this could be very powerful," Sharada continues, "because the myth grew out of sustaining the land and your dependence on it. This is an agricultural country. We are very much dependent on the land. The ecology of the land is woven into our basic mythology."

Mythology and ecology hand-in-hand. Could belief in a sacred Ganga translate into respect for nature, and therefore for sustainable development? You cannot stop development. India needs the energy, the land needs irrigation. But you can respect it. An awful lot of this debate about Ganga anyway is probably not really about mythology at all. It's basically people fighting over an economic resource. Ganga is indeed a symbol in the debate of rape versus respect of nature, about the misuse of resources, the loss of respect for the river as life-giver, of its irreparable effect on the lives of people. Destroy Ganga and you will therefore destroy the essence of India.

The greatest danger to the river comes from the goddess herself. I believe that the faith in the ability of goddess Ganga to cure herself leads to avoiding the life and death issues the river faces.

I think the other threat to the goddess may be less from within India than from outside India. I worry that India may be changing too fast. Like many others I worry that these changes may not take into account the delicate fabric of traditional and rural India.

I used to think none of this would really matter. India has suffered many physical and cultural invasions down through the centuries — Aryans, Moghuls, British — and in each case bent and absorbed them, "Indianizing" them. It's a comforting scenario, part and parcel of the Indian concept of circular time. But what if it doesn't work this time? There's no law of physics that states time must always be circular, that it can never experience a linear deviation. Can one go too far, beyond the point of no return? Can the river Ganga effectively die?

How to convince those who worship the goddess that the physical deterioration of the river can affect her essence?

It may be possible, but it will require ordinary Indians to make that link, not just the members of its elite or outsiders.

~

Tivari returns from bathing. If Sagar's sons can get back their lives then we all can. Here on the beach at 6:30 in the morning on Makar Sankranti, we look back at our many months spent together on Ganga. We're nearing the end of this yatra down Ganga. But I think both of us also realize this could also be the swan song of a working relationship that's lasted now twenty years.

"This is the end of our yatra," I say.

"Yes this is the end." He looks suddenly solemn, almost sad.

I ask Bijoy which has been the single most memorable occasion on this trip. He thinks a few minutes, lists all the tirthas he bathed at.

"Which one? Actually each place has its own significance. But the most important was Prayag. This is also a very important and historical tirtha. That's why people come, because they believe that their souls will be freed if they have a bath here."

Shivering, Bijoy looks seriously at me:"Chief, what a great journey we have made."

Indeed we have. It's hard not to think in clichés. This really is an extraordinary mass of humanity: the whole of India really does seem to be here. Fitting that our yatra down Ganga should end here on this day. I really wouldn't have missed this for the world.

We have to pack up and get back to the ferry, the mainland and Kolkata. Slowly and reluctantly I move away back to the dry sand. I cross the path of a man rattling off the names of gods — great and small. The mobile phone rings.

"Hello. Who is it?"

"It's Martine, your wife. Calling from America. Remember me? I need to check something on your Visa bill."

"Can you phone back later?" I tell her. "It's Makar Sankranti. I need a few moments alone. It's the end of a wonderful journey."

*****

Glossary

aarti (arthi)	a small lamp which is fueled by oil or clarified butter (ghee) and used as part of the pooja ceremony. Also refers to the pooja ceremony itself and is characterized by the circling of oil lamps before the divine image.
acharya	spiritual guide, learned man
adivasi	Indian tribal or aboriginal
aerobic	requiring oxygen
Agni	the Vedic fire god; also the fire itself
ahimsa	the refusal to hurt or kill others, often associated with Jainism
AIWPS	Advanced Integrated Wastewater Pond Systems
Akbar	late sixteenth century emperor of the Mughal dynasty
akhara	wrestling ground
Akshay Tritiya	another name for Ganga Dussehra
aloo	potato
amrit	nectar
anaerobic	not requiring oxygen
alpana	decorative floor designs made from rice paste and created for special occasions
andolan	mass movement
ashram	religious retreat, often in forests, dwelling places of sages, yogis and their students
Ashwamedh yagna	the Vedic horse-sacrifice, usually performed at consecration of a king
Asi	the stream that borders Varanasi at its south and enters Ganga at Asi Ghat
asthis	ashes
asuras	demons
asvaccha	clean
atman	the essence or soul
atta	flour
avatar	incarnation, another form of

ayurveda	traditional form of herbal medicine
bacteria	a single cell life form that can reproduce and live in both aerobic and anaerobic conditions
bacteriophage	a micro-virus
Badrinath	a place of pilgrimage in the Himalayas
bauls	mystic wandering musicians from West Bengal, often dressed in distinctive multicolored clothes
Bhagavad Gita	the "song of the lord," from the sixth book in the *Mahabharata*. Arjun laments he must fight his friends; Krishna convinces him that battle is an act of devotion and duty.
Bhai dooj	day after Divali
bhajan	popular religious hymn, usually about Ram and Sita or Krishna and Radha.
bhakti	the heart's devotion and love towards God
bharal	blue mountain sheep
Bharat	the ancient name for India
bhatiali	folk songs sung by boatmen in Bengal
bidi	hand-rolled cigarette made from bidi leaves
biryani	a dish of rice, saffron, and (usually) marinated lamb
BOD	Biological Oxygen Demand
bodhisattva	Buddhist term referring to someone who has attained enlightenment but postpones nirvana to help others in the process
Brahma	the creator god of the universe: one of the great trinity along with Shiva and Vishnu
Brahman	the Absolute, the ultimate God, the one reality, the essence of life, the reality which is source of all being and knowing
Brahmapurana	a very old Vedic account of a rivalry between two families. It lists thirteen actions that one should not perform near Ganga.
brahmin	a member of the priestly class, one of Hinduism's four varnas or castes
bustee	a small poor village
caste	a Portuguese term for group, race or kind of people (in Hindi jati). Castes are organized from the most ritually pure to those considered polluted. Traditional society is also divided into classes or varnas based on occupation or skin

	color.
Centre	political shorthand for government in Delhi
CETP	Combined Effluent Treatment Plant
chaan	cowshed, seasonal shelter made of thatch
chappal	sandal
chappati	unleavened wholewheat flatbread
char	sandbar
charpoy	string cot
chatti	shelter or stop along a pilgrimage route
chawal	rice
cholera	(*Vibrio cholera*) infectious disease caused by bacterial infection of intestines, characterized by severe vomiting and diarrhoea, leading to dehydration, often death
choola	hearth
chowkidar	night watchman
crore	ten million
cusecs	units measuring flow in cubic feet per second, ft^3/sec. An old British unit, it is still used in India, now replaced by cumecs (m^3/sec), the metric adaptation of cusecs.
dacoit	bandit
dal	lentils
dalit	untouchable
damaum	small tambourine-like drum
darsan	to be in the presence of or to view the deity: seeing the divine image is the single most common and significant element of Hindu worship
Dasasvamedha	a tirtha and one of most famous ghats in Varanasi
Dussehra	festival celebrating the final victory of Lord Rama over the demon king Ravanna, in other words the triumph of good over evil (in Bengal it marks the climax of Durga Pooja)
deva, devi	god, goddess (also refers to Great Goddess called Devi or Mahadevi)
Dev Bhoomi	abode of the gods
dhama	the abode or dwelling of god
Dhanuk	another name for dhoms in Uttar Pradesh
dharma	moral and religious duty of individual: also the special duties and obligations to be performed accordingly to carefully formulated codes of

	behavior and according to one's position in life
dharamshala	rest house for pilgrims
dhobi	a sub-caste whose occupation is usually laundering
dhol	two-sided drum (esp in West Bengal)
dhom	untouchable who carries out cremations
dhoti	a piece of cloth worn by men and tied either in the form of pants or worn as a wraparound
distributary	a river that flows out of a main river down to the sea. A tributary is a river that flows into a main river.
Diwali	also Divali and Deepavali. A five day Hindu festival, often referred to as the Festival of Lights, that celebrates the end of one year and the start of the new year in the lunar calendar. The day after Divali is called Bhai dooj.
DO	Dissolved Oxygen
dumroo	small drum
Durga	same as Kali, a manifestation of Parvati or Devi, very popular in Bengal
Durga Puja	a Hindu festival in honor of Durga symbolizing the triumph of good over evil, celebrated for ten days
effluent	waste
Ganesha	the elephant-headed son of Shiva and Parvati, to be honored at the beginning of any venture
gand, gandagi	waste matter
gandhak	sulphur
Ganga Dusshehra	installation of Ganga in her temple in Gangotri
Ganga jal	water from Ganga
Ganga Lahiri	song of Ganga written by Jagannathan in seventeenth century
ganja	hashish
Gauri	another name for Parvati, Siva's wife
gaushala	stable for cows
Gaya	about 100 km south of Patna, not to be confused with nearby Bodhgaya, a major Buddhist pilgrimage center. Gaya is considered to be one of the three most sacred places in Hinduism — the sangam and Varanasi are the others. Vishnu gave Gaya the power to absolve sinners and his

footprint is believed to lie inside the temple.

ghat	steps leading down to a river
ghee	clarified butter
Godavari	one of India's seven sacred rivers in the Deccan in central India
goonda	thug
Gupta	great north Indian empire from fourth-sixth centuries AD
guru	teacher or spiritual guide
gurudakshina	symbolic gift such as a small sum of money or sweets or flowers, which a student gives to a guru to acknowledge the pricelessness of learning
gurudwara	Sikh temple
Hanuman	monkey god, famous as faithful servant of Ram, and helped him free Sita from captivity
harijan	untouchable, literally "child of god"
Harishchandra	legendary king famous for his righteousness, ghat in Varanasi named after him
havan mundan	head-shaving ceremony
Hexavalent Chromium	Cr(VI), highly toxic form of chromiun produced in tanning leather
High Command	slang/shorthand for final authority in an organization
hilsa	Bengali fish
hookah	water pipe
hydrology	science dealing with water on or under earth's surface and in its atmosphere
Indra	king of the gods, the Vedic warrior god, wielder of thunderbolts
Jagannath	"lord of the universe"— Jagannathan is a seventeenth century poet, author of the *Ganga Lahiri* (song of the Ganges)
jal	water
jati	caste or sub-caste. Marriage partners are usually chosen from the same jati. There are thousands of jati. Local customs and practices frequently determine the precise relationship of one jati to another.
jhoola	swing
Kabir	famous fifteenth- to sixteenth-century Varanasi

	poet who taught a synthesis of Hinduism and Islam
karamandal	gourd water pot in which Ganga was born (according to some legends)
kajal	black eye-liner
Kala-azar	subtropical disease carried by sand flies causing emaciation, enlargement of the spleen and liver and fever
Kali	the Mother Goddess, also wife of Shiva and malevolent form of Durga.
Kali Yuga	fourth "age" of the world. The first is krita — the perfect age of the beginnings of time; the last is kali — the age of strife, degeneracy, and immorality.
Kar sevak	volunteer
karma	the sum total of the ethical consequences of one's thoughts and actions, which determine a person's destiny in his or her existence
Kartik	the eighth month in the Hindu lunar calendar
Kashi	beloved name for Banaras or Varanasi, literally "city of light"
kavar	pilgrims who carry Ganga water on foot
khadi	handloom cloth, usually cotton
kheer	rice pudding
kingfisher	(*Alcedo atthis*) small bird with long beak and brilliant blue and orange plumage, feeding on fish that it captures by diving
Krishna	an avatar or form of Vishnu, but also worshipped in own right, as the playful lover of milkmaids (and Radha) in his native homeland near Mathura
kumbha	a round water pot
Kumbh Mela	a great religious fair held once every twelve years at Prayag or Allahabad. There are four different kumbhs: Prayag (Allahabad), Haridwar, Nasik, and Ujjain. The annual Magh kumbh is held in Allahabad during the month of Magha (January-February), the Ardh Kumbha mela every sixth year in one of four sites where nectar was spilled during a cosmic struggle; the Purna every twelfth year, and the Maha kumbh every twelve Purnas or 144 years. The last Maha was held in 2001.
kund	pool, usually sacred for bathing
kurta	long-sleeved tunic worn by men
Kurukshetra	site of great war described in the *Mahabharata*

lakh	one hundred thousand
Laxman	brother of Ram, who accompanied him into exile to seek Sita
Lakshmi	goddess of wealth
langar	communal kitchen
lingam	stone, phallic representation of Shiva
maala	garland
Mahabharata	huge epic body of stories, myths, and folk tales based on legends of Vedic gods and the struggle between two families for the possession of northern India
mahant	a religious superior
mahseer	freshwater fish (*barbus tor)* found in northern plains and in the Himalayas
Makar Sankranti	the day in the solar calendar when the sun moves from the Tropic of Cancer to the Tropic of Capricorn, marks the end of the winter solstice
mali	gardener
Mandakini	a Himalayan river that rises near Kedarnath, the abode of Shiva, also name of a lake in Kashi, named for Ganga
mandala	circular diagram which is also a schematic map of sacred universe in paintings and temples
Manikarnika	one of two cremation ghats at Varanasi
mantra	sacred phrase or chant
mandir	temple
masala	in Indian cooking masala refers to a mixture of spices used in a specific dish. In general usage it simply means a mixture, a hodge podge.
Mathura	one of India's seven sacred cities, located on Yamuna river in northern India and birthplace of Krishna
maya	illusion
mela	fair, especially religious festival to which people come long distances on pilgrimage
moksha	release from the cycle of rebirth, therefore final liberation
mull maas	thirteenth month in Hindu lunar calendar that occurs every third year
murti	form or likeness

mukti	freedom, release from
nadi	river
naga	ancient serpent deities, today refers to ascetics who are naked and keep warm by smearing their bodies in ashes
nala (nallah, nullah)	wastewater drain
narayan	god
Nataraj	another name for Shiva, Nataraj is the lord of dancers who eternally dances in the circle of fire and thus maintains the rhythm of the world
neem	(*Azadirachta indica*), a tree valued for its leaves and bitter bark which are used medicinally, and for oils from which a soap is made
Nirvana	the highest spiritual goal, freedom from all earthly attachments and desires
nitya puja	daily bathing ritual especially in Ganga at Varanasi
Om (Aum)	the sacred syllable, the supreme mantra — the seed or source of all wisdom
pakka	neat, accurate
pakoras	any vegetable fried in batter
paan	betel nut for chewing
paap	past sins
Panchganga	a ghat and tirtha in Varanasi; literally means "the five Gangas"
Panchkrosi	a circular pilgrimage route round Varanasi, which takes five days to complete
Panchatirtha	five tirtha pilgrimage in Varanasi, including Asi, Dashashvamedha, Adi Keshava, Panchganga, and Manikarnika ghats
panchayat	an elected Indian village council
panda	slang for purohit (see below)
pandit	a learned person
paratha	fried flatbread usually stuffed with vegetables
Pandavas	the five brothers whose struggle with their cousins forms the subject of the *Mahabharata*
parikrama	circular journey around a place: you can make a parikrama of a building, a town or Ganga (up and down its entire length)
Parvati	"daughter of the mountain," wife of Siva
pathogen	a micro-organism that causes disease

phool	ash and unburned bits of bones left after cremation, colloquially called flowers
pinda daan	offering of the ashes and bones after cremation
pradusan	pollution
prasad	food first offered to a deity then, once consecrated, returned to the devotee
prayag	a confluence and place of sacrifice; also a famous tirtha at the confluence of Ganga, Yamuna, and mythical Saraswati rivers at Allahabad
puja (pooja)	ritual worship
pujari	a brahmin priest responsible for worship in a temple
pradhan	headman
Purana	one of the collections of "ancient stories" that preserve traditions of myth, legend and rite
purnima	the full moon day of the Hindu lunar calendar, hence Kartik purnima — the purnima in the month of kartik
purohit	brahmin who serves as a pilgrim priest
PWD	Public Works Department
Radha	a shepherdess who was the great lover of Krishna
rakshas	demon
Rama	virtuous king and hero of the epic *Ramayana* (Rama is said to embody the ideals by which a man, warrior, and king must live), also an avatar of Vishnu
Ramayana	epic poem originally written over 3,000 years ago in Sanskrit by Valmiki, subsequently retold in Hindi by Tulsi Das in Varanasi, telling the story of Ram, prince and later king of Ayodhya
ran singhar	serpent-shaped hunting horn
rickshaw wallah	a man who pulls a rickshaw
Rig Veda	ancient Hindu religious text consisting of 1028 hymns to various gods probably composed between 1500 and 900 BC
rishi	monk, sage
roti	wholewheat flatbread fried in oil
Rudra	Vedic god
sabji	vegetable
sadhu	holy man, ascetic, person who has renounced world

salwar kameez	loose pantaloons and long shirt (worn by women)
samosa	fried pastry with savory filling
samsara	passage, never-ending cycle of birth, death, and rebirth
sanatana dharma	eternal religion, eternal truth
sangam	confluence of rivers
sankalpa	a vow of intent taken before any ritualistic activity
sant	a holy man
sanyas	renunciation of the material world
sanyasi	someone who has left behind worldly attachments for a life of contemplation and asceticism
sari	garment worn by women, made of unstitched fabric
Sarnath	site just north of Varanasi where the Buddha began his teaching career
Sati	a wife of Shiva who burned herself to death because of her father's insult to Shiva (hence, the "good wife" who dies on her husband's funeral pyre), commonly used as noun to refer to self-immolation, practice banned by the British in early nineteenth century
Shakti	power, creative energy, usually related to the goddess
Shankacharya	respected Hindu religious leader
shastra	sacred text
Shigella	bacteria that cause intestinal diseases, especially dysentery
Shitala	goddess of smallpox
shraddha	rites for the dead performed after cremation to nourish the deceased for passage to the world of the ancestors
shudra	the lowest of the four castes, usually servants
sindur	powder made from red lead and used for anointing images of local deities; also used by women in the central parting of their hair
Sita	the beautiful, chaste, and faithful wife of Ram, kidnapped by Ravana and rescued from Lanka by Ram with help of Hanuman
Shiva	one of the great trinity of Hindu gods, along with Vishnu and Brahma (also Siva or Shiv). Shiva is the god of destruction. But once something has been destroyed it can then be created again. So

Shiva is also considered the god of re-creation. Along with Vishnu believed responsible for bringing Ganga down to this earth. His followers are called Shaivites.

sloka	a verse from the Vedas or any other poetic utterance or metric phrase that contains a single thought
snan	ritual bathing
STP	Sewage Treatment Plant
stupa	Buddhist monument, shaped like a dome, to honor earthly remains of the Buddha
suddha	pure
susu	Gangetic dolphin
tantra	esoteric religious movement, emphasizing union of opposites, usually symbolized by male and female
tapas	heat
tapasya	meditation
tirtha	ford, crossing, sacred place of pilgrimage
tirthayatra	the journey (yatra) to a sacred place; a pilgrimage
thali	tray
tahr	mountain goat
tilak	mark on forehead to signify completion of worship
trishul	trident, carried by devotees of Shiva
triveni	meeting of three rivers
tulsi	basil plant sacred to Vishnu (not sweet like European basil)
Tulsi Das	late sixteenth century poet, author of Hindi interpretation of the *Ramayana*, known as *Ramcharitmanas*
UASB	Upflow Anaerobic Sludge Blanket
Upanishads	sacred texts from which Hindu philosophy derives; Hindu scriptures that represent early Hindu beliefs about the soul and are part of the Vedas
vaviyas	traditional Bengali folk song
varna	there are four varnas or classes of Hindu society — brahmin, kshatriya, vaishya, shudra — and thousands of jati or subcastes
Vedas	the Vedas are the oldest Hindu scriptures. They appear in four formats — Samhita (prayers and

hymns), Brahmanas (prose explanations of sacrifice), Aranyakas (instructions for meditation), and the Upanishads. Most important is the Rig Veda.

virus	a parasite that doesn't breathe move or grow; it can only reproduce in a host cell and in the process kills its host.
visaryana	submersion of the ashes of a departed relative
Vishnu	one of the trinity of supreme gods; the epitome of goodness and mercy and maintains the order of the universe: followers called Vaishnavites
vrata	vow, religious observances done in fulfilment of a vow
wallah	someone who sells
yagna	fire
yaksha	animist deities in pre-Hindu India, usually associated with nature and animals
yatra	pilgrimage
yatri	pilgrim
yoni	female sexual organ
Yuga	the ages of the Hindu world — Krita, Treta, Dvapara, and Kali. Since recorded time man has always been living in the fourth age — the Kali Yuga — the age of degeneracy and disaster.
zamindar	landowner

Bibliography

Abbasi, S.A.
> *Water Quality, Sampling and Analysis*. New Delhi: Discovery Publishing House. 1998.

Adel, M. M.
> "Effect on Water Resources from Upstream Water Diversion in the Ganges Basin," *Journal of Environmental Quality*. 30 no 2, (2001): 356-368.

Adhikarni, K.D. et al (eds)
> *Cooperation on Eastern Himalayan Rivers: Opportunities and Challenges*. New Delhi: Konark Publishers Pvt. Ltd. 2000.

Agarwal, P.K.
> *Environment Protection and Pollution in the Ganga*. New Delhi: MD Publications Pvt. Ltd. 1994.

Ahmed, Sarah.
> "Whose Concept of Participation? State-Society Dynamics in the Cleaning of the Ganges at Varanasi". *Water and the Quest for Sustainable Development in the Ganges Valley*. London, New York: Mansell. 1995. 141-162.

Ahmad, Q.K. et al (eds).
> *Converting Water into Wealth: Regional Cooperation in Harnessing the Eastern Himalayan Rivers*. Dhaka: Academic Publishers. 1994.

> *Perspectives on Flood 1998*. Dhaka: The University Press Ltd. 2000.

> *Ganges-Brahmaputra-Meghna Region: A Framework for Sustainable Development*. Dhaka: The University Press Ltd. 2001.

Aitken, Bill.
> *Seven Sacred Rivers*. New Delhi: Penguin Books India. 1992.

Ali, Mir M. et al (eds).
> *Bangladesh Floods: Views from Home and Abroad*. Dhaka: The University Press Ltd. 1998.

Ali. M.Y.
> "Openwater Fisheries and Environmental Change." *Environmental Aspects of Surface Water Systems of Bangladesh*. Eds. A.A. Rahman, S. Huq and G.R. Conway. Dhaka: University Press Ltd 1990. 145-165.

Alley, Kelly D.
> "Idioms of Degeneracy: Assessing Ganga's Purity and Pollution." *Purifying the Earthly Body of God - Religion and Ecology in Hindu India*. Ed. Lance E. Nelson. New York: Suny. 1998. 297-330.

> "Urban Institutions at the Crossroads: Judicial Activism and Pollution Prevention in Kanpur." *Urban Anthropology*. 25 (4), 1996. 352-383.

> "Ganga and Gandagi: Interpretations of Pollution and Waste in Benares." *Ethnology*. 33. 1994. 465-88.

> *On the Banks of the Ganga: When Wastewater Meets a Sacred River*. Ann Arbor: University of Michigan Press. 2003.

Alter, Stephen.
> *Sacred Waters: A Pilgrimage Up the Ganges River to the Source of Hindu Culture*. New York, San Diego, London: Harcourt. 2002.

Ameer, K.M.
> *Rain and River*. Dhaka: Nabeela Books. 1991.

Anderson J.
> *Anatomical and Zoological Researches: Comprising an account of zoological results of two expeditions to western Yunnan in 1868 and 1875; and a monograph of the two cretacena gera Platasista and Orcella*. London: B. Quaritch. 1878.

Archer, Mildred.
> *Early Views of India - The Picturesque Journeys of Thomas and William Daniell 1786-1794*. London: Thames & Hudson. 1980.

Bandopadhyaya, Manik.
 Padma River Boatman. Australia: Queensland University Press.
 1973.

Banerjee, Brojendra Nath.
 Can the Ganga Be Cleaned? New Delhi: B.R.Publishing
 Corporation. 1989.

Banerjee, Manisha.
 "A Report on the Impact of Farakka on the Human Fabric. (A
 Study of the Upstream and Downstream Areas of Farakka
 Barrage). A Submission to World Commission on Dams. A
 Thematic Review: Flood Control Options." (2001) www.irn.org/
 programs/reviews/submissions/SANDRP.Farakka.html.

Barman, Advaita Malla.
 A River Called Titash. London & Delhi: Penguin. 1992.

Basham, A.L.
 The Wonder That Was India. London: Sidgwick & Jackson. 1954.

Bhattacharya, Deben, Editor and Translator.
 The Mirror of the Sky: Songs of the Bauls from Bengal. Hohn
 Press, London: 1999.

Bernstein, Henry T.
 *Steamboats on the Ganges: An Exploration in the History of
 India's Modernization Through Science and Technology.*
 Hyderabad: Orient Longman. 1987.

Bertocci, Peter.
 "Notes Towards an Ethno-sociology of the Bengal Sundarbans."
 From a workshop: The Commons in South Asia: Societal
 Pressures and Environmental Integrity in the Sundarbans, held
 at the S. Dillon Ripley Center, Smithsonian Institution,
 Washington, D.C. November 20-21, 1987.

Berwick, Dennison.
 A Walk Along the Ganges. UK, Dorset: Javelin. 1986.

Bhargava D.S.
 "Psuedoism in Environmental Education." *Journal of the IPHE,*

India. 4, 1999, 38-42.

"Sacred but Unclean." *Asia Water Environment*. Water Environment Federation. 1998. 13-16.

"Foolproof Pollution Control of Indian Rivers." *Indian Journal of Engineering and Materials Sciences*. 5, 1998. 162-166.

"River BOD Prediction Under Non-Point Discharge Conditions." *Indian Journal of Engineering and Materials Sciences*. 1, 1994. 35-40.

"Why the Ganga Could Not Be Cleaned." *Environmental Conservation*. 19. 1992. 170-172.

"Nature and the Ganga." *Environmental Conservation*. 14 (4). 1987. 307-318.

"DO SAG Model for Extremely Fast River Purification." *Journal of Environmental Engineering*. 112 (3). 1986. 572-585.

"Expression for Drinking Water Supply Standards." *Journal of Environmental Engineering*. 111 (3). 1985. 304-316.

"Most Rapid BOD Assimilation in Ganga and Yamuna Rivers." *Journal of Environmental Engineering*. 109 (1). 1983. 174-188.

"Use of a Water Quality Index for River Classification and Zoning of Ganga River." *Environmental Pollution Series B*. 6. 1983. 1-17.

Bhaskar, Roy.
  A Realist Theory of Science. London and New York: Verso. 1997. (1975).

Bolstad, Trygve & Jansen, Eric G.
  Sailing Against the Wind - Boats and Boatmen of Bangladesh. Dhaka: The University Press. 1992.

Brown, Joyce.
  "A Memoir of Colonel Sir Probey Cautley, F.R.S., 1802-1871

Engineer and Palaeontologist." *Notes and Records of the Royal Society of London*. Vol. 34. 1979-80. 185-225.

Centre for Science and Environment Indo Gangetic Links.
A Directory of Environmental Experts in the Indo Gangetic Plains. New Delhi. 2000.

Chakrabarti, Dilip K.
The Archaeology of Ancient Indian Cities. Calcutta, Chennai, Mumbai: Oxford University Press India. 1997.

Chapple, Christopher Key & Tucker, Mary Evelyn (Eds).
Hinduism and Ecology - The Earth, Sky and Water. Cambridge: Harvard University Press, MA. 2000.

Chapman, Graham P.
"'Other' Cultures, 'Other' Environments and the Mass Media." *The Daily Globe: Environmental Change, The Public and the Media*. Joe Smith (ed.) London: Earthscan. 2000. 127-150.

"The Ganges and Brahmaputra Basins." *Water and the Quest for Sustainable Development in the Ganges Valley*. London, New York: Mansell Publishers. 1995. 3-24.

"Flood Mitigation in West Bengal." *Dept of International Development*. R8092 (London): 2002.

Chapman, Graham P. & Rudra, Kalyan.
"Society and Water: Bengal's Millennium Flood". *Transactions*. Institute of British Geographers and Geography Journal (forthcoming)

Chapman, Graham P, Keval Kumar, Caroline Fraser and Ivor Gaber.
Environmentalism and the Mass Media: The North-South Divide. London: Routledge. 1997.

Chaudhari, Nirad C.
The Autobiography of an Unknown Indian. Reading, MA: Addison-Wesley Publishing Company, Inc. 1989.

Choudhary, UK.
The Living Similarity between the Ganga and the Human Body.

Varanasi: The Ganga Lab oratory. 2003.

Choudhury, Anyradha Roma.
"Attitudes to Nature." *Themes and Issues in Hinduism*. Ed. Paul Bowen. London and Herndon, VA: Cassel. 1998.

Central Board for the Prevention and Control of Water Pollution.
(CBPCWP) *Basin Sub-basin Inventory of Water Pollution: The Ganga Basin Part II*. Ministry of Environment and Forests, Government of India. 1984.

Central Pollution Control Board.
An Inventory of Major Polluting Industries in the Ganga Basin and Their Pollution Control Status. Ministry of Environment and Forests, Government of India. New Delhi, 1995.

Status and Trend of Water Quality of River Ganga (1983-1989). Ministry of Environment and Forests, Government of India. New Delhi, (no year of publication given).

Water Quality Status and Statistics (1988-1989). Ministry of Environment and Forests, Government of India. New Delhi, 1990/91.

Water Quality Status and Statistics (1993-1994). Ministry of Environment and Forests, Government of India. New Delhi, 1996.

Water Quality Status and Statistics (1996-1997). Ministry of Environment and Forests, Government of India. New Delhi, 1999.

Central Water Commission/ River Data Directorate.
Water Quality Studies Ganga System Status Report. Government of India. New Delhi. 1992.

Cole, W. Owen with Peggy Morgan.
Six Religions in the Twentieth Century. Cheltenham: Stanley Thornes (Publishers) Ltd. 1984.

Crow, Ben and and Nirvikar Singh.
"Impediments and Innovation in International Rivers: the waters

of South Asia." *World Development*. 28:11. 2000. 1907 - 1925.

Crow, Ben with Alan Lindhurst and David Wilson.
Sharing the Ganges: The Politics and Technology of River Development. New Delhi, Thousand Oaks, London: Sage Publications. 1995.

Cumming, David.
The Ganges Delta and its People. East Sussex: Wayland. 1994.

Daniell, Thomas & William.
Oriental Scenery: One hundred and Fifty Views of the Architecture, Antitiquities and Landscape Scenery of Hondoostan. London: Logman, Hurst, Rees, Orme and Brown. 1812-1816.

Darian, Steven G.
The Ganges in Myth and History. Honolulu: The University Press of Hawaii. 1978.

Darian, Steven G.
A Ganges of the Mind - A Journey on the River of Dreams. Delhi: Ratna Sagar Publishers. 1988.

Das, N.K. and R.K. Sinha.
"Pollution Status of River Ganga at Patna (Bihar), India." *Journal of Freshwater Biology*. 6(2). 1994. 159-164.

"Assessment of water quality of the Ganga river, Bihar, India." *Environment and Ecology* 11 (4). 1993. 829-832.

Dasa, Jaya Vijaya.
Our Merciful Mother Ganga. New Delhi: Padayatra Press. 2000.

Dasgupta, Subhayu.
Hindu Ethos and the Challenge of Change. New Delhi: Arnold-Heinemann. 1977.

Davis, Joel.
Alternate Realities: How Science Shapes Our Vision of the World. New York, London: Plenum Press. 1997.

Dey, Kumar Tapan.
Sundarban at a Glance. Deputy Conservator of Forests, Divisional

forest Office, Sundarban Division, Khulna. (one copy), November 2000.

Dharwadker, Vinay & Ramanujan, AK (eds).
The Oxford Anthology of Modern Indian Poetry. Delhi: Oxford University Press. 1994

Dimock, Edward C., Jr., Editor.
The Thief of Love: Bengali Tales from Court and Village. Chicago: The University of Chicago Press. 1963.

Dhole, V.
"Environmentalism and the Mass Media in India: Diffusing North-South Divides." Paper presented to the workshop for International Communication and Environmentalism, Lonavala, India, 1997.

Doniger, Wendy, Translator.
Hindu Myths. New York: Penguin. 1984.

Dutta, Krishna and Robinson, Andrew (eds),
Selected Letters of Rabindranath Tagore. Cambridge, UK: Cambridge University Press. 1997

Rabindranath Tagore - The Myriad-Minded Man. London: Bloomsbury. 1995.

Dutta, Krishna and Robinson, Andrew, Translators.
Glimpses of Bengal. London: MacMillan. 1991.

Dutta, Krishna and Lago, Mary, Translators.
Rabindranath Tagore - Selected Short Stories. London: MacMillan. 1991.

Dwivedi, O.P.
"Editor's Introduction: Administrative Heritage, Morality and Challenges in the Sub-Continent Since the British Raj." *Public Administration and Development*. Vol. 9, 1989, 245-252.

Eaton, Richard M.
The Rise of Islam and the Bengal Frontier 1204-1760. Berkeley, Los Angeles, London: University of California Press. 1996.

Eck, Diana.
Banaras City of Light. New York: Knopf. 1982, 1999.

Darsan: Seeing the Divine Image in India. Pennsylvania: Amina Books. 1981.

EGIS.
Environmental and Social Impact Assessment of Khulna-Jessore Drainage Rehabilitation Project. Ministry of Water Resources, Government of Bangladesh, September 1998.

Environment Baseline of Gorai River Restoration Project. Ministry of Water Resources. Government of Bangladesh, May 2000.

Environmental Impact Assessment of Alternative Flow Regimes for Gorai River Restoration Project. Ministry of Water Resources, Government of Bangladesh, September 2000.

Embree, Ainslie T., Editor.
Sources of Indian Tradition: Volume One: From the Beginning to 1800. New York: Columbia University Press, 1988.

Faruqui et al.
Water Management in Islam. Tokyo, New York, Paris: United Nations University Press. 2001.

Flood, Gavin.
An Introduction to Hinduism. Cambridge: Cambridge University Press. 1996.

Freeman, Rich.
"Forests and the Folk: Perceptions of Nature in the Swidden Regimes of Highland Malabar." *Pondy Papers in Social Sciences.* 15, 1994. Pondicherry.

Fuller, C.
The Camphor Flame: Popular Hinduism and Society in India. Princeton, NJ, Princeton University Press. 1992.

Gardner, Katy.
Songs at the River's Edge - Stories from a Bangladeshi Village. London: Pluto Press. 1997.

Goel, Radhey Shyam.
Environmental Impacts Assessment of Water Resources Projects:

Concerns, Policy Issues, Perceptions and Scientific Analysis. New Delhi, Calcutta: Oxford and IBH Publishing Co. Pvt. Ltd. 2000.

Ghose, N.C. and C.B. Sharma.
Pollution of the Ganga River. New Delhi: Ashish Publishing House. 1989.

Godden, Rumer.
The River. Calcutta: Rupa Paperback. 1991.

Golding, Paul R & Singh, Virendra (trans).
Tales of Banaras - the Flowing Ganges. Delhi: Book Faith India. 1997.

Gorai River Contractors.
Gorai River Re-excavation Project Pilot Priority Works. PPW Second Season. Government of the Peoples' Republic of Bangladesh, Bangladesh Water Development Board, May 2000.

PPW Final Report. Government of the Peoples' Republic of Bangladesh, Bangladesh Water Development Board, June 2000.

Briefing Report on the Occasion of the Visit of the Honourable Vice Minister of Transport, Public Works and Water Management of the Netherlands. The Government of Peoples' Republic of Bangladesh, Ministry of Water Resources, Bangladesh Water Development Board, Nov 2000.

Gosling, David L.
Religion and Ecology in India and South East Asia. London, New York: Routledge. 2001.

Grepin, Georges.
Integrated Resource Development of the Sundarbans Reserved Forest Bangladesh. Draft Final Report Consultant Mangrove Ecology. United Nations Development Program/ Food and Agriculture Organization of the United Nations, Khulna, June 1995.

Gupta A.

Post-colonial Developments: Agriculture in the Making of Modern India. Durham, North Carolina: Duke University Press. 1998.

Guha R.
"Radical American Environmentalism and Wilderness Preservation: A Third World Critique." *Environmental Ethics*. 11 (Spring),1998. pp 78-83.

Hamilton, Walter.
East-India Gazeteer. (2 vols), Delhi: Low Price Publications. 1993 (originally published 1828).

Hans RK, Farooq M, Babu GS, Srivastava SP, Joshi PC, Viswanathan PN
"Agricultural Produce in the Dry Bed of the River Ganga in Kanpur, India - A New Source of Pesticide Contamination in Human Diets." *Food and Chemical Toxicology*. 37(8). 1999. 847-852.

Hawley, John Stratton and Wulff, Donna Marie, Editors.
Devi: Goddesses of India. Berkeley: University of California Press, Motilal Barnarsidass: Delhi.1996.

Hay, Stephen, Editor.
Sources of Indian Tradition: Volume Two: Modern Indian and Pakistan. New York: Columbia University Press. 1988.

Hebner, Ganesh and Osborn, David.
Kumbha Mela: The World's Largest Act of Faith. California: Entourage Publishing. 1990.

Heiderer, Tony.
"Sacred Space: India's Kumbh Mela." *National Geographic Magazine*. May 1990.

Hillary, Edmund.
From the Ocean to the Sky. New York: Viking Press. 1979.

Hollick, Julian Crandall, and Tomalin, Emma.
"Making a Radio Documentary on the River Ganges." *Contemporary South Asia*. 11:2. July 2002.

Iyer, Ramasway R.
"Conflict Resolution: Three River Treaties." *Economic and Political Weekly*. June 12, 1999. 1509 - 1518.

Jain, C.K.
"Absorption of Zinc on Bed Sediments of the River Ganga: Absorption Models and Kinetics." *Hydrological Sciences Journal*. 46(3). 2001. 419-434.

"A Hydro-chemical Study of a Mountainous Watershed: The Ganga, India." *Water Research*. 0. 2001. 1-13.

Jansen, Erik G. et al (eds)
The Country Boats of Bangladesh: Social and Economic Development and Decision-Making in Inland Water Transport. Dhaka: University Press Ltd. 1994 (1989).

James, E. O.
The Cult of the Mother Goddess: An Archeological and Documentary Study. London: Thames & Hudson 1994.

Jhingran.
Fish and Fisheries of India. Delhi, India: Hindustan Publishing Corporation. 1982.

Johari, Harish.
The Birth of the Ganga. Vermont: Inner Traditions. 1998.

Kabir, Humayun,.
Men and Rivers. Bombay: Kulkarni Publishers. 1945.

Kannan K, S. Tanabe, R. Tatsukawa and R.K. Sinha.
"Biodegradation Capacity and Residue Pattern of Organochlorines in Ganges River Dolphins From India." *Toxicological Environmental Chemistry*. 42. 1994. 249-261.

Kannan K, Senthilkumar and Sinha R.K.
"Sources and Accumulation off Butyltin Compounds in Ganges River Dolphin, Platanista Gangetica." *Applied Organometallic Chemistry*. 11. 1994. 223-230.

Kannan, K., Sinha R.K., Tanabe, S., Ichihashi, H. and Tatsukawa R.
"Heavy Metals and Organochlorine Residues in Ganges River Dolphin from India." *Marine Pollution Bulletin.* (26)3. 1993.159-162.

Kanjilal, Tushar.
Who Killed the Sundarbans? Kolkata: Tagore Society for Rural Development. 2000.

Kaul, H.K. and Sangeeta Kaul.
E-mail Directory of Institutions in India. New Delhi: Virgo Publications. 2000.

Khan, Tauhidul Anwar.
"Management of Sharing of the Ganges." *Natural Resources Journal.* 36(3). 1996. 455-480 (Natural River Basins Part II).

Kipling, Rudyard.
Collected Stories. London: Everyman's Library. 1906.

Khilnani, Sunil.
The Idea of India. London: Penguin Books. 1997.

Klostermaier, Klaus.
A Survey of Hinduism. New York: State University of New York Press. 1994.

Kramsjo, Bosse.
Bangladesh a Quest for Reality. Dhaka: Shamunnay. 2000.

Krishna Murti C.R., K.S. Bilgrami, T.M. Das and R.P. Mathur (Eds.).
The Ganga: A Scientific Study. Published for the Ganga Project Directorate (Ministry of Environment and Forests, Government of India, New Delhi), 1991.

Kumari, Amupma, R.K. Sinha amd Krishna Gopal.
"Organochlorine Contamination in the Fish of the River Ganges." *Aquatic Ecosystem Health and Management.* 4. 2001. 505-510.

Kumra, V.K.
"Water Quality in the River Ganges." *Water and the Quest for Sustainable Development in the Ganges Valley.* Eds. Graham

Chapman and Michael Thompson. London, New York: Mansell. 1995. 130-140.

Kurz, Paul (Ed).
Science and Religion - Are They Compatible? New York: Prometheus Books. 2003.

Lane, Stuart, Keith S. Richards and Sudanshu Sinha and Shuang-ye Wu. "Screw the Lid Even Tighter? Water Pollution and the Enforcement of Environmental Regulation in Less Developed Countries." *Water Quality: Processes and Policy.* Eds. Stephen T. Trudgill, Des E. Walling and Bruce W. Webb. Chichester, New York: John Wiley and Sons Ltd. 1999.

Larson, Gerald James.
"Conceptual Resources in South Asia for Environmental Ethics." *Nature in Asian Traditions of Thought: Essays in Environmental Philosophy.* Eds. J. Baird and Roger T. Ames. New Delhi: Sri Satguru Publications. 1991, 207-278.

MacLeod, Roy and Deepak Kumar (Eds.).
Technology and the Raj: Western Technology and Technical Transfers to India, 1700 -1947. New Delhi, Thousand Oaks, London: Sage Publications. 1995.

Mahajan, Jagmohan (Ed).
Ganga Observed - Foreign Accounts of the River, Varanasi, India: Indica Books. 2003.

Mahajan, Jagmohan.
The Ganga Trail - Foreign Accounts and Sketches of the River Scene. Varanasi, India: Indica Books. 2004.

Mani, V.G.T. and S.K. Konar.
"Chronic Effect of Malathion on Feeding Behaviour, Survival, Growth and Reproduction of Fish". *Environmental Ecology.* 4(4). 1975. 517-520.

Markandya, A. and M.N. Murty.
Cleaning Up the Ganges: A Cost-Benefit Analysis of the Ganga Action Plan. New Delhi: Oxford University Press. 2000.

Ministry of Environment and Forests, India.
   An Action Plan for the Prevention of Pollution of the Ganga. Delhi.
   1985.

   National River Action Plan. 1994.

   Evaluation of Ganga Action Plan. Government of India. New
   Delhi. 1995.

Moddie, A.D.
   The Brahmanical Culture and Modernity. Bombay: Asia
   Publishing House. 1968.

Moorhouse, Geoffrey.
   Calcutta: The City Revealed. New York: Penguin. 1971.

Nelson, Lance E. (Ed.).
   *Purifying the Earthly Body of God - Religion and Ecology in
   Hindu India*. New York: SUNY. 1998.

Newby, Eric.
   Slowly Down the Ganges. London: Picador. 1983 (1963).

Novak, James.
   Bangladesh: Reflections on the Water. Bloomington, Indiana:
   University Press. 1993.

O'Reilly, James and Habegger, Larry.
   India, Travelers' Tales. San Francisco: Travellers' Tales Guides.
   1995.

Pandey, Kamala.
   Rakshata Gangam. Varanasi, India: Shree Mata Publications.
   2000.

Patkar, Medha (Ed).
   River Linking: A Millennium Folly? Mumbai, India: National
   Alliance for People's Movements. 2004.

Peavey, Fran.
   "Working with the Waters." *By Life's Grace: Musings on the
   Essence of Social Change*. Philadelphia: New Society of
   Publishers. 1994.

"Would You Do This to Your Mother?" *Heart Politics*. Philadelphia: New Society Publishers. 1995.

Pederson, Poul.
"Nature, Religion and Cultural Identity: The Religious Environmentalist Paradigm." *Asian Perceptions of Nature: A Critical Approach*. Eds. Ole Bruun and Arne Kalland. Richmond, Surrey: Curzon Press. 1995. 258-276.

Pollard, Michael.
The Ganges. London: Evans Brothers Ltd. 1997.

Prakash, Gyan.
Another Reason: Science and the Imagination of Modern India. Princeton, New Jersey: Princeton University Press. 1999.

Putnam, John and Singh, Raghubir.
"The Ganges, River of Faith." *National Geographic*. October 1971.

Radice, William, Translator.
Tagore: Selected Poems. London: Penguin. 1987.

Tagore: Selected Short Stories. London: Penguin. 1994.

Rahman, Atiur.
Beel Dakatia: The Environmental Consequences of a Development Disaster. Dhaka: University Press Ltd. 1995.

Ray, Satyajit.
Apu Trilogy: The World of Apu, Aparajito, Panther Panchali. Columbia: Tristar. 1996.

Rice, Edward.
The Ganges - A Personal Encounter. New York: Four Winds Press. 1974.

Rudra, Kalyan.
"The Encroaching Ganga and Social Conflicts: The Case of West Bengal, India." Independent Broadcasting Associates, Littleton, MA, 2004.

The Palaeo Channel and Wetlands of Southern Deltaic West Bengal. Landforms Processes and Environment Management. Ed. By S. Bandyopadhyay et. al. New Delhi: Concept Publishing House. 2002.

"The Saga of Bank Erosion: Malda and Murshidabad."(Bengali) *Mrittika.* Calcutta. 2002.

"The Flood in West Bengal September 2000." *NAPM* Calcutta, 2001.

"Will the Ganga Outflank the Farakka Barrage?" (Bengali). *Desh.* 9.12. 2000, 58-68, ABP Publications, Calcutta.

"Living on the Edge: The Experience Along the Bank of the Ganga in Malda District, West Bengal." *Indian Journal of Geography and Environment.* 5, 2000, 57-67.

"The Farakka Barrage - An Interruption to Fluvial Regime." *Indian Journal of Landscape System and Ecological Studies.* Vol.19, No.2, 1996, 105-110

"Problems of River Bank Erosion Along the Ganga in Murshidabad District of West Bengal. *Journal of Geography and Environment.* 1. 1996. 25-32.

"Encroaching Ganga in West Bengal." *Indian Journal of Landscape System and Ecological Studies.* Vol.16 , No.2, 1993.

"Exploration to the Bhagirathi Off-take." (Bengali) *Biswabiksha.* Vol. 2, No. 2, 1992.

"Quaternary History of the Lower Ganga Distributaries" *The Geographical Society of India.* Calcutta. 49(3). pp. 38- 48, 1987.

"Locational Dispute Over Two Ancient Ports of Bengal." *Geographical Review of India.* Vol.48, No.1. pp 32-37, 1986.
"Identification of the Ancient Mouths of Ganga As Described by Ptolemy." *Geographical Review of India.* Vol.43, No.2. pp 97-104. 1981.

Rudra, Kalyan (jointly with M. K. Bandyopadhyay).
"Dating of Ancient Outlets Of the Bhagirathi River." *Indian Geographical Studies*, Vol. 15, 1980. 1-8.

Sachchidananda.
Social Dimensions of Water Supply and Sanitation in Rural Areas: A Case Study of Bihar. New Delhi: Concept Publishing. 1999.

Saith, Sanjeev & Kesavan, Mukul.
A Journey Down the Ganga. Delhi: Lustre Press. 1989.

Sampat, Payal.
"The Ganges: Myth and Reality." *World Watch*. Vol. 9, No. 4. July/August 1996.

"Myth and Reality: Cleaning the Ganges River in India." Masters Thesis, Tufts University, 1995.

Shreider, Helen & Frank.
"From the Hair of Shiva." *National Geographic*. October 1960.

Schjolden, Ane.
"Leather Tanning in India: Environmental Regulations and Firms' Compliance." *F.I.L. (Forurensende Industri-Lokalisering)* Working Papers, No. 21, 2000.

Segal, Ronald.
The Crisis of India. Ringwood, Victoria, Australia: Penguin Books. 1965.

Senhilkumar, Kannan, Sinha, Tanabe and Giesy.
"Bioaccumulation Profiles of Polychlorinated Biphenyl Congeners and Organochlorine Pesticides in Ganges River Dolphins." *Environmental Toxicology and Chemistry*. 18 (7), 1999.1511-1520.

Shiva, Vandana and Bandyopadhyay.
"The Large and Fragile Community of Scientists in India." *Minerva*. 18(4). 1980. 575-594.

Shukla, AC & Vandana.
Ganga: A Water Marvel. New Delhi: Ashish Publishers. 1995.

Singh, H.P., J.P. Mishra and L.R. Mahaver.
"Observation on Biochemical and Chemical Oxygen Demands of Certain Polluted Stretch of River Ganga". *Journal of Environmental Biology*. 20(2). 1999. 111-114.

"Impact of Industrial and Sewage Wastes on Water Qualities in Middle Stretch of River Ganga from Kanpur to Varanasi." *Journal of Environmental Biology*. 20(3). 1999. 279-285.

Singh, Jyotsna.
Colonial Narrative, Cultural Dialogues: 'Discoveries' of India in the Language of Colonialism. London, New York: Routledge. 1996.

Singh, Ragubhir.
The Ganges. London: Thames and Hudson. 1992.

Singh, Raghubir & Newby, Eric.
Ganga: Sacred River of India. Hong Kong: Perennial Press. 1974.

Singh, Rana PB (ed).
Banaras (Varanasi) - Cosmic Order, Sacred City, Hindu Traditions. Varanasi, India: Tara Book Agency. 1993.

Singh, Rana PB.
Towards the Pilgrimage Archetype - The Pancakrosi Yatra at Banaras. Varanasi, India: Indica Books. 2002.

Cultural Landscapes and the Lifeworld - Literary Images of Banaras. Varanasi, India: Indica Books. 2004.

Singh, Rana PB & Rana, Pravin S.
Banaras Region - A Spiritual & Cultural Guide. Varanasi, India: Indica Books. 2002.

Singh, Vijay.
Jaya Ganga. Paris: editions Ramsay. 1985.

Smith, Brian, A.K.M. Aminul haque, M. Shakhawat Hossain and Anisuzzaman Khan.
"River Dolphins in Bangladesh: Conservation and the Effects of Water Development." *Environmental Management*. 22(3). 1998. 323-335.

Smith, W. Cantwell.
The Meaning and End of Religion: A New Approach to the Religious Traditions of Mankind. New York: New American Academy. 1964.

Spear, Percival.
A History of India, Volume Two: From the Sixteenth Century to the Twentieth Century. London: Penguin Books. 1990 (1965).

Srivastava, Manish.
Pollution of Ganga River: A Limnological Study at Hardwar. New Delhi: Shree Publishers. 2000.

Stille, Alexander.
"The Ganges' Next Life". *The New Yorker*. January 19, 1998.

Stone, Ian.
Canal Irrigation in British India: Perspectives on Technological Change in a Peasant Economy. Cambridge, London: Cambridge University Press. 1984.

Subba, Bhiman.
Himalayan Waters: Promise and Potential, Problems and Politics. Kathmandu, Nepal: Panos South Asia. 2001.

Sur, Abha.
"Aesthetics, Authority, and Control in an Indian Laboratory: The Raman-Born Controversy on Lattice Dynamics." *Isis*. Vol. 90, 1999. 25-49.

Swami, Lokanath.
Kumbh: The Festival of Immortality. Delhi: Padayatra Press. 2001.

Robinson Andrew, Krishna Dutta.
Rabindranath Tagore - The Myriad-Minded Man. London: Bloomsbury. 1995.

Tagore, Rabindranath.
Quartet (Chaturanga). Oxford: Heinemann. 1993.

The Wreck. New Delhi: Macmillan. 1999.

Tare, Vinod, Purnendu Bose and Santosh K. Gupta.
"Suggestions for a Modified Approach Towards Implementation and Assessment of Ganga Action Plan And Other Similar River Action Plans in India." *Eco-Friends Reports*. Kanpur, India. 2004.

"Critical Evaluation of Ganga Action Plan: Suggestions for a Modified Approach." (Unpublished Paper). 2001.

Tare, Vinod, Ajay Veer Singh Yadav and Purnendu Bose.
Analysis of Photosynthetic Activity in the Most Polluted Stretch of River Ganga. (Unpublished Paper), 2001.

Tomalin, Emma.
"Transformation and Tradition: A Comparative Study of Religious Environmentalism in Britain and India." (unpublished PhD thesis), Lancaster University. 2000.

Tsai, Chu-fa and M. Youssouf Ali (Eds).
Openwater Fisheries of Bangladesh. Dhaka: The University Press Ltd. 1997.

UNEP.
"Tanneries and the Environment: A Technical Guide to Reducing the Environmental Impact of Tannery Operations." United Nations Environment Programme, Industry and Environment, Programme Activity Centre (UNIDO, IE/PAC), Paris, 1991.

Valmiki.
Ramayana. Translated by Makhan Lal Sen. New Delhi: Munshiram Manoharlal Publishers. 1976.

Verghese, B.G.
Waters of Hope: From Vision to Reality in Himalaya-Ganga Development Cooperation. Dhaka: The University Press Ltd. 1999 (1990).

Westcoat, James.
"Common Law, Common Property, and Common Enemy: Notes on the Political Geography of Water Resources Management for the Sundarbans area of Bangladesh." http://www.smartoffice.com/tiger/pi.htm. From a workshop: The Commons in South Asia: Societal Pressures and Environmental

Integrity in the Sundarbans. Held at the S. Dillon Ripley Center, Smithsonian Institution, Washington, D.C. November 20-21, 1987.

Wiegant WM, Kalker TJJ, Sontakke VN, Zwaag RR.
"Full Scale Experience with Tannery Water Management: An Integrated Approach." *Water Science and Technology.* 39(5), 1999. 169-176.

Wu, Kegang and John B. Thornes.
"Terrace Irrigation of Mountainous Hill Slopes in the Middle Hills of Nepal: Stability or Instability." *Water and the Quest for Sustainable Development in the Ganges Valley.* Eds. G.P. Chapman and M. Thompson. London and New York: Mansell Publishing Limited. 1995. 41-63.

Yadav, Hira Lal.
Floods in Eastern UP. New Delhi: Radha Publications. 1999.

Index

Acknowledgments

Ganga is the fruit of twenty years of living and working in India. I have tried to remember all the people who have put up with my foibles and guided and helped me to understand Ganga. Inevitably, I will have forgotten someone. It is not intentional. Put it down to creeping senility and accept my profound apologies.

In India and Bangladesh — Indu and Vijay Agarwal, Q.K. Ahmed, Anish Andheria, Vandana Asthani, Rana Behal, Ravendra Swaroop Bhargava, Bimal and Bipin, Raja Chatterjee, Abhijit Choudhary (ADM, South 24 Parganas), Shebana Coelho, Saurajit and Chittaranjan Das, Suman Dubey, Thoma and Jayant Gokhale, Sachcha Gopalji, the Indian Embassy in Washington DC, and the XP division of the Ministry of External Affairs in Delhi.

Monirul Islam (Chhutu), C.K. Jain, Rakesh Jaiswal, B.D. Joshi, Vidhyeet and Vidhya Katagarde, R.C. Kesarwani, Hasan Mansur, Gita Mithal, Rakesh Mishra, Veer Badre Mishra, Sharada Nayak, Ainun Nishat, Veena and Philip Oldenburg, Mohammed Owais, Sheela Patel, Triyogi Prasad.

Attiur Rahman, Jay Ramachandran, Krishna Rao at the Rajiv Gandhi Foundation, Binayak Rath, Dr. Tej Razdan, Kalyan and Gouri Rudra, Bittu Sahgal, Sourav Sarangi, Radhika Sareen, Jay Sen, Monatosh Shah, Nidish Sharma and his wife Kalyani, Nidish's Garhwal crew — Bhagwat Prasad, Pushker Singh, Nandan Singh, Dalbir Singh.

Mr. Sheshan at Ganges View Hotel, Rana B. Singh, all the Singhs great and small from "The Attic," Raj Pal Singh, Ravindra Kumar Sinha, the crew from Patna to Kolkata — Khalid, Mahesh, Subhash, Raju, Arjun, Mohan, all the Sircars of Townshend Road, Sudhir Subedhar, D.K. Sundd, Vinod Tare, Adhiti Thorat, Bijoy Tivari, Manoj Tivari, Anil Yadav, and Rinku in Varanasi.

In Britain and the USA — Kelly Alley, James Ashby, Richard Bannermann (BBC), Chris Beacock, Constance Bertka, David Black, Bob Blanchette, Graham and Annegerd Chapman, John Cort, Krishna Dutta, Diana Eck, Roberta Farrell, Hyman Field, Mithu Gupta, Neal Jackson, Valentina Kass.

Bob Malesky, Karen Miles, Tina Morris, Michael Putnam and Melody Lawrence, Sally Robbins, Andrew Robinson, Fernando Ruiz del Prado, Shubha Sankaran, Jack Schmidt, Brian Silver, Hugh Stevens, Emma Tomalin, Sandra Welch(National Science Foundation), and Jonathan Williams.

Special thanks to Sarah Jane Freymann, my patient literary agent in New York, to Deepti, Krishna, Parul, and all the other staff at Random House in Delhi, to my first editor Shakti Bhatt, who bought the book, to Rajni George for seeing the book through its final birth pangs, and above all to Chiki Sarkar for her intelligence, wit, patience, and editorial competence. She has turned a manuscript into a book. No one has the right to ask for more.

To my family — my late mother who always wanted but never got to come to India; Margot, who edited so many of the technical papers I could never hope to understand; Jerome, who was at his happiest throwing cow dung patties with other kids (Indians) in Kashmir; Francesca, Coco and Durga, who know who they are.

And above all, to Martine (Kali ma*)* who has loved me and shared me with Ganga and India. She has been as much a friend, lover, companion, and wife as any man could hope for. I hope I have been half as much for her. It is not for nothing that Indians call her both Shakti and Kali. I think she also has been enriched as a person by India and Ganga.

Finally, to India and her people — what serendipity brought me to India I will never know. Indu Agarwal says I was obviously an Indian in a previous life. I have no idea. All I do know is that without India I would not be who I am today. They say a wife makes a man. I have been lucky enough to have two — Martine and India. A country can also make a man.

I once met someone in Marseille who told me that where you want to be buried tells you where your real homeland is. I sat and thought about this and realized I wanted my ashes to be shared between certain vineyards in France and places along Ganga that have meant so much to me, not always famous places, often little villages or places where we spent days and nights. I hope Ganga will look kindly many years from now on the person who has to execute my wishes!

Some people are going to wonder at my fabulous recall of what villagers and other ordinary Indians said to me on the street, in fields, on the river and at melas and other festivals associated with Ganga. My answer is certain and twofold: first, it was all recorded for radio. People really did say what I write they say! The tapes exist.

Second, it was all transcribed by two Indians — Indu Agarwal and Shahana Gupta who are both fluent in Hindi, Bengali and a few other languages. Indu and Mithu have been correcting my mistakes for more than fifteen years. They are the two most fabulous (unofficial) editorial assistants anyone could ever ask to have; without them all my radio work in India, and this book, would not have been possible.

To all of you with love and gratitude.

Julian Crandall Hollick
Vaison-la-Romaine, November 20, 2006

About the Author

Julian Crandall Hollick is an award-winning producer and writer of radio documentaries about Islam and South Asia. Co-founder of Independent Broadcasting Associates Inc., a non profit media production company based in Massachusetts, he has also been an independent radio producer for NPR, BBC Radio Four and World Service and CBC in Toronto. He has broadcasted a weekly programme on Radio Midday in Mumbai, written on India in *Smithsonian* magazine and *New Republic,* and been a columnist for *The Times of India* and *The Hindu*. Currently, he divides his time between Massachusetts and Provence.

About Island Press

Island Press is the only nonprofit organization in the United States whose principal purpose is the publication of books on environmental issues and natural resource management. We provide solutions-oriented information to professionals, public officials, business and community leaders, and concerned citizens who are shaping responses to environmental problems.

Since 1984, Island Press has been the leading provider of timely and practical books that take a multidisciplinary approach to critical environmental concerns. Our growing list of titles reflects our commitment to bringing the best of an expanding body of literature to the environmental community throughout North America and the world.

Support for Island Press is provided by the Agua Fund, The Geraldine R. Dodge Foundation, Doris Duke Charitable Foundation, The Ford Foundation, The William and Flora Hewlett Foundation, The Joyce Foundation, Kendeda Sustainability Fund of the Tides Foundation, The Forrest & Frances Lattner Foundation, The Henry Luce Foundation, The John D. and Catherine T. MacArthur Foundation, The Marisla Foundation, The Andrew W. Mellon Foundation, Gordon and Betty Moore Foundation, The Curtis and Edith Munson Foundation, Oak Foundation, The Overbrook Foundation, The David and Lucile Packard Foundation, Wallace Global Fund, The Winslow Foundation, and other generous donors.

The opinions expressed in this book are those of the author(s) and do not necessarily reflect the views of these foundations.